IN1
PE[

Introdi   )her
Mikh: 1ose
studyi   ɔgic
schola   ung
childr   ʒing
and re   ling
and e
    Th   1 to
suppc   ugh
ethica   d of
the y   :t of
adult:
    K(

-]   uca-
  1   ility;
- (1es;
- Theorising a range of approaches   e, as
  pedagogy.

This accessible and readable guide offers sound theoretical principles with practical suggestions for early years settings. The book is supplemented by an extensive
online video resource website that will provide a visual means of contemplating the
potential for these ideas in practice.

E. Jayne White is an Associate Professor at the University of Waikato, New
Zealand.

INTRODUCING DIALOGIC PEDAGOGY

Provocations for the Early Years

E. Jayne White

Routledge
Taylor & Francis Group

LONDON AND NEW YORK

First published 2016
by Routledge
2 Park Square, Milton Park, Abingdon, Oxon OX14 4RN

and by Routledge
711 Third Avenue, New York, NY 10017

Routledge is an imprint of the Taylor & Francis Group, an informa business

© 2016 E. J. White

British Library Cataloguing in Publication Data
A catalogue record for this book is available from the British Library

Library of Congress Cataloging-in-Publication Data
White, E. Jayne.
  Introducing dialogic pedagogy : provocations for the early years /
E. Jayne White.
     pages cm
  1. Bakhtin, M. M. (Mikhail Mikhailovich), 1895–1975. 2. Early childhood education—Philosophy. 3. Children—Language. I. Title.
  LB775.B1752W45 2016
  372.21—dc23
  2015002979

ISBN: 978-0-415-81984-8 (hbk)
ISBN: 978-0-415-81985-5 (pbk)
ISBN: 978-1-315-71000-6 (ebk)

Typeset in Bembo
by Apex CoVantage, LLC

This book is dedicated to my late father,
Norman Gellatly (1940–1997),
a teacher who devoted his life to education
and who understood the importance of
laughter and love in the life of a child.

CONTENTS

LIST OF VIDEO FOOTAGE

ACKNOWLEDGEMENTS

Without the generosity of the children and teachers who feature throughout this book – in research, video and practice – I could not possibly have completed this project. In particular to Zoe, Jayden, Lola, Harrison, Harry from anonymous New Zealand early years centres, and Zen, Clayton, Selina, Cory, Gemma, Jacob, Te Arai, Haukore from Kidicorp Kids-to-Five Bader Street, Hamilton. To you and your families I am enormously indebted. To early years teachers Alicia, Rachel, Lynnette and Jayde, I also thank you from the bottom of my heart: it is not easy to have one's practice – normally such a private affair – laid bare in this manner. I am in awe of your commitment to the early years profession and have enjoyed our many dialogues about the possibilities of dialogism for twenty-first-century pedagogy.

I thank my early childhood students and colleagues at University of Waikato who urged me to develop these ideas in ways that would bring much-needed provocations to the early years in a contemporary context of accountability and certainty. I am forever indebted to Bridgette Redder for her never-ending optimism and support in putting the footage together and checking the text so diligently. To Alistair for his stalwart library work too. Special thanks to Tracey Lowndes for, once again, helping me bring it home.

To all my Bakhtin friends across the world who encouraged me to take on this challenge, I owe a great deal. In this regard I want to especially thank Eugene Matusov, Mikhail Gradovski and Beth Fernholt for their critical readings of initial drafts; and other members of the dialogic community who continue to challenge, inspire and encourage me through our dialogue across the miles. I thank Ana Marjanovic-Shane for our many late-night Skype meetings between America and New Zealand over the last four years, based on a shared passion for these ideas and their relevance to the early years.

I am indebted to Craig Brandist at Sheffield University for graciously hosting me during the critical final period of writing this book and for sharing resources that enabled me to gain a deeper appreciation of the texts at my disposal. Spending time with Craig and other scholars of Russian theory at Sheffield returned me to the complexity of the ever-widening Bakhtin Circle's ideas in an increasingly mono-logic contemporary Western world. Throughout the writing of this text I have had these Bakhtinian friends on my shoulder, reminding me not to trivialise ideas, isolate concepts from their contextual origins or abuse my outsider privilege (and serious limitations as a non-Russian speaker). It is with this deep sense of humility that I present the text that follows.

Paperback cover art work by Alexander Benfante, Olle Erliden, Linea Fransson Nordén, Tyra Isidorsson, Tuva Idebäck, Maja Larsson, Elton Nilsson, Janice Nguy, Tiago Pedraza Carlholt, Helinn Polat, Doris Peterson, Malte Rönneke, Eskil Sundh, Livia Borgmark, Cornelis Mrak and TheoPalmér.Preschool HallonEtt, Jonkoping, Sweden. The image was made by a three-year group in 2010. It was chosen for this book because it so beautifully captures some of the many dialogues that take place for young children in early years settings – often when the teacher is nowhere in sight but nevertheless present in one way or another.

INTRODUCTION

Challenges and provocations

As its title suggests, this is a book about dialogic pedagogy and the provocations it offers for the early years. I should say, from the outset, that this is not a book about any and all kinds of dialogic pedagogy – we would need a whole series for that! Ideas about the role of dialogue and teaching are evident as early as Plato and can be traced through to recent theorists such as Paulo Freire in his emancipatory work with literacy in Brazil. This book takes a different turn by offering a persistent focus on dialogic pedagogy that is based on the inspiration of a Russian philologist and thinker called Mikhail Bakhtin (1895–1975). Bakhtin's approach – through a set of ideas that can be summarised as 'dialogism' – provides tremendous scope to consider pedagogy well beyond traditional classrooms or even spoken language (*slovo*). His emphasis on aspects of human encounter that unashamedly embrace emotion, the body, the developing consciousness and a celebration of human agency is particularly relevant for early years teaching and learning. Thinking about these concepts in relation to pedagogy provides a great deal of scope to consider the role of love, laughter and play in educational settings for the very young. Here, Bakhtin's pedagogical inspiration is less concerned with popular concepts such as 'emancipation', 'empowerment' or 'enculturation' than with the effort of understanding and appreciating the potential of meaning-making encounters between subjectivities, and what this means for the developing consciousness.

Why Bakhtin?

It may, at first, seem rather strange to bring Bakhtin into conversation with early years pedagogy. After all, Bakhtin never studied young children specifically. Unlike popular theorists for early years practice – such as Vygotsky, Bruner and Piaget – Bakhtin was not interested in providing explanations for child development and learning. In contrast to Malaguzzi, Bakhtin did not set out to innovate early years practice or to generate truths about how young children think. He was not interested in cognition (*poznanie*) as a primary function of education, and it is highly likely – perhaps even certain – that he would have rejected the idea that children ought to be brought into certain specific ways of thinking about the world. In short, Bakhtin sits at odds with many of his predecessors, outrightly rejecting what he describes as 'monologic' (one-dimensional) claims of truth and resisting 'you versus me' divides.

While Bakhtin does not advocate for 'one truth' he makes the important claim that what is true for each of us is granted legitimacy in the lived moment of exchange. Truth differs across time and space and may be very different from one moment to the next – even for a group of people who share an experience at exactly the same time. For this reason Bakhtin is often described as 'two-faced' because he looks in spaces that resist certainty yet at the same time seeks to interpret these as an important process of meaning-making. For this reason, a book that draws on his insights may be deeply unsatisfying for the student or teacher who seeks recipes for their practice in these pages. Bakhtin does not let us off the hook so easily!

When you consider the location of his texts across time and space – spanning over 50 years during the twentieth century – the challenge becomes even greater. The fact that his works were published out of order, in secret collaborations with other writers, in Russian and often in fragments is only half the battle. His orientation towards literature and language may seem remote from human experience, let alone the work of those who live, laugh and love in the early years. Early years scholars will find little support from Bakhtin for any kind of reified practice, framework or system. His dialogic entreaty suggests that, as with any language form, methods lose their significance once they become an authority that must be adhered to by all. As such, we need to be careful not to exploit or isolate one of Bakhtin's ideas without an appreciation of its location in the wider body of work. To employ the ideas in such a manner would violate the very principles of Bakhtin himself, who believed that creativity could only thrive in places where knowledge is viewed as a lively debate or encounter with other points of view. His own texts are full of such contradictory meetings.

And yet, if one reads carefully across the texts Bakhtin and his colleagues have left for us to ponder, there are many riches to be found. Burrowing deeper into these works it becomes evident to the patient reader that Bakhtin never talks about any word or text without first considering its relationship with people in time and space. He is concerned with the use of language as a route to all meaning. For Bakhtin, the significance of meaning is not only found in its shared understanding (or intersubjective potential), but also in its potential to disrupt interpretation (what he calls its *alteric* potential). It is here Bakhtin offers us significant provocation in a concept best known as *dialogism* – a place where subjectivities encounter one another in the social act of communication. Under this interpretation dialogism can be described as a rich process of inexhaustible possibilities that exist in spoken and unspoken dialogues (real or imagined), characterised by voice (*golos*), gesture, posture, movement and motion. Located in the flux of time and space, the notion of dialogism captures the heart of Bakhtin's work as a means of expanding the possibilities for human existence in social encounters with 'other'. This is an important agenda for early years pedagogy.

Why early years pedagogy?

"That's all very well," I hear you ask, "but why should I bother to read a book that attempts to bring dialogism to bear on early years pedagogy?" Believe me, this is a question colleagues have often posed over the months of contemplating this text and its relevance to their practice. And yet I am continually tantalised by Bakhtin's provocations in my work as an early years scholar even though there is, at the time of writing, very little precedent to support my curiosity from the field. His ideas offer significant challenges to many deep-seated claims that are made by theorists who dominate the profession regarding communication, culture and relationships – all of which lie at the heart of early years pedagogy. Bakhtin prompts us to examine the dominant discourses that shape our practice, while simultaneously stripping us of any excuse (or alibi) for our actions. His insistence on the 'lived' nature of language – beyond merely words or text – leaves us with an obligation to look and listen carefully, to suspend certainty and to position ourselves at the centre of learning. His moral attitude provides a serious challenge to any practice that is not in the best interests of 'other', implicating teachers at all levels of exchange. This is not a provocation for the faint-hearted.

Though it could be argued that an explicit focus on pedagogy is not a prominent theme in Bakhtin's texts, he cannot be dismissed as a pedagogue in his own right. As a secondary teacher himself Bakhtin was critical of what he called processes of 'schoolification' that dulled students' attention to creative potential and established authoritative regimes that did not allow for alternative views. His descriptions of classroom practice, in tandem with his sustained emphasis on dialogue as an event-of-being, leave us in no doubt of his pedagogical commitment. Bakhtin reminds us of the importance of individual agency and of resisting authoritative supremacy. He is also concerned with core principles of freedom, imagination, creativity and potential in learning. His attention to the aesthetic (*esteticheskii*) aspect of experience alerts us to the dangers of speaking on behalf of others, and to the role of *authorship* in learning – both as those who author others and those who retain the right to author themselves. For Bakhtin, there is no alibi in this regard – we do both whether we realise it or not.

What is dialogic pedagogy?

The term dialogism can be loosely described as a way of exploring the social event of 'voice' (or rather voices, plural) as learning. The spoken and unspoken dialogue that takes place between those involved – directly or indirectly – is of interest here because, for Bakhtin at least, this is where meaning is generated. It makes sense, therefore, that dialogic pedagogy emphasises learning dialogues that take place in social settings. In actual fact all pedagogy can be thought of as dialogic, because no matter what happens in the classroom – for better or for worse – learning of some sort is taking place. A Bakhtinian approach to dialogic pedagogy is not, therefore, concerned with particular methods or approaches, but rather accepts that dialogue is a fact of life whether or not we embrace its significance and potential. However, when we take these meaning-making encounters seriously, we can pay attention to the limitations as well as the possibilities of understanding 'other' in dialogue with the very young, and the importance of ourselves in this relationship. In doing so there are opportunities to consider pedagogy as a meeting place for learning. Implicating oneself so deeply is, perhaps, the biggest challenge of all.

Dialogic pedagogy thus advances the idea that teaching is a shared act or deed and, as such, the learner has a strong agentic role to play in their own learning and even in the learning of the teacher as an event-of-being (that is, *sobytie*). Following on from this point it is no surprise that the role of the teacher is expanded to consider the interplay of their subjectivities with those of the learner. In an era of increased accountability on the part of teachers, such a view provides a refreshing antidote to authoritative strongholds that are increasingly evident in the early childhood sphere internationally. In many contemporary early years settings worldwide, teachers are pressured to 'know' what children are thinking and, by extrapolation, learning – with the ultimate view of establishing learning outcomes that will be achieved on this basis. The idea that teachers can preplan or control learning, magnanimously granting children agency through such endeavours, is rejected in a dialogic approach. For Bakhtin, when one is fully known they are also finalised, with no room for creativity or growth. This book thus makes the bold claim that learning is less a known product for teachers to achieve than a series of open points of wonderment for teachers to enjoy with learners.

Taking this approach Bakhtin offers a means of reconceptualising education as a relational exchange that involves the body, the mind, the heart and the soul in relationship with other. Dialogic pedagogy celebrates the personality of a learner in the here and now rather than as some future potential contributor to society. For Bakhtin there is no novice to be enculturated into the stagnant reality of the well-meaning adult-expert, but a human being who is deeply engaged with others in a mutual encounter. In this regard, the book offers an interesting counter-response to the popular cultural-historical theories of Vygotsky, and the poststructuralist claims of writers such as Foucault, Deleuze or Merleau-Ponty, by providing an alternative springboard for students to explore – rather than commit to, suspend or simply ignore – alternative standpoints. The opportunity readers have to consider the implications of such a stance offers an important challenge to practices that are often located in traditional 'schooling' models of certainty in psychological frameworks that claim to know how children think or lodged in monocultural (that is, exclusive ways of approaching pedagogy that are often based in the West) theories. Dialogic pedagogy is thus an important agenda for the early years.

An agenda for the early years

In an era of difference and diversity, marked by new and emerging understandings about the experience of even the youngest infant and the way they might be seen (through such routes as neuroscience that reveal a far greater appreciation of infant capability than previously realised), Bakhtin allows us to theorise early years teaching as mutual social exchange. Here dialogue does not merely contribute to learning, it *is* learning. Through such means we are freed from the heavy emphasis on top-down assessment of individual children in isolation of 'other' and standardised measurement of universal learning outcomes – both of which now characterise (and in my view seek to legitimise) professional early childhood practice. From a dialogic standpoint, the teacher must suspend such certainties and lovingly linger long enough to gain a deep appreciation of the learner as a personality in their own right. Located in the here and now of the event rather than seeking to determine children's potential as future citizens in the service of society or culture, dialogism invites us to enjoy the many riches learners bring to the educative experience. Given all that we now know about the importance of relationships for learning and well-being in the early years this should not be too difficult to swallow.

Bakhtin's attention to 'other' is equally well aligned to emerging propositions in early childhood theory that suggest the very young child is less a product of their inheritance than a subject who is deeply influenced by those around them. Bakhtin shares the view that the young child is initially shaped by others through language and its emotional significance. Bakhtin's few words on this topic are evidence of his treatment of the infant as a social partner. Here teachers, as those who work with the child, are severely implicated:

> Everything that pertains to me enters my consciousness, beginning with my name, from the external world through the mouths of others (my mother, and so forth), with their intonation, in their emotional value assigning tonality. I realize myself initially through others: from them I receive words, forms, and tonalities for the formation of the initial idea of myself. . . . Just as the body is formed initially in the mother's womb (body), a person's consciousness awakens wrapped in another's consciousness.
>
> *(Bakhtin, 1986, p. 138)*

Had Bakhtin taken his ideas further into an investigation of young children, as I did, he would also have discovered how quickly very young children move from being shaped to shaping in a reciprocal manner. Yet taking into account Bakhtin's later work on the novel where dialogue is located within and between discourses, it is possible to interpret the experience of infants as dialogic partners who not only receive language as an emotional experience but also employ that language strategically in relationships with others. This is a particularly important idea in contemporary early years pedagogy since infants, toddlers and young children move between multiple social settings in their education experience. Through dialogic exchange the young child entering the early years learning context can now be seen as orienting themselves within unknown worlds that are forever altered by their presence (and, of course, this is reciprocal). This is very different to the experience of being enculturated by others into an existing world that is merely passed over to the infant as a cultural package. Here, there is potential for individuals to transgress such boundaries.

How to get the most out of this book

Like other books in this series, a whole new set of ideas and associated words are introduced to the vocabulary of early years pedagogy through the exploration of dialogic pedagogy. Since, for Bakhtin, words convey meaning in the moment of their delivery, as well as their aftermath, it is especially important to explain the interpretations that have been given to these in this book. I should state from the outset that these are my interpretations of the ideas based on what I have read and learnt from others.

Given the Russian origin of Bakhtin's texts this book contains several words that may be new to the reader and which draw from this particular set of ideas. These are defined in the glossary at the end of the book and feature throughout. At times the original Russian word is used where there is no English equivalent or where the original term best explains the concept. I accept the fact that, as an English speaker, my translation is likely to be primitive to the Russian reader and apologise in advance for this.

Engaging with polyphonic video

This book employs images, vignettes and an accompanying video companion as a means of bringing the ideas that are presented to life. Every time you see an image representing a video still you are invited to turn to the video companion and view the footage. I hope this forms the basis of some lively debates in your early years settings and classrooms as you consider your interpretations of the events captured, based on the dialogic provocations offered.

The images are mostly presented as time-synchronised split-screens to convey the multiple visual standpoints of each event and are accompanied by a vignette and/ or explanation. They draw from my own research involving very young children from education and care settings located in the North Island of New Zealand over the past six years. I do not apologise for the fact that most of the images emphasise the experiences of under 2 year olds, since this age group is so often overlooked or presented as an afterthought based on trickle-down, third-party assertions in early years research. Throughout this book infants and toddlers have a central role to play alongside their older peers. Although extracts of 3–4 year old children's dialogues are included, they draw mostly on other people's research and are therefore unac-companied by video except in a few cases. In such cases transcripts of dialogues are provided where possible, alongside footage taken by teachers for this book.

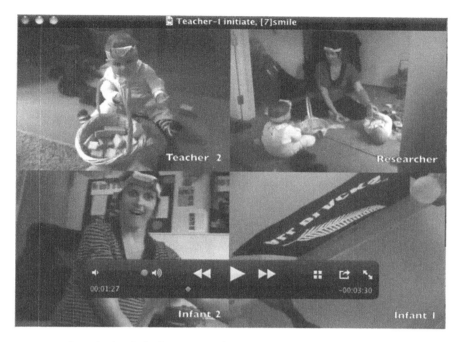

FIGURE I.1 Introducing Lola, Harrison and Rachel

The image in Figure I.1 shows a still from video footage that introduces you to the visual perspective of 8-month-old infant Lola (Infant 2), 4-month-old infant Harrison (Infant 1), Lola's key teacher Rachel (Teacher 2), and me (Researcher). Each screen is labelled so you can see whose lens is whose.

In these studies I sought to interrogate events from the visual and interpreted perspective of the child, the teacher and the researcher (myself) in an effort to try to understand the experience from each standpoint. I call this approach *polyphonic* video – based on Bakhtin's (1984) inspiration from the Russian novelist Fyodor Dostoevsky. This author employed a similar artistic device in his writing that allowed the voice of each character to speak for themselves (rather than being spoken for by others). In this image, if you look closely, you can see tiny nano-pod cameras on headbands worn by each of the participants. These allowed us to 'see' events through the eyes of each person, providing opportunities to contemplate very different insights accordingly. As you read on you will learn why this particular way of looking at events is so important in providing 'visual surplus' (*izbytok*). It is not simply a case of putting a camera on someone's head and assuming that what I see represents the finalised 'truth' of or for another, but a means through which dialogue can be generated and interpretation expanded. While this approach does not solve the problem of adults speaking on behalf of children, it does open up possibilities to see anew or, at the very least, to complicate previously held truths concerning the lives of our youngest. Critics of this method suggest adults can never really 'know' infants because they do not necessarily share the same understanding or experience. Yet adults (especially early years teachers in many parts of the world) are called to account for their perspectives because they are now considered to shape the nature of engagement, and by association, learning itself. Bakhtin's imperative makes trouble for any certainty of knowing but at the same time does not ignore the central and unavoidable significance of interpretation in dialogue.

Despite the limitations and risks of any finalising assertion about what can be seen, there are some things we can learn through this kind of engagement. If you look really closely at Figure I.1 you can see that Lola and her teacher are exchanging a look as Lola offers her teacher a block. Harrison, lying on the floor next to both of them, does not appear to share in this exchange. As far as we can tell from this image his eye is drawn, instead, to the All Blacks poster and balloons on the ceiling – a sociocultural clue to the time and space of this study, which was during the Rugby World Cup tournament in New Zealand in 2011 (an event of great significance to many New Zealanders at the time). But my access to his visual field is limited. From my viewpoint as the researcher I cannot easily see what Harrison sees or experiences – he is lying on his back on the floor facing away from me. I do not have access to the three-way nature of this exchange, nor do I claim to know what each person is thinking. But I can readily see that although the teacher is smiling at Lola, and her eye seems fixed on her, she is simultaneously passing a block to Harrison. I can see that Lola's gaze is not directed to her teacher at this moment, but instead in the direction of Harrison. Already there is a sense that more than a two-way encounter is taking place. Each visual perspective offers a different insight into the event. Collectively we have an expanded view of the experience because it is not seen from any one standpoint exclusively – instead there is a chorus of 'voices' at play. Whether we realise it or not, these insights will influence the way we see one another, the way we understand we are seen and the way such insights impact on us as individuals. By discussing the significance of these insights we are more likely to move into a deeper appreciation of one another, even if we can never know exactly what is going on for each individual.

Through such polyphonic means I argue that the voice of each research participant begins to have the opportunity to contribute in some way to the overall interpretations that are made – indeed the act of trying to make sense of each other (consciously or unconsciously as occurs in everyday life) is central to learning about oneself and 'other'. What is of interest here is not only how they are communicating but also the strategic nature of their use of language in all its many forms. The teachers I have worked with on these projects share the view that the visual surplus of polyphonic footage gives them tremendous insights about what is happening for children in their early years settings and, by association, what pedagogies are being promoted.

These methods have the potential to provide teachers with unique opportunities to gain important insights into their own practice. For example, in polyphonic footage taken with 18-month-old Zoe and her teacher Alicia we came to 'see' the central significance of the early years teacher as a compass for Zoe's strategic orientation towards engagement with another. I also discovered that Zoe seemed to be equally and expertly orienting her teacher. The footage that accompanies this image is presented in chapter 4 but, for the moment, I draw your attention to the close physical proximity of Zoe to Alicia – a stance that was consistently evident in footage with young children during their early years experience and one which dialogic pedagogy draws our attention towards.

Paying attention to what can be seen by a variety of participants, as well as what might be heard, is very important for parents too. What might be interpreted as an everyday random or even deviant act from the perspective of one person (often an adult who draws from a very different place) might be viewed very differently when understood with the benefit of additional insights. I have found myself constantly amazed at the remarkable creativity of very young children in strategically orienting themselves through the watchful eye of others – adjusting their language to alter the social event. This is also a principle Bakhtin applied to his work, drawing on the inspiration of writers, artists, poets and dancers to summon a visual approach to understanding that pays attention to both the form and content of any social event, but which also pays heed to the subtle nuances of everyday events as creative potential in the discourse. You will learn more about this as you read on.

FIGURE I.2 Introducing Zoe and Alicia

Engaging with the text

The book is structured in a way that invites a cover-to-cover read of the unfolding concepts and ideas that underpin dialogic pedagogy, supported by examples and models where possible. Chapter 1 begins by providing a contextual background for the ideas that are later explored, and key concepts are introduced. In chapter 2, dialogic pedagogy and its manifestation in contemporary education is presented by drawing from recent research in schools and universities across the world. Chapter 3 explains the relevance of these ideas for early years pedagogy specifically – introducing the small but growing body of research that has been undertaken recently in ECE contexts applying Bakhtin's ideas. The following three chapters explain three important aspects of dialogic pedagogy that are of particular relevance to early years pedagogy, and which I think offer significant provocation to twenty-first-century teachers. Chapter 4 explores the radical idea of 'teaching with love' – a contentious notion for professional teachers to contemplate, while chapter 5 deals with more familiar ideas associated with play in the early years. Don't be fooled into thinking that this chapter is yet another depiction of play as a means of 'knowing' or manipulating learning on the part of the teacher as is the common trend in many countries today. There are some surprises in store here! Chapter 6 juxtaposes the idea of playfulness with seriousness through an examination of one of Bakhtin's most exciting contributions regarding the role of laughter as a form of *carnivalesque*. Finally, chapter 7 examines notions of accountability in the early years by summoning Bakhtin's idea of *heteroglossia* as a route to engaging with diversity in all its forms. The book concludes with a brief summary of the key ideas presented and their provocations for early years teachers. I hope that this final chapter will form the basis for many lively discussions about these ideas and their provocations for you!

As you make your way through the text, I hope you are not distracted by some of the language that I use to convey key ideas. As a pakeha New Zealander I employ terms that reflect my unique social context, which may not be shared by everyone.[1] For instance, when I refer to 'the infant' I mean a nonwalking (or toddling) baby; by 'toddler' I mean a walking young child under the approximate age of two; and by 'young child' I mean anyone between approximately two years and school age. The New Zealand early childhood curriculum, *Te Whāriki*, distinguishes between these age groups but they may be located in the same early years space, and often are. When I speak of a teacher I mean any nonfamilial adult who works with infants, toddlers and young children in formal or informal education and care arrangements. While most teachers are officially qualified in early years pedagogy, some are not. It is important for you to know that all the teachers who feature in this book and video accompaniment are qualified (three years' study), registered (two years' provisional supervision) professionals with several years of teaching experience. They do not approach their work lightly, but at the same time they do not present themselves as perfect either.

By using the term 'key teacher' I refer to the system whereby the infant, toddler or young child is cared for by one or, perhaps, two adults specifically. In the United

Kingdom the key teacher (or primary caregiver as this role is sometimes described) is now legislated in early years settings with infants, but at the time of writing the system is still a choice for New Zealanders. You may have different names for these roles but they are all concerned with the promotion of well-established adult–child relationships based on intimate and consistent communication – a process that is so central to the idea of dialogic pedagogy in the early years.

Finally, I use the term 'early years setting' to refer to a broad range of provision – from the home of the infant, toddler or young child to the education and care centre where most of my filming took place. This does not suggest that these are the only early years settings in the world. Indeed, as societies continue to diversify it is likely that early years settings will expand to places still unimagined. It is in these locales of diversity and difference that I predict Bakhtin's ideas will bear even more fruit, promising stories that are yet to be told.

As a student teacher or someone who works with young children on a daily basis, you may wish to consider the ideas presented in the chapters that follow as an opportunity and provocation to revision your own teaching in your own early years context and in your own time. From a dialogic perspective, such considerations are a provocation for further dialogues, not a set of rules that are to be adhered to. This is a point you will return to again and again through this book.

You are now invited to explore each chapter in terms of its significance to you by responding to a series of provocations throughout and hopefully generating some of your own. As you consider the significance of these ideas to the early years pedagogical experience you are encouraged to consider *your* point-of-view – a position that is essential for you as a dialogic partner. Whether you agree or disagree is less of a priority than the fact that you are thoughtfully engaging with the text, contemplating the significance or potential of the ideas or seeking to deeply understand your response. In my view this is the only way to read Bakhtin – as a living encounter with 'other' – in this case that 'other' is *you*.

Note

1 'Pakeha' refers to people whose ancestors have settled in New Zealand. I am a fourth-generation pakeha with ancestry in Scotland and England.

1

TOWARDS DIALOGISM

By now you may have realised that the term *dialogism* is laden with meanings that expand well beyond the study of dialogue as merely a verbal exchange. While language is indeed central to Bakhtin's thinking, his ideas concerning dialogism are not merely related to the study of verbal conversation and its composition – though such investigation is certainly an important part of his work. Nor are they simply an add-on to other dialogic theories that exist in the work of educationalists. This opening chapter sets the scene for an encounter with dialogism that spans a large part of the last century. Like the ideas he explored over his lifetime, you will discover how Bakhtin's ideas deepen as a result of his willingness to think across disciplines and philosophies during an unrivalled historical era of political change. Beginning with an overview of his fascinating life spanning 80 years in Soviet Russia, this chapter attempts to examine the complex background to what has now come to be known as Bakhtin's overarching theory of dialogism. The central tenets of this theory will be briefly introduced to establish some of the important themes of Bakhtin's work. They are by no means the sum total of all that Bakhtin has to offer but they do set the scene for the particular approach to dialogic pedagogy that underpins this book.

I hope that by the time you have finished this chapter you will realise that Bakhtin's original orientation is towards a philosophy of human development rather than a more rigid psychological or educational approach. Bakhtin raises a persistent philosophical question again and again throughout his texts concerning human consciousness which forms the basis of what we have come to describe as a particular type of dialogic theory:

> The position occupied by consciousness while creating an image of the other and while creating an image of one's own self. At the present time this is the central problem of all philosophy.
>
> *(Entry in wartime notebooks by Bakhtin, published in 1992,*
> *cited in Emerson, 1994, pp. 206–226)*

Bakhtin's quest is therefore not to set about creating a theory that will provide answers but, instead, to raise provocations about the assumptions each person brings to their relationships with others and the consequences of these. You may be left with more questions than answers about the nature of learning, what should be learnt and how it ought to be taught, but this is not Bakhtin's quest. Instead you will be introduced to some of Bakhtin's key ideas that offer fresh provocations for early education concerning relationships, interpretation, 'other' and the profound task of living in an uncertain, polyphonic world. To understand the origin of this philosophical approach I begin with a brief biography of Bakhtin, followed by an introduction to the ideas that underpin his ideas concerning dialogism. I hope that by understanding a little about Bakhtin and the world in which his ideas developed you will gain important insights into his unique approach to dialogism, and why an expanded view of pedagogy plays such a central role to his thinking. As you work your way through this chapter it may be helpful to take note of key terms and associated ideas that emerge. Many of them may be new or unfamiliar to you. But you will revisit these time and time again throughout this book so it is worth taking a bit of time to understand the provocative role each of these ideas plays in thinking about dialogic pedagogy and all that it might mean for the early years.

The life of Mikhail Bakhtin (1895–1975)

Caryl Emerson (1995), one of the people responsible for bringing Mikhail Bakhtin's ideas to the West, believes that "a major thinker [such as Bakhtin] deserves to be known in his genesis" (p. 107). Since his death in 1975 many people have tried to claim the 'real' Bakhtin, only to discover the many loopholes that lie in their wake. I do not make any such claim but, instead, attempt to piece together identified fragments from Bakhtin's life as a means of trying to locate the ideas in time and space. For this reason it is important to begin at the beginning of Bakhtin's long life on 16 November 1895 in the town of Orel, south of Moscow, in the Russian Empire. His childhood was spent in Vilnius and Odessa where he was the second in a family of five children. At nine years of age Bakhtin contracted a serious case of osteomyelitis, a bone infection that led to the amputation of his right leg 33 years later. The lifelong pain he suffered as a result must have been excruciating and perhaps explains why his work, especially in the early years, places a great deal of emphasis on the body.

Born to parents who held liberal views and the means to instil these in their children through education, Bakhtin enrolled as a 'free attendant' (someone who attends lectures but does not complete exams) at Novorossjskjj University in Odessa (1913–1916) and then at the University of Petrograd (1916–1918) where he studied classics and philology. Though it is uncertain if he ever graduated (some scholars even suggest he lied about his qualifications) both subjects are evident throughout his lingering emphasis on the relationship between literature and language, words and their meanings.

Bakhtin was also a teacher for a good part of his life – working at the Mordovian State Pedagogical Institute in Saransk for many years as Department Head of World

Literature. In his classrooms he was able to bring both interests together and engage his students in many lively encounters with text and each other's ideas. It is perhaps unsurprising that his students held him in high esteem – the efforts they went to in order to preserve his ideas in adverse situations are testimony to this fact.

It is important to understand the political situation in which Bakhtin found himself at various points in his life. Many of Bakhtin's friends were executed for their beliefs during the Soviet Union's totalitarian years (the 1930s and '40s) when ideas were closely controlled by the state. It is hardly surprising that one of Bakhtin's most important ideas concerning monologism and heteroglossia (described in Russian in terms such as *raznorechie*, *raznogolosie* and *raznojazyie*) conveys the message that any thought or act that has ultimate supremacy over others, shuts them down or denies their right to speak stifles all forms of creativity and life. This idea was to form the basis of Bakhtin's emphasis on culture as a boundary concept. By this he meant that culture only exists when experienced alongside 'other'; without 'other' Bakhtin believed that culture was dead because it had no lived meaning – a dangerous idea in the Soviet Union at this time. It has been surmised that Bakhtin escaped a tragic death only because of his ability to write in riddle or to contradict ideas. Other scholars suggest it is due to the vigilance of those around him, who sought to protect him and his ideas.

Even with such strategies Bakhtin did not escape being sentenced to exile on Solovetsky Island in the arctic seas of northwestern Russia for a short period following his arrest in 1929 on the charge that he was engaged in an underground Russian Orthodox Church movement. Whether or not this is true remains a mystery, but we do know that he actually served his sentence in Kustanai, Kazakhstan. His deteriorating health kept Bakhtin in Kustanai even after he had completed his sentence, and it was during this 11-year period that several of his key texts were conceived.

Although initially rejected at a doctoral candidate degree level in 1946, Bakhtin's doctoral thesis – on laughter – was subsequently awarded a PhD in English in 1952. However, under the repressive regime of the 1940s and early '50s, he could do very little to promote his work outside of the classroom. Indeed, had it not been for a group of his students discovering his manuscripts and publishing them in the period known as 'the Khrushchev thaw', you might not be reading this book. The remarkable humility of Bakhtin, the man, is underscored by his equally remarkable life – a life that was lived as a thinker who played with ideas and, somewhat ironically, answered to no one.

Bakhtin's writing first arrived on the scene in the West in 1968. By this time his thesis was not only published in English, but some of his work had also been translated into Italian and French – establishing an international thirst for more. The gradual introduction of his texts over subsequent years meant that his ideas were now accessible to many parts of the world, except Russia where his work was not formally published until 1979 and even then as heavily censored fragments. By his death in 1975 Bakhtin had become internationally renowned – serving as a symbol of post-Stalinist hope and optimism in an increasingly diverse and globalised world – yet he never saw his work celebrated in his own country. His continued influence reflects the strength of his work not so much in finding solutions or creating theories, but in its examination of, and response to, serious philosophical problems that are still relevant today.

Bakhtin's key informants

Reading Bakhtin can be challenging for a number of reasons. One is that he does not stick to one discipline or consistent philosophical orientation; instead he is somewhat of a two-faced Janus because his work is often located at the intersections, or boundaries, between ideas. By this I mean that he looks one way towards his formalist Kantian heritage and the other to poststructuralist thought – never settling in one place or the other completely. I concur with Daphna Erdinast-Vulcan's (1997) explanation of Bakhtin's work and its location "not in its neat dovetailing into postmodernism, but in a self-conscious threshold position, that is, its fundamental unresolved ambivalence" (p. 252). A further frustration is that his texts are not necessarily neatly finished. Indeed, as I mention earlier, he was not always responsible for their publication. The stories of his manuscripts make for interesting reading – some used as paper for cigarettes, others lost and yet others compiled by his students in later years. As a result, much of his work is in fragments that make them challenging to read. His ideas, read in isolation and often out of order, do not seem to follow a logical sequence, repeating many of the same thoughts through different routes over time.

It is also not always clear that you in fact are reading Bakhtin. Like several other scholars of his era, Bakhtin was notorious for borrowing ideas from writers, poets and philosophers he had met or read about. He has been described, perhaps not altogether unfairly, as a master plagiariser because he does not always fully acknowledge the contributions of others in his writing. However, of known and substantial significance to his theory of dialogism are several German philosophers including Kant and the poet Goethe, Russian writer Dostoevsky and French writer Rabelais to name a few. Each, in their own way, played a shaping role in the development of Bakhtin's work – as antagonists or collaborators alike – with apologies to those many others who have not made it to these pages.

Johann Wolfgang von Goethe (1749–1832): An orientation that Bakhtin developed towards the idea of interpretation through and with 'other' was deeply implicated by the German poet and philosopher Goethe. In particular, Bakhtin was very influenced by Goethe's notion that one should give way to the work of the eye as a means of understanding. Goethe's notion of 'great time' – one that takes account of the past, present and future was to form the basis for his own theory of visual surplus drawing on the German concept of *Bildungsroman*, or becoming (White, 2014a). The idea that seeing is an authorial gift to 'other' is enshrined in Bakhtin's notions of answerability (*otvetstvennost*) and authorship – both of which we explore later in this chapter.

Immanuel Kant (1724–1804): Kant was responsible for Bakhtin's emphasis on the moral aspects of human behaviour and the importance of context on how this is viewed. Bakhtin was also heavily influenced by members of the neo-Kantian Marburg School, such as Hermann Cohen, Paul Natorp and Ernst Cassirer, and most especially those who reacted against their ideas (including Martin Heidegger and Friedrich Nietzsche). Bakhtin's good friend, Matvei Kagan, was a student from the Marburg School. Through these important dialogues Bakhtin was able to go beyond what he saw as a very limiting Kantian view of morality when considered as a universal concept. For Bakhtin there was always an opportunity to move past any imperative 'norms' or 'oughts' because it was possible for individuals to take concrete steps beyond their present way of being in response to others. Here originates the ideas of 'self-other' and ethics we discuss in chapter 4, and of *postupok* – a concept we will explore in detail in chapter 5.

Fyodor Dostoevsky (1821–1881): A well-known Russian novelist from the 1800s, Dostoevsky wrote in a way that avoided speaking on behalf of his characters. Bakhtin was tantalised by this artistic device, called *polyphony*. He devoted one whole book to this and related ideas called *Problems of Dostoevsky's Poetics* (1984). Dostoevsky's own writing often focused on human suffering. His attention to emotions such as love and pain probably made sense to Bakhtin, who placed heavy emphasis on human acts in his early work. *Problems of Dostoevsky's Poetics* was the first of Bakhtin's books to be published, not long before his arrest in 1929. We explore emotion specifically in chapter 4 and revisit polyphony time and time again throughout this book.

François Rabelais (1494–1553): Central to Bakhtin's thesis on laughter was the writing of French humanist François Rabelais. Writing about Middle Age peasant culture and the influence of Renaissance on its legitimacy, Rabelais provided Bakhtin with a context through which he could expand his thinking by introducing a genre called *carnivalesque*. In this genre officialdom is suspended in order to unsettle authoritative dogma. Laughter is a primary source of language utilised in carnivalesque as a kind of de-crowning of hierarchy and power (Bakhtin, 1968). Here Bakhtin's consideration of discourse flourished – providing a means of exploring alternative ideas in an era where they were very dangerous to entertain. We will examine carnivalesque and associated concepts in chapter 6.

Max Scheler (1874–1928): In contrast to Kantian laws of morality, Scheler advocated for a very different values base to human relations (Scheler, 1954). Scheler separated feelings from values, arguing for the presence of value-facts (i.e. based on what can be seen) and the problem of relativity that creates diverse ways of responding. His distinction between the spirit and the psyche formed the basis to his approach of sympathy as a perceived response. Scheler's suggestion that engagement with other (as an act or deed of love, or hate for that matter) is imbued with our own feelings and experiences and sets the scene for a view of 'other' in the lifelong development of self. This was an important influence in Bakhtin's interpretation of aesthetic love, which will be discussed in chapter 4.

There are many other philosophers, scientists, thinkers and writers that Bakhtin drew upon in developing his dialogic philosophy over the years. Appreciating the legacy of his ideas and their relationship to the past lends much to our thinking about their meaning both today and in the future.

The Bakhtin Circles: As was often the case in early twentieth-century Russia, Bakhtin spent many evenings in the company of like-minded thinkers in 'circles' that met regularly to discuss and debate important ideas. The influence of members of what is now described as the Bakhtin Circle cannot be understated in the development of his ideas. Todorov (1984) describes one formulation of the Bakhtin Circle as an eclectic group of artists, writers and philosophers who met in Nevel following the 1917 Russian Revolution. A second circle met in the nearby centre of Vitebsk (1919–1920) and still another in Petrograd in 1924. During this time in Russian history there was a short period of political freedom heralded by the overthrow of capitalism and the promise of freedom. Not only was there a radical shift in geographical,[1] ideological and artistic boundaries, but these were deliberately encountered, indeed welcomed, in public open dialogues where Bakhtin and his friends met to explore their ideas.

We can see the influence of these circles on Bakhtin's ideas in many ways and several Bakhtinian scholars have explained the significance of each of the circles on Bakhtin's thinking (see for example edited volumes by Brandist, 2002, and Shepherd, 1998). Their contributing ideas are important in the development of Bakhtin's earliest ideas concerning I-thou relationships, aesthetics, answerability and authorship but can also be traced forward to his later writing (Nikolaev, 1998). Among others, linguist Valentin Voloshinov (1895–1936), neo-Kantian Matvei Isavich Kagan (1889–1937), Pavel Medvedev (1891–1938) and Lev Pompianskii (1891–1940) contributed to these groups and offered Bakhtin many provocations – as he did them. Bakhtin's lingering interest in ideas that relate to the details of interpretation and seeing (among other concepts that underpin dialogism) were fuelled throughout this unprecedented period of creativity in Russia and can be summarised as "an aesthetics of verbal interaction" (Zima, 1989, p. 98) that was to later form the basis of dialogism.

An important idea that later arose from the circles was the notion that every cultural act lives essentially on the boundaries. Gaining inspiration through art, literature and life, consciousness was revisioned as a series of polyphonic events that live in the flux of otherness – both in terms of people and time/space dimensions. The idea was that when an artistic position becomes too fixed, as the formalist approaches that were privileged at the time promoted, culture could not survive because it lost its creativity (something Bakhtin and his friends had seen happening in reality in Russia under autocratic rule). This principle lay at the centre of Bakhtin's sustained philosophical interrogation of neo-Kantianism (in a nutshell, the idea that understanding is produced by the subject not by some preordained categories), phenomenology (emphasizing lived encounter at the heart of understanding) and *Lebensphilosophie* (locating understanding as a lifelong process of going beyond the limits of oneself).

As you may have guessed, this era of thought marks the early beginnings of post-formalist thinking that was to develop over the next century in Europe and, later, in America post–World War II. Although Bakhtin never completely abandoned his postformalist origins, his work took another turn in his eventual attention to discourse throughout his later texts. Scholars do not agree on the extent to which his later work reflects his earlier ideas, not helped by their out-of-order publication; but I agree with Deborah Hicks (2000), who suggests that although there was a certain shift towards discourse as opposed to language in his later work, Bakhtin never abandoned the original ideas completely. In particular, she suggests that the intentionality of language that framed the early work of the circle reappeared as *genre* in his later texts, and that his early attention to self–other relationships is evident in his later orientation towards discourse. Bakhtin's moral entreaty permeates all his work even though its emphasis shifts over time.

It was during the 'circle' encounters, where Bakhtin was introduced to diverse cross-disciplinary ideas in a climate of 'free' speech, that he played out many of the dialogic principles we will discuss throughout this book. Such encounters not only provided a rich groundswell of thinking during this period in Russian history, but they also set the scene for radical thought concerning creativity itself. Taken together they make up the complex theory of dialogism that encapsulates all of Bakhtin's thinking. Notwithstanding Craig Brandist's (2002) cautionary note concerning a criticial engagement "with the work of the Circle rather than simply adopt[ing] any of their specific formulations" (p. 5), there are many provocations arising from these important ideas.

The Marxist influence: In my view there can be little doubt that, due to the era in which he lived and his association with other Marxists, Bakhtin was also influenced by the ideas of Karl Marx (1967). Even though Bakhtin rejected outright the communist regime that was to unfold in his country during Stalin's reign, the original work of Marx and Engels in *The Communist Manifesto* would have been at his disposal. Several members of the Bakhtin Circle, who profoundly influenced Bakhtin's work, were known Marxists. Their ideas on the sociocultural nature of language were part of a much larger school of thought emanating from, among other influences, German philosopher Georg Wilhelm Friedrich Hegel, who influenced Marx himself. While Bakhtin drew on these ideas, in particular in his writing with Voloshinov (1929/1973) and Medvedev (1978), who applied them to the study of language, he differed markedly in his rejection of systems, dualisms and, with this, the idea of material dialectics that was so central to Marxist thought. Bakhtin was deeply suspicious of organised political activity, systems or dogma because it had the potential to represent another form of totalitarianism (or what he described as *monologism*). For Bakhtin there always needed to be a dialogue that was accessible to the individual speaker, who held personal, ethical accountability, rather than a distanced political stance that allowed others to speak on their behalf.

Unlike many scholars who have since employed Marxist ideas to make claims about politics and democracy, Bakhtin did not concern himself directly with issues of social justice or human rights. He was deeply conservative and suspicious of any ideology that had the potential to dominate and silence another. He has been harshly criticised and, I think, as a result dismissed in many contemporary postrevolutionary education contexts for this. But it is important to realise that Bakhtin's orientation was not towards events that occurred as collective activities but rather as individual responses and interactions as events. His ideas implicate people for their action or inaction in response to what is placed before them, rather than any isolated event that they are initially faced with. Bakhtin suggests there is no excuse for indifference because each is responsible for his or her own acts and has the opportunity to make choices accordingly. This is a theme that has great significance for education too, as we shall see in the chapter that follows.

Bakhtin today

Since Bakhtin's death a great many scholars have built on these ideas in various ways. Some have taken aspects of Bakhtin's ideas and aligned them with others – for instance, you can read a lot of claims in sociocultural texts that suggest Bakhtin is a kind of sequel to Lev Vygotksy's sociocultural theories – an idea that is hotly contested (see the educational work of Matusov, 2011; Roth, 2013; Wertsch & Smolka, 1994; and White, 2014b, to name a few). Martin Buber and Emmanuel Levinas are often summoned in discussions of dialogism alongside Bakhtin due to their emphasis on I-thou relationships but, while they share an emphasis on relationships, Bakhtin takes a very different approach (see Perlina, 1984). Some scholars have added seemingly incompatible ideas to Bakhtin's thinking as a means of disruption, while others try to understand the ideas in context. Still others have creatively employed seemingly unconnected ideas to make sense of Bakhtin. A recent example is offered by Rupert Wegerif (2013) when he utilises Maurice Merleau-Ponty's notion of 'chiasm' to suggest that the in-between space in dialogue promoted by Bakhtin is like a 'hinge' that allows us to explore contradiction as creativity (see also Shotter, 2012). This may be a useful metaphor to employ when thinking about some of Bakhtin's ideas but it does not replace them by any means. For this reason, the section that follows focuses on Bakhtin's work solely, though it is important to remember his persistent dialogue with other points of view – an approach that not only characterises his own thinking but underpins the very nature of Bakhtin's dialogism.

Bakhtin's dialogism

Dialogism, which attempts to span all of these complex ideas concerning language and meaning, can be loosely described as a kind of 'in-between-ness' because it is always concerned with the social space between people. Meaning is not rooted in people's self-contained statements and it cannot be generated outside of the social space because, from this point of view, meaning represents complex, often contradictory or confusing interpretations of 'lived truths' as they are encountered in each moment. Hence meaning is a process rather than a fixed idea that gets handed down or passed from one person to the next – the idea changes according to those who are exploring it, the time of their discoveries, their context and their way of looking at the world. In this flux Bakhtin suggests there are opportunities for *transgradience* – that is, the capacity to 'see' more than would otherwise be accessible and to be enriched by the discoveries.

This social space exists as a kind of essential border through which one can appreciate another without being fully consumed by them. Here, and only here, is where meaning is revealed – not in the heads of individuals who deliver or receive information but in the living act of dialogue itself. In Russian this is called *pravda* or 'lived knowing'. Ideas only become real when they are grounded and experienced in the social world, not passed over from one person or text to another. Meaning can thus be encountered through everyday struggles with language in all its many forms, as it is shared with 'other'. Such is the central thesis of dialogism.

Key principles of dialogism

Although the umbrella term 'dialogism' captures all of Bakhtin's ideas in one, it is helpful to understand some of the important principles that underpin this term and its use throughout this book. The interpretations here are my own, based on ideas I have gained from reading Bakhtin's own extensive work (as well as members of the circles) and the scholarship of others who have since shared an interest in understanding his ideas. My informants are primarily those writing in the West since, as a non-Russian speaker, I do not have access to Russian texts. As a twenty-first-century reader of English translations of Bakhtin and the work of the circles, I have been able to read texts chronologically rather than in the order they were published. I am particularly drawn to Bakhtin's early philosophical works as the basis for an examination of human intersubjectivity which, in my view, has great relevance to early years pedagogy.

While I distinguish between this emphasis on relationships in the early writing of the circle, and the linguistic 'turn' heralded by Voloshinov's (1929/1973) emphasis on language more specifically, I concur with several writers who suggest that some fundamental principles remained throughout the lifetime of Bakhtin's work. I draw on my own subjective reading of the text accordingly, as well as on those who have variously discussed Bakhtin's significance in a historical, political and philosophical context (see for example, Shepherd, Brandist, Todorov, Emerson, Holquist Tihanov; see also Zbinden, 2006). Navigating one's way through this complexity and the different orientations of each is no mean feat. But in the end this interpretation is my own. For readers who want a more complex analysis of the various epochs of Bakhtin's work, they will need to turn to my esteemed peers for further insight.

Notwithstanding this cautionary note, here are the main ideas you will encounter as you read on. They are by no means all of the important ideas Bakhtin has to offer, but they are ones you will need to take with you as you journey through the text. Each is discussed in the next section.

1. Answerability
2. Becoming
3. Aesthetics
4. Authorship
5. Polyphony

1. Answerability (otvetstvennost)

This concept is first introduced in Bakhtin's earliest works where he describes the ethical process of trying to understand 'other' as an unrepeatable, nontransferable act of evaluation through answer and response. Bakhtin takes considerable time to explain this process as both an intimate act of love (insider stance) and an external act of accountability (outsider stance). Both, he says, are necessary. He uses a range of helpful metaphors to explain the absolute necessity of 'other' in any individual's life. Bakhtin's imagery of someone trying to pull oneself up by one's own hair conveys the importance of others in the way we see ourselves. It makes sense when you think about how much we are all influenced by what others say about us. A look, gesture or sound, as easily as a word, can convey meaning that we interpret against our own experience.

What we have learnt from our very earliest experience – words spoken, the tone in which they were spoken, actions and even looks – have traces of influence throughout our lives. In this sense we are all shaped by one another and therefore, Bakhtin suggests, answerable for each other's lives.

Thinking about answerability in the early years provides a means through which we can consider the significant impact of our acts on the lives of infants, toddlers and young children, whether we recognise this or not. Of course this goes both ways, and we can think about the extent to which very young children influence us – sometimes in very subtle ways. Answerability brings with it accountabilities and responsibilities to ourselves and for others. For Bakhtin, it is a moral imperative. Answerability is therefore an important concept to think about when we talk of early years pedagogy, as we most certainly will in various ways throughout the chapters that follow.

2. Becoming (stanovienie)

If we accept the idea that we are answerable to others and, in turn, influenced by them in profound ways, it is hardly surprising to learn that Bakhtin promoted the idea that we are always in a state of becoming (well, at least until the point of death, where there is no further opportunity for engagement!). He borrowed the term *Bildungsroman* from Goethe to capture this idea of constant evolvement. In this lifelong process of becoming, each individual is always on the border between transitory states with the potential to be other than what they seem. Seen in this way there is no such thing as a fixed person who stays the same regardless of their circumstances, moving unaffected from one life event to another. Instead each of us is seen as a complex personality who emerges through experiences over time, place and encounters with 'other'. Without 'other', Bakhtin suggests, subjectivity is limited. We always have the opportunity to exercise agency through relationships with others since diverse ways of thinking and doing can be revealed in ways that alter the way we are thought of by others, and perhaps even ourselves. Chapters 5, 6 and 7 look at this idea in various ways.

No doubt you will already be beginning to see the importance of this idea for early years practice where infants, toddlers and young children are so often 'assessed' according to standards that do not bear any significance to their own. From a dialogic stance we are invited to maintain an openness to our understanding of children and their potentialities. This idea is repeated throughout the book in relation to important early years concepts such as pedagogy, play and learning, culminating in chapter 7.

3. Aesthetics (esteticheskii)

Aesthetics as a central means of appreciating other was very important to Bakhtin in his early works. But understanding language acts in terms of their form and interpreted meaning was never enough for him. He was equally concerned with the emotional-volitional (*emotsionalaniy no volevoi*) tone that accompanies voice and its lived experience. For Bakhtin this was a route to *axiology* – the value that sits behind judgements. Axiology is both an ethical (asking "what is right or good?") as well as an aesthetic (asking "what is beautiful or worthy?") stance.

What sets Bakhtin apart, and was to form his subsequent scholarship, was his resistance to dichotomies such as 'you' versus 'me' – suggesting that it is not a case of either self or other but 'us' in aesthetic relationships. In other words the self *needs* other to be the self in all its complexity. In this depiction intersubjectivity is more fully realised because communicating subjects recognise themselves and their ideas while giving feedback to their social partners. Identity becomes a plural concept here because our understandings of ourselves are constantly altering and altered in relations with others – what Susan Petrelli describes as a logic of otherness where "subjectivity is not given once and for all" (2013, p. xxv). Language is therefore expressed rather than being delivered by one to the other (as if each were uninfluenced by the event in which the language takes place). Hence there is not one but two phenomena at play here – the first is the event itself (or the semantic), while the second is the event of narrating itself (or the pragmatic). Each subject, both author and interpreter alike, is formed through dialogue in everyday life; each event is unique and never to be repeated due to these complexities.

Aesthetics is thus an ideological event of becoming that takes place between people and, in this sense, betrays and portrays meaning. Gary Morson and Caryl Emerson (1990) suggest four ways of engaging in Bakhtin's aesthetics:

a.   physical perception,
b.   recognition,
c.   contextual significance and
d.   active dialogic understanding (p. 99).

Dialogic understanding occupies much of Bakhtin's thought, as it will ours throughout this book. To achieve such understanding Bakhtin believed that individuals needed to try to understand 'other' by suspending their own truths. It was this thinking that formed the basis of his understanding of authorship as creative, aesthetic understanding. Chapter 4 looks at this idea closely in the context of loving contemplation.

4. Authorship

Bringing together notions of answerability and aesthetics, the idea behind authorship conveys the principle that relationships with 'other' are not simply chance encounters that occur in isolation as a given event. As people engage with each other they are also evaluating each other and acting on these evaluations – whether we realise it or not. Authorship is thus an essential aspect of being human, and everyone is implicated. To author each other, as answerable subjects in dialogue, we need to take the time to understand one another as individuals in a particular moment in time and space. Bakhtin offers a cautionary note here though. If the balance between intimate engagement and external, perhaps impartial, accountability shifts too much in one direction or the other, authorship turns into a form of submission or manipulation. With no distance between author and hero (the subject of our evaluation), he argues that the individual whom we are trying to understand (the hero) may be consumed by the 'other' (that is, the author), who is working hard to interpret according to their assumption of sharedness (or intersubjectivity). Alternatively, if the author is too removed from the hero, they are unable to appreciate the fuller creative potential of meanings in these acts – through which they themselves are implicated. Neither extreme is a desirable stance, suggests Bakhtin, yet both feature (often tenuously) in the authorship process and warrant our attention.

Understanding that authorship is concerned with subjectivities in relationship with each other presents significant provocation. For Bakhtin, unlike many of his contemporaries, there is no 'object' of dialogue. There are only mutual subjects who are capable of speaking for themselves in communication with others. Thus what can be interpreted and how it is interpreted is just as important as what is discovered. Voice lies at the heart of this entreaty and invites us, as early years scholars, to consider the opportunities we provide for infants, toddlers and young children to be seen and heard as complex subjects in their own right – not merely objects to be manipulated for adult purposes or unknown entities. Moreover, it provides opportunities for adults to contemplate the extent to which they too are authored in relationships. This idea is keenly excavated in chapter 3 where we analyse voice(s) – in all their many forms – as a source of wonderment, responsibility and responsivity.

5. Polyphony

In his later works Bakhtin takes the idea of authorship further to describe the 'other' of the authoring self as an addressee. Here he introduces the notion that each of us uses multiple voices to speak, and that these draw from our past, present and imagined futures. The dialogic event is now characterised by a polyphonic chorus of voices – each competing and jousting for a place. In this sense we are always answerable to ourselves, each other and to those voices that shape (or shaped) our experience. This is also a deeply ethical stance that, Bakhtin argues, leads to a choice-making personality who is capable of making moral judgements beyond any prescribed 'ought'. In this way Bakhtin offers a view of life as a responsive act to events that we cannot necessarily prevent but which we can encounter in a number of ways. This is a very powerful idea that promotes individual agency in all circumstances. For the early years we can see its significance in the multiple voices each child brings to their experience – voices from the family, the community, culture, the corporeal lives of our youngest and perhaps even distant voices from the womb. That we cannot always 'see' these, or their significance in any event, makes them all the more provocative.

Studying dialogism

Because Bakhtin was able to develop his ideas over a long period of time he was also able to provide the means through which they might be studied. His orientation is clearly towards language in all its many forms, and it is important to remember that when Bakhtin speaks of language he is not simply talking about words. He also invokes the body in all its forms. Though very fragmented, in his last book, *Speech Genres and Other Late Essays* (1986), Bakhtin offers five key strategies for a dialogic interrogation of language events:

   1. Utterance (*vyskazyvanie*) refers to the two-sided act of dialogue that shares territory. It is comprised of a series of language forms that combine to form a particular stabilised speech genre (*zhanr*) that makes a response possible. It is a constant struggle to enact answerability that characterises utterance in dialogue. For this reason utterance is described by Bakhtin as "the language of life" (1986, p. 63). Bakhtin suggests that words (as well as other forms of language) need to be understood as utterance, not in separate parts but as links in a communicative chain.

   Many dialogic researchers employ utterance as the unit of analysis, taking into account not only the event itself but also the point of view of participants regarding that event. Meaning is generated from diverse ideological standpoints rather than some sort of collective response that is achieved through consensus. In my research with Zoe, Lola and Harrison, I asked the adult participants – teachers and parents – to contribute their interpretations on what they saw or experienced as a central means of understanding the infants' meaning-making in the social world. In this way I avoided speaking on their behalf and took responsibility for the additional interpretations I made along the way as a result of the significant surplus now at my disposal. There were many moments where each of us – parents, teachers and myself as a researcher – saw the same event very differently, even with polyphonic footage that showed us the same images. I came to appreciate that our interpretations were deeply informed by the ideologies we brought to our seeing. Each added a different layer to our understanding but did not (and could not) resolve the philosophical tensions of Bakhtin's dialogic entreaty. Appreciating this complexity is an especially important pedagogical imperative for the early years, as we will explore in the chapters that follow.

   2. Speech genre (*zhanr*) are relatively stable combinations of language forms and their meaning in dialogue. They make utterance visible by revealing the way language can be interpreted by 'other' based on a shared set of conventions. They are made up of form (the kind of language combinations that are used) + content (their interpreted meaning) that draw from the past but exist in the present. Bakhtin suggests that there are two types of genre. The first, primary genre, refers to simple, unmediated language combinations that develop through everyday dialogues. Secondary genre are already developed forms of cultural communication, such as professional jargon. Utterance reveals their value in dialogue, but they retain their meaning in certain cultural contexts. As Bakhtin explains: "Genre serves as an external template, but the great artist awakens the semantic possibilities that lie within it" (1986, p. 5). James Cresswell and Ulrich Teucher (2011) address some of its significance in the early years:

> As a child experiences more speech genres, her actions undertaken at the nexus of these demands are experienced as a collision of emotional–volitional world-shaping tones. In other words, she finds herself in a condition where she is compelled to act to satisfy juxtaposed obligations and respond to others in kind. For example, a child would be compelled to respond to the caregiver from a speech genre learned at daycare and be compelled to respond to the daycare worker from the blue-collar maleness speech genre. Each emotional–volitional tone is lived and experienced such that each could apprehend the other as wrong. Children are brought into the full polyphony of others that includes a compellingness to respond to other communities as wrong.
>
> *(p. 116)*

   There are several implications that arise from the positioning of some speech genres as 'wrong' when young children enter in and out of dynamic spaces, such as early years settings. These are considered throughout the book in terms such as 'professionalisation' and 'pedagogicalization'.

   3. Chronotope (*khronotop*) is the place that ultimately determines how meaning is made. It is made up of three central and interrelated features:

a.   time,
b.   space and
c.   axiology.

In essence chronotope defines the significance of any particular genre and its use according to the time and place of its delivery. It offers a way of making sense of meaning and its relevance at a particular point in history.

We can think of many examples of genre that might hold more meaning in one time and place than another. In education we might examine aspects of curriculum, styles of teaching and their relationship to one another as a way of understanding which genres are valued in any particular setting (White, 2013). For example contemporary early years pedagogy in many countries today places a great deal of value on photographs of children or other forms of documentation, such as selected artwork or depicting moments of perceived significance through the use of portfolios. This genre is valued in our contemporary ocular-centric age because we now have access to image-producing devices and we live in an era that is oriented towards the visual. What makes up this chronotope, however, is not merely the portfolio itself but its use in describing aspects of children's learning that are valued by those who compile it. This intensive use of documentation has, I think, altered the nature of early years experience: teachers are taking photographs or collecting artwork that indicates its value to the child, to the parent and to society as a form of pedagogy. Children quickly understand the value of these images to others and often ask for their photo to be taken when they have something they wish to share (conversely a teacher recently told me about two boys who hid their artwork from the teacher because they thought she was going to take a photograph of it). Within this chronotope, learning appears to be valued when, and only when, it can be captured visually as a source of evidence. Twenty years ago, or even 20 years into the future, learning might be seen very differently depending on what is valued at the time, by whom and for what purpose.

In the next few chapters you will learn about other chronotopes researchers have examined in early years settings. For Bakhtin chronotope gets really interesting when one contradicts, co-exists or collides with another, causing friction or perhaps cracks in its armour. His concept of chronotopic thresholds is of great interest here – suggesting a means of understanding how events where people draw from different ideological spaces have the potential to act as a means of *transgradience* – that is, a way of seeing more than one's own limited point of view. Thresholds are important meeting places in pedagogy too, where clashes and collisions are an essential component of learning. There are many potential threshold encounters in early years settings to be explored.

4. Visual surplus (*izbytok*). As we have already established, Bakhtin viewed the 'seeing eye' as the highest authority in any interpretation. What can be seen and how it can be seen takes precedence over any third-person report or interpretation. However, it is important to recognise that when he speaks of 'seeing' Bakhtin is not talking of merely a cursory look or a glance (what the Greeks called *eidos*) or a manipulative type of observation, but seeing that is "saturated with all the complexity of thought and cognition" (1986, p. 27). Bakhtin argues that we cannot

see ourselves in the way that another person can. We cannot step outside of ourselves as it were. Therefore what another person can offer us through their seeing
is additional insight, or authorial gift, into ourselves that we would not otherwise
have access to. Due to the deeply ethical nature of such an act, Bakhtin (1986)
cautions readers not to interpret visual surplus as "a chance to sneak up and attack
from behind" (p. 299). It is very important that in the first instance any insights are
honestly and openly expressed to those involved. It is their lives that are implicated,
after all.

You will see that we have come full circle and are also referring to the significance of answerability. I took this concept very seriously in my research, developing
a method I called 'polyphonic video' which allowed me to metaphorically see the
world through the eyes of other by inviting different visual and interpreted perspectives on the same event. The purpose of this method was not merely to see
differently but to see with a view to building a richer picture of experience as a
dialogic event. By now you will understand that this approach is an attempt to
operationalise all the principles discussed in this chapter in a philosophical as well
as an empirical sense.

5. Heteroglossia (*raznojazycie*). Given Bakhtin's emphasis on interpretation
it is no surprise to discover that he also conceptualised a means of understanding
its complexity. The concept of *heteroglossia* captures this complexity by examining
colliding and competing polyphonic voices, as discourse – the "concrete, living
totality" (1984, p. 181) of language – that exists in utterance. Heteroglossia was, of
course, not the word Bakhtin used. Busch (2014) explains that the term is better
captured in his concepts of *raznojazycie* (meaning linguistic variation or multiplicity of languages) and *raznogolosie* (meaning diversity of individual voices). Taken
together they depict heteroglossia as "embracing multifaceted and multilayered
plurality" (p. 24). Remember that the key idea of dialogism is to suspend certainty,
never allowing any one voice (this includes any internal or external voice that is
employed by an individual) to completely take over or consume others, so it is no
surprise that this principle led Bakhtin to his own interrogation of utterance across
different contexts including everyday communication. He attends to this through
the study of intersections between *authoritative discourse* (which he describes as the
unchanging "voice of the fathers" that is passed down to us) and *internally persuasive
discourse* (which refers to the evolving ideas people bring from the discourses they
are part of). For Bakhtin neither should take precedence but play out in the heteroglot, challenging and resisting one another in a constant ideological battle. Unlike
many democratic processes it is not a question of winners and losers, synthesis or
dialectical understanding, but of generating meanings as a source of insight. He
uses the scientific metaphor of *centripetal* (unifying) and *centrifugal* (de-centralising)[2]
forces to convey the process of jostling for meaning, suggesting that both intersubjectivity (shared meaning) and alterity (dissensus of meaning) are necessary for this
to occur.

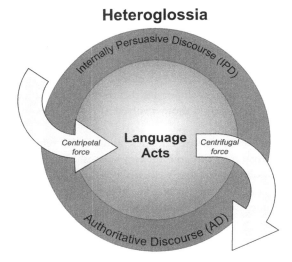

FIGURE 1.1 Heteroglossia

Heteroglossia offers us a way of thinking about dialogue in contemporary regimes of accountability which demand certainty in the early years. Heteroglossia reminds us to examine the extent to which voices are shut down or invited to join the chorus and warns us of the dangers in monologic ways of engaging with other. It allows us to become much more critical of meaning as received knowledge or truth. In a dialogic world, diversity is not only necessary but essential. It is not something that we strive for – it already exists in all language.

Bringing the ideas together

It may be helpful to use a beginning example to highlight these ideas. Watch the footage of Lola eating, or at least trying very hard to eat, popcorn at morning tea in her early years setting. This footage (see '01 Single screen from infant visual field' in the video companion) is taken from her own camera view.

Watch the footage of this event.
    What can you see through Lola's lens?
    Now watch the same event taken from a polyphonic standpoint – the camera view of Lola, her teacher, her 4-month-old peer Harrison and me as the researcher.

FIGURE 1.2 Single screen from infant visual field

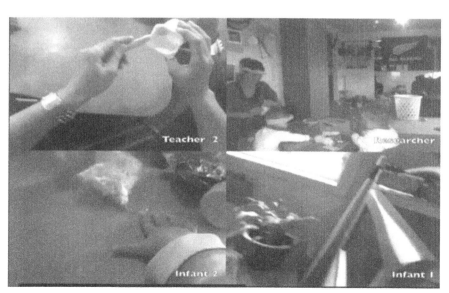

FIGURE 1.3 Polyphonic split screen from four visual fields

What more can you see? How does the added visual perspective expand on your understanding of the experience? What did you notice about the teacher? About Harry, Lola's 2-year-old peer who is 'sharing' her morning tea? Did you:

- think about the genre (plural) in use and their orientation?
- reflect on the chronotope that gives this event meaning to you (or which you cannot access and which makes you wonder what its meaning might be)?
- consider the competing voices at play in the wider setting (or heteroglot)?
- pay attention to your own competing discourses (professional, personal or both) either in your head or in dialogue with others?

What ideologies (ideas, assumptions, assertions from the discourses you draw from) do you bring to your seeing and why? What alternative ways could you look at this event? What does this footage reveal to you about Lola – as a creative agent in her own life, as a personality? Moreover, what does this footage reveal about *you*?

In asking these questions I am inviting you to contemplate the complex, irreconcilable nature of human relationships that call for meaning while simultaneously evading interpretation. In the moment of their delivery we are summoned to a response while at the same time deeply implicated in whatever the reply. Welcome to the theory of dialogism!

Looking back, looking ahead

Dialogism and its related concepts have been employed by many researchers across disciplines such as linguistics, literature, art, religious studies, health and psychology as a means of trying to understand the lived experience of human beings. For Bakhtin this experience is approached through the study of language in action, as an *event*. Although this is most certainly a pedagogical imperative, the dialogic quest is not to discover what learning has been 'achieved' or received but to better understand and appreciate personality and creative potential. Education in the twenty-first century offers a rich landscape for such investigation, since our lives are increasingly characterised by diversity and difference. Learners come to classrooms from many different backgrounds – each with their own authoritative and internally persuasive discourses that interlocute with those that are valued by the teacher and/or the state. In this way thinking is viewed as "a dance of positions in the dialogic space of possible positions" (Wegerif, 2007, p. 13). This dance posits learning as a mutual encounter in dialogue regardless of the context in which it takes place. An investigation of the potential for dialogism in the pedagogical spaces offered to us in and through education forms the basis of the next chapter.

Notes

1 During this period the Pale of Settlement restricting where Jews could live in Russia was revoked, allowing Jews and other minority cultures to live in the larger cities.
2 Visit this website for a further discussion of centrifugal force: http://www.jove.com/science-education/5019/an-introduction-to-the-centrifuge?utm_source=homepage

References

Bakhtin, M. M. (1968). *Rabelais and his world* (H. Iswolsky, Trans.). Cambridge, MA: MIT Press.

Bakhtin, M. M. (1984). *Problems of Dostoevsky's poetics* (C. Emerson, Trans.). Minneapolis: University of Minnesota Press.

Bakhtin, M. M. (1986). *Speech genres and other late essays* (C. Emerson & M. Holquist, Eds.; V. W. McGee, Trans.). Austin: University of Texas Press.

Brandist, C. (2002). *The Bakhtin circle: Philosophy, culture and politics.* London: Pluto Press.

Busch, B. (2014). Building on heteroglossia and heterogeneity: The experience of a multilingual classroom. In A. Blackledge & A. Creese (Eds.), *Heteroglossia as practice and pedagogy* (pp. 21–40). Dordrecht: Springer.

Cresswell, J., & Teucher, U. (2011). The body and language: M. M. Bakhtin on ontogenetic development. *New Ideas in Psychology, 29*(2), 106–118.

Emerson, C. (1994). The making of M. M. Bakhtin as a philosopher. In J. P. Scanlan (Ed.), *Russian thought after communism: The recovery of a philosophical heritage* (pp. 206–226). Armonk, NY: M. E. Sharpe.

Emerson, C. (1995). Bakhtin at 100: Looking back at the very early years [Review of the book *Toward a philosophy of the act*, by M. M. Bakhtin, V. Liapunov, & M. Holquist]. *Russian Review, 54*, 107–114.

Erdinast-Vulcan, D. (1997). Borderlines and contraband: Bakhtin and the question of the subject. *Poetics Today, 18*(2), 251–269.

Hicks, D. (2000). Self and other in Bakhtin's early philosophical essays. *Mind, Culture and Activity, 7*(3), 227–242.

Marx, K. (1967). *The communist manifesto.* Harmondsworth: Penguin.

Matusov, E. (2011). Irreconcilable differences in Vygotsky's and Bakhtin's approaches to the social and the individual: An educational perspective. *Culture and Psychology, 18*, 109–120.

Medvedev, P. N. (1978). *The formal method in literary scholarship: A critical introduction to sociological poetics* (A. J. Wehrle, Trans.). Baltimore, MD: Johns Hopkins University Press.

Morson, G., & Emerson, C. (1990). *Mikhail Bakhtin: Creation of a prosaics.* Stanford, CA: Stanford University Press.

Nikolaev, N. (1998). The Nevel school of philosophy (Bakhtin, Kagan and Pumpianskii) between 1918 and 1925: Materials from Pumpianskii's archives. In D. Shepherd (Ed.), *Studies in Russian and European literature: Vol. 2. The contexts of Bakhtin: philosophy, authorship, aesthetics* (pp. 29–39). Amsterdam: Harwood Academic.

Perlina, N. (1984). Bakhtin and Buber: Problems of dialogic imagination. *Studies in Twentieth Century Literature, 9*(1), 13–28.

Petrelli, S. (2013). *The self as a sign, the world, and the other*. New Brunswick, NJ: Transaction.

Roth, W.-M. (2013). An integrated theory of thinking and speaking that draws on Vygotsky and Bakhtin/Vološinov. *Dialogic Pedagogy: An International Online Journal, 1*. Retrieved from http://dpj.pitt.edu/ojs/index.php/dpj1/article/view/20/28

Scheler, M. (1954). *The nature of sympathy* (P. Heath, Trans.). London: Routledge & Kegan Paul.

Shepherd, D. (Ed.). (1998). *Studies in Russian and European literature: Vol. 2. The contexts of Bakhtin; philosophy, authorship, aesthetics*. Amsterdam: Harwood Academic.

Shotter, J. (2012). Agentive spaces, the 'background', and other not well articulated influences in shaping our lives. *Journal for the Theory of Social Behaviour, 43*(2), 133–154.

Todorov, T. (1984). *Mikhail Bakhtin: The dialogic principle*. Minnesota: University of Minnesota Press.

Voloshinov, V. (1973). *Marxism and the philosophy of language* (L. Matejka & I. R. Titunik, Trans.). Cambridge, MA: Harvard University Press.

Wegerif, R. (2007). *Dialogic education and technology: Expanding the space of learning*. New York, NY: Springer.

Wegerif, R. (2013). *Dialogic: Education for the internet age*. Abingdon: Routledge.

Wertsch, J. V., & Smolka, A.L.B. (1994). Continuing the dialogue: Vygotsky, Bakhtin & Lotman. In H. Daniels (Ed. & Trans.), *Charting the agenda: Educational activity after Vygotsky* (pp. 69–92). London: Routledge.

White, E. J. (2013). Circles, borders and chronotope: Education at the boundary? *Knowledge Cultures, 1*(2), 25–32.

White, E. J. (2014a). Bakhtinian dialogic and Vygotskian dialectic: Compatibilities and contradictions in the classroom? *Educational Philosophy & Theory, 46*(3), 220–236.

White, E. J. (2014b, November). *A philosophy of seeing: The work of the eye in early years education*. Paper presented to the Philosophy of Education and Theory Conference, Hamilton, New Zealand.

Zbinden, K. (2006). *Bakhtin between East and West: Cross-cultural transmission*. London: Modern Humanities Research Association & Maney Publishing.

Zima, P. (1989). Bakhtin's young Hegelian aesthetics. *Critical Studies: The Bakhtin Circle Today, 1*(2), 77–94.

2

INTRODUCING DIALOGIC PEDAGOGY

Bakhtin's emphasis on philosophy and language through seemingly obscure inter-actions with literature and art may, at first glance, seem to have very little to do with pedagogy. Yet on closer examination of Bakhtin's use of *Bildung* (becoming) it becomes apparent that the study of the social conditions of life underpinning his work *is* pedagogy. Bakhtin was also, by all accounts, a highly successful teacher in his own right. He taught mostly in the provinces, where his students described him as a charismatic secondary and tertiary teacher who would lecture for hours on end, summoning poetry and prose to illuminate his ideas. He is reported to have held high standards for teaching, emphasising student engagement with the text and low tolerance of unpreparedness on their part. Although he taught for many decades, Bakhtin only ever wrote one essay (in 1945) specifically on the topic of teaching, based on a grammar lesson he took with 14–15-year-old students. It is here Bakhtin first introduces the term dialogic pedagogy.

In this chapter you will be introduced to dialogic pedagogy as it is most often located – in the classroom with older learners, focusing on verbal language between teachers and students. This is not surprising given Bakhtin's orientation. Up until now dialogic pedagogy in the early years has received very little attention. In my view there is much that can be gained from examining its treatment in these more tradi-tional educational spaces. As you read through this chapter I invite you to consider the provocations these ideas offer to early years pedagogy. Perhaps there are some aspects of dialogic pedagogy in classrooms that hold less relevance for the early years, while others may be absent altogether. Maybe there are topics of tremendous relevance that have not previously been considered in this way. See what you think as you read on.

Bakhtin's dialogic pedagogy

So what is dialogic pedagogy? Perhaps the definition given by Bakhtin in that 1945 essay offers the most useful starting point:

After all, language has a powerful effect on the thought processes of the person who generates it. Creative, original, exploratory thought that is in contrast with the richness and complexity of life cannot develop on a substrate consisting of the forms of depersonalized, clichéd, bookish language. The further fate of a student's creative potential, to a great extent, depends on the language he takes with him out of high school. And this is the instructor's responsibility.

(Bakhtin, 2004, p. 24)

Let's look at this quote in detail. Suspending the pedagogical topic of inquiry (it could be any topic at all for our purposes) it is immediately evident that Bakhtin wants to draw our attention towards the generating properties of language as meaning-making. We have explored this idea in the last chapter with related concepts of answerability and aesthetics. It is not by chance that Bakhtin makes use of the term 'creative' more than once in this excerpt; it highlights the essential point of language as creative act, not a means of acquiring endpoint knowledge. The route to creativity, as Bakhtin explains, is through living encounter, not transferred ideas that are valued by the teacher (or the academy or society for that matter). It is here that we can see the notion of *Bildung* take prominence since, for Bakhtin, emphasis is given to the formation of individual personality through social interaction.

Although pedagogy of this nature is by no means confined to formal pedagogical institutions, Bakhtin leaves teachers with a strong sense of accountability for their acts of authorship. In Bakhtin's classroom it is clear that students also play an authorship role as they engage with ideas that are relevant to their lives. They have an opinion that they are encouraged to contribute in careful interrogation with the ideas they are confronted with. In this sense dialogic pedagogy is not merely about disagreement. As Gary Morson and Caryl Emerson (1990) explain, "Agreement is just as dialogic as disagreement" (p. 132) when it is characterised by complex interaction rather than imposition. Agreement and disagreement are equally welcome in a dialogic classroom – the point is to keep them both in lively interplay. The emphasis is on the dialogues that take place, not the institution, buildings or set curriculum, for it is in the dialogues that meaning is created. As with all Bakhtin's entreaties, there is nowhere for the teacher to hide in a classroom like this!

By now you will see how many of the ideas Bakhtin explored during his lifetime under the broad theory of dialogism have potential for theorising and practising classroom pedagogy. It is hardly surprising, then, to discover many educational theorists employing these ideas today in a variety of ways. For some, dialogism provides a route to what Emerson (2000) describes as "anarchy in the classroom" (p. 22), providing for resistance and autonomy on the part of the student. For others it prioritises certain styles of teaching over others, arguing for approaches that eliminate the teacher altogether and thus calling into question the notion of pedagogy itself. These extreme views sit oddly against Bakhtin's own experience as a teacher – he never dismissed the authoritative voice of text or teacher but instead invited active engagement with both. Charles Bazerman (2005), who has attempted to interpret Bakhtin's pedagogical practice, describes this as a facilitation of "the birth of the student's individual language" (p. 338). In his classroom, Bakhtin advocated for lively and interesting disagreements, disputes and debates about the language of everyday life as an antidote to 'schoolification', but he *never* set out to replace one way of thinking with another. This idea is central to Bakhtin's notion of dialogic pedagogy.

Audra Skukauskaite and Judith Green (2004) suggest that Bakhtin's approach to teaching can be conceptualised as a series of inquiry cycles whereby information is collated, analysed and then used to guide pedagogy at each point. They describe the way Bakhtin supported his students to question valued knowledge by analysing points where there was a "frame clash" (p. 68). These were the moments of most significance to learning because they required students to question received knowledge against their own points of view. Students take on the role of author who can argue with other ideas, even authoritative ones, and generate new understandings. In this way there is no longer a gap between theory and practice, often described as a divide that must be breached even in contemporary education, but instead "by examining how a teacher can construct a theoretically and pragmatically grounded practice, [Bakhtin] demonstrated how inquiry and practice relationships form the foundation for this new approach" (p. 71).

Dialogic pedagogy today

Bakhtin's legacy has left a rich platform for us to think about in relation to pedagogy today. He approached learning as a social experience between people and a journey towards selfhood that is never fully achieved (but always strived for). His quest for such encounter was therefore less concerned with 'cognition' in an intellectual or conceptual sense, as psychology defines it, but rather as form-shaping consciousness. By this Bakhtin invites us to consider the socially imbued nature of human beings and our engagement with ideas. He can therefore be approached both epistemologically and ontologically. Epistemological approaches to dialogism view the communicative act as interdependent from other acts, in dialogue with other aspects of the context and as a constructed process of meaning-making (Wegerif, 2007).

Epistemological approaches to dialogism might ask:

- How is knowledge conceptualised? By whom? How will I know?
- What knowledge matters? To whom and in what contexts?
- Am I prepared to be challenged on this topic? Why? Why not?

Ontological approaches to dialogism suggest that the ways we come to know the world are central to inquiry. Such 'knowing' is not only dependent on the nature of dialogue, its context and participants but also dimensions of time and space that impact on what can, or cannot, be considered meaningful or relevant.

Ontological approaches to dialogism might ask:

- How will this learner's participation in this dialogue affect his or her life?[1]
- Why should we discuss this topic rather than do something completely different?
- What is meaningful to this learner at this moment? How will I find out?

Adam Lefstein and Julia Snell (2014) suggest that dialogic pedagogy is a democratic process because it invites learners into thinking about learning with others:

> We engage in dialogue because we are interested in what our interlocuters – including children and pupils – have to say . . . We engage in dialogue because we do not know everything. And we engage in dialogue because we are social animals, who cherish and take pleasure in the company of others.
>
> *(p. 21)*

In a dialogic classroom teachers do not simply deliver or receive ideas (or curriculum) as if they were a neat package of information to be adopted without question. Meaning is never fixed because it relies on individual interpretation that draws from many different influences. Each person brings their different perspectives to the classroom and these become the source of dialogic pedagogy through shared inquiry. Of course this doesn't mean that the teacher, who brings important ideas to the classroom, doesn't have an important role to play. However, their role requires some adjustment in a classroom that is committed to dialogic pedagogy.

Dialogic pedagogy emphasises the idea that dialogue *is* learning, not merely a means to learning. Seen in this way dialogic pedagogy focuses on learner engagement with ideas, questions and provocations rather than answers. Consider the following principles that underpin this approach:

Dialogic pedagogy is:

- an infinite space of possible meanings
- a place where curriculum is dialogue
- contingent responsiveness to 'other'
- characterised by lively discussion about ideas of importance to learners
- interested in valued knowledge from a range of sources
- resistant of end points; interested instead in points of wonder
- not afraid to set challenges or respond to those posed by others
- concerned with ideas, not correct answers
- welcoming of uncertainty
- respectful of the pace and style (forms) of communication learners bring to the classroom

- underpinned by relationships that take time to try to understand others
- influenced by what can be seen and what is unseen but nevertheless important
- respectful of diverse ideas and ideologies
- encouraging of debate, dissensus and perhaps even silence
- interested in insider and outsider perspectives on topics
- at times lots of fun and at other times potentially painful. Sometimes both!

The extent to which these principles are shared with other approaches to teaching and learning is of interest here. You might argue that *all* educational experiences should be characterised by these fundamental ideas, yet clearly they are not. As early as Plato we can see the tendency for education to want to shape learners into certain ways of thinking, doing and being. A common way of describing Socratic styles of teaching is to employ the metaphor of a midwife whose task it is to bring important knowledge into the light, for illumination. But who decides what is important knowledge? In a dialogic classroom this is very much a negotiated position and so is curriculum or syllabi. As Peter Renshaw (2004) explains, dialogism leads us to a "pedagogy of possibility . . . not a question of either/or . . . but rather both/and, a stance that entails a commitment to on-going engagement in dialogue and mutual answerability" (p. 6).

Some dialogic pedagogues go as far as to suspend their lesson plans altogether, as Eugene Matusov did in his university class. Despite his best dialogic intentions, Eugene (alias Edward as he calls himself in the text) describes the way he was misunderstood by his students as being manipulative. The following web post highlights the perspective of one of his students:

> Well this was Edward's entire experiment, be it pre-planned or not. One day out of the blue we went from having a relatively traditional class regime where we had assignments to do (weekly mini-projects, readings, webtalk postings, etc.) to something of an academic anarchy. Edward declared the new regime to be that there was no longer a regime. The early result was people just not doing assignments because they didn't feel like it or altering assignments to suit themselves. The later result was crazier shit like Jane and I's mid-class miniature cover band. Not to mention lots of existential self-questioning prompted by Edward and propagated across the WebTalk. This existential questioning brought on by Edward led me to suggest that he (or perhaps more broadly high dialogic philosophy) was acting as somewhat of a puppet master, controlling each of us.
>
> *(Reflective web, Summer 2009, in Matusov & Brobst, 2013)*

Eugene has spent many years trying to understand dialogic pedagogy. He now views it as deeply challenging and distinct from other forms of educational practice today, even within sociocultural theories. His experiences within his own class-rooms coupled with extensive scholarship have led him to assert dialogic pedagogy as a highly challenging, distinct, approach to teaching and learning. In saying this, Eugene makes a clear distinction between different pedagogical approaches that might be called dialogic – you can read about these in a paper he writes with Kiyo Miyazaki (Matusov & Miyazaki, 2014). Together the authors discuss different types of pedagogies that teachers might present in their classroom practice and the extent to which they represent dialogic pedagogy. If you are really keen, you can also read some of the responses to their views by others in the same journal issue – in doing so you will see that there is no 'one' view of dialogic pedagogy. That's what makes it so interesting!

The role of the teacher in dialogic pedagogy

Alexander Sidorkin (1999) refers to the role of the teacher in dialogic pedagogy as one that supports the breakability of classroom discourse – remaining open and welcoming of different ideas that create a crack or fissure in deeply held truths. Through such means he and others argue that possibilities truly exist for transgradi-ence as learners (here I am referring to teachers too) revise their thinking in light of new and potentially confronting ideas. The point of the exercise is not necessarily to change points of view, or to make everyone think the same, but to create more complex thinking. An example is offered by Sara Pollack and Yifat Ben-David Kolikant (2011) in an online history lesson between Arab and Jewish Israeli students, who held very different political beliefs. By placing students with diverse groups into online pairings, and inviting them to examine historical texts and share perspectives, students began to examine their own point of view with the benefit of other insights on the same events. The following excerpt is taken from an online discussion between Arab and Jewish students:

AP: And I hate you because you occupied and destroyed our land.
JP: You should stop blaming the Jews. We can blame u (you) too.
(Pollack & Kolikant, 2011, p. 144)

When Sara and Yifat examined their own pedagogy through these examples of online student dialogue, they concluded that it is simply not enough to chal-lenge student viewpoints through dialogue with others. They determined that their role should also be to support student access to a variety of information sources that would assist them to re-examine, expand or challenge their argument. This is an important idea for teachers, especially in societies where diverse voices are increasingly present – whether or not they are *heard* is the challenge of the dialogic teacher. We could argue that it is also a very important principle for any serious dialogue – especially where views are potentially polarised as they were for these students. Since education is always ideologically driven (Saljo, 2003) the task of dia-logic pedagogy is to interrogate the dilemmas that arise as a result of ideologies. In this way teachers can support learners to generate new insights that are important for them through classroom dialogues of difference.

Olga Dysthe (2011) has also tried to understand the role of the teacher in dialogic pedagogy. Her investigation took her into an American classroom with a teacher who was trying to work with national standards that, on the face of things, did little to promote the kind of teaching she valued. Like Bakhtin in his pedagogical demonstrations in 1945, this teacher invited her students to explore text in ways that invited lively encounter. Olga explains admiringly the strategies this teacher employed to involve all learners – even those who were less likely to pass the external 'test'. These included reading provocative text, interviewing family members and reporting back, recording journal entries and sharing ideas with others formally and informally. At the same time this teacher did not dismiss the currency of the 'test' and its related significance to students and their families. She helped her students to understand its genre – how to answer multi-choice questions, how to prepare for the test, and so on. The engagement of this teacher with both the test (valued curriculum) and the personally relevant responses of the students to the text that was being tested (underground curriculum) supported learners to approach the educational challenge as an opportunity. Though we are not told how well these students eventually did on the test, Olga leaves us with some statements from students that reveal the significance of this kind of teaching for students' lives (which is, arguably, equally as important as passing tests). Here is one of them:

> Val: Most of the time we're too busy trying to tiptoe around the rules and regulations that they give us to live by to really understand what they're about . . . The interview contained many things which I couldn't put into my essay because they were too hard to put into words.
>
> *(Dysthe, 2011, p. 79)*

What this student highlights is the important point that not everything that is in the official curriculum matters most (or necessarily at all) to learners. Tests or assessments do not necessarily capture all aspects of learning or life. Yet at the same time they are important because they play a vital role in authoring the future of students – influencing access to scholarships, jobs and so on. The teacher's response was to provide a means through which students could engage with both personal and authoritative interests in ways that dismissed neither their own insights nor the answers required by the state. These findings support Helen Rothschild Ewald's (1993) claim that "if Bakhtin has been helpful to those who seek to escape convention-driven pedagogies, he is becoming useful to those for whom there is no escape, no exit" (p. 337). Olga Dysthe (2011) has termed this optimistic approach to dialogic pedagogy an "opportunity space" (p. 86) which can assist teachers in bridging the different chronotopes that exist and impact in and out of the classroom.

A similar pedagogical insight is provided by Maren Aukerman (2013) in a reading comprehension class where she describes a teacher working with student hypotheses about the water cycle by seeking their point of view in tandem with textbook information. Through this dialogic process the teacher confesses her own thinking has been reshaped:

> I thought that paragraph made it pretty clear to me just what drove the water cycle. Now after having the discussion that we've had, I see that it's much more complicated than that, and *maybe the question is not nearly as important as the discussion you've had about it.*
>
> *(Mohan, 2008, p. 63, cited in Aukerman, 2013, my emphasis)*

The complexity for teachers in trying to live out the principles of dialogic pedagogy is clearly challenging. Part of the work of contemporary dialogic pedagogy is to try to understand the kinds of classrooms and contexts that give rise to rich dialogue and which open up (rather than close) opportunities for student contributions. Adam Lefstein and Julia Snell, in their recent book *Better Than Best Practice* (2013), provide several examples of classroom pedagogy followed by a series of diverse commentaries on the extent to which each might be dialogic (you can check out their examples online at http://dialogicpedagogy. com). Analysis of classroom dialogues highlights the significance of not only the language forms (e.g. who spoke, how they spoke and so on) but also the content of the dialogues (that is, what was its significance to the learners themselves). The orientation here is to ensure that lessons are relevant to those for whom they are targeted – whether that lesson responds to the priority of passing a text or understanding a personally challenging issue. In an ideal world we might hope that the latter took precedence but we cannot dismiss the significant authority of assessment in the lives of learners.

Challenges for dialogic pedagogy

Critics of dialogic pedagogy have suggested that it is only suitable for privileged groups of learners who share an understanding that they have a right to express their own opinion. I think this is a gross misunderstanding. While it is true that different learners approach dialogue differently, a primary role of the dialogic teacher is not to simply facilitate verbal debate as a means of self-assertion. In my view the central principle of dialogic pedagogy is to understand the ways ideas are best explored for each learner as well as the ideas themselves. There is no singular way to engage in dialogue – it is as dynamic as those who engage in it.

As we have seen by these examples, dialogic pedagogy is by no means a 'soft' or easy option for teachers. There are many challenges teachers face in contemporary educational regimes that do not always place value on the process of learning rather than the product. The suspension of closely guarded truths in the dialogic classroom is not a comfortable stance for many teachers who have built their careers based on their expertise in a chosen topic rather than as pedagogue. This should not come as a surprise. So much of curriculum, especially today, is oriented towards knowledge end points rather than processes of learning. Coupled with the requirement for certain standards that characterise many educational systems in the world, it can be difficult for teachers to emphasise dialogues of difference over outcomes. Do you think this is also true for the early years?

Dialogic pedagogy classrooms may also be scary or unsettling places for learners who have grown accustomed to receiving rather than generating knowledge. Eugene Matusov goes so far as to suggest that learners who have endured years of teaching that does not take dialogic principles into account (or pays lip service to them) may need to undergo a detoxification process in dialogic classrooms. He and others argue strongly that many classrooms today are far from a dialogic reality – perhaps we can understand why.

In the end, however, it seems that the extent to which classrooms reflect the principles of dialogic pedagogy – or not – is in no small way influenced by the teacher. This is a point we will consistently return to throughout this book. From a Bakhtinian perspective we are always answerable for our acts and these lie at the heart of pedagogy. There is no curriculum, no method, no technology, equipment or programme that can erase this central tenet. The teacher, in dialogue with learners, *is* the curriculum in a dialogic classroom. In accordance with this principle, Eugene Matusov (2009b) suggests three important qualities for the dialogic teacher:

1. **Intellectual courage:** A readiness to revise our own beliefs when presented with alternatives;
2. **Intellectual honesty:** An ability to change a belief if presented with a good reason to do so; and
3. **Wise restraint:** An ability to examine alternatives carefully before changing beliefs, and to encourage others to do the same. (p. 277)

If we accept that these qualities are important for a dialogic teacher, it is hard to ignore the central moral tenets of Bakhtin's thinking. And so we come full circle to the idea that teaching, like all human experience, is a dialogic event. The extent to which teachers recognise and respond to these principles is the extent to which such pedagogies can be realised in the classroom.

Looking back, looking ahead

Dialogic pedagogy is not for the faint-hearted. It requires an openness to other and an associated willingness to embrace uncertainty – often in conditions where teachers are pressured towards authorial goals that go against these principles. There is often very little support for this type of pedagogy in mainstream contemporary schools and universities; and there is no pedagogical manual that can tell teachers how to do it (to do so would violate the dialogic tenets of Bakhtin against finalisation). The extent to which practice can claim to be dialogic relies on the ethical and aesthetic agency of individual teachers who are committed to understanding what really matters to their students rather than to any one method or technique. How this 'looks' in real life pedagogy is a matter for ongoing consideration.

Based on these provocations many educationalists have asked themselves, "What kind of relationship should I share with learners in teaching contexts that are characterised by dialogic pedagogy?" and "How do I go about it?" You can read more about the way scholars in formal schooling classrooms have gone about this, or continue to challenge their pedagogy in this way, by sourcing some of the authors mentioned in this chapter. There are also two very helpful websites you can go to if you wish to learn and see more:

http://dpj.pitt.edu/ojs/index.php/dpj1/index

and

http://dialogicpedagogy.com/

But since this is a book about *early years* pedagogy it is now time to turn our focus towards early childhood 'classrooms' or, as I shall refer to them from now on, 'settings'. The questions asked by educationalists in their dialogic examination of classroom pedagogy are no less significant for those who work with very young children. But they do take on a slightly different emphasis, as you will soon see.

As you prepare to move into the next chapter, pause for a moment and think of the kinds of relationships you have shared with teachers or as a learner yourself. To what extent were they dialogic or monologic? How do you know?

Then think about the implications of everything you have read so far for your practice as a teacher yourself. You will then be in a position to consider the importance of dialogic pedagogy to the complex domain of early years practice and theory – which lies at the heart of this book.

Note

1 These first two questions are borrowed from Eugene Matusov (2009a), p. 8.

References

Aukerman, M. (2013). Rereading comprehension pedagogies. *Dialogic Pedagogy: An International Online Journal, 1*. Retrieved from http://dpj.pitt.edu

Bakhtin, M. M. (2004). Dialogic origin and dialogic pedagogy of grammar: Stylistics in teaching Russian language in secondary school. *Journal of Russian and East European Psychology, 42*(6), 12–49.

Bazerman, C. (2005). An essay on pedagogy by Mikhail Bakhtin. *Written Communication, 22*(3), 333–338.

Dysthe, O. (2011). Opportunity spaces for dialogic pedagogy in test-oriented schools: A case study of teaching and learning in high school. In E. J. White & M. A. Peters (Eds.), *Bakhtinian pedagogy: Opportunities and challenges for research, policy and practice in education across the globe* (pp. 69–90). New York, NY: Peter Lang.

Emerson, C. (2000). The next hundred years of Mikhail Bakhtin (The view from the classroom). *Rhetoric Review, 19*(1/2), 12–27.

Lefstein, A., & Snell, A. (2014). *Better than best practice: Developing teaching and learning through dialogue.* London: Routledge.

Matusov, E. (2009a). Guest editor's introduction to parts I and II. *Journal of Russian & East European Psychology, 47*(1), 3–19. doi:10.2753/RPO1061–0405470100

Matusov, E. (2009b). *Journey into dialogic pedagogy.* Hauppauge, NY: Nova Science.

Matusov, E., & Brobst, J. (2013). *Radical experiment in dialogic pedagogy in higher education and its Centauric failure: Chronotopic analysis.* New York, NY: Nova Science.

Matusov, E., & Kiyozaki, K. (2014). Dialogue on dialogic pedagogy. *Dialogic Pedagogy: An International Online Journal, 2.* Retrieved from http://dpj.pitt.edu

Morson, G. S., & Emerson, C. (1990). *Mikhail Bakhtin: Creation of a prosaics.* Stanford, CA: Stanford University Press.

Pollack, S., & Kolikant, Y. B.-D. (2011). Fostering dialogue in a context of socio-political conflict: An instructional model. In E. J. White & M. A. Peters (Eds.), *Bakhtinian pedagogy: Opportunities and challenges for research, policy and practice in education across the globe* (pp. 129–157). New York, NY: Peter Lang.

Renshaw, P. (2004). Dialogic learning teaching and instruction: Theoretical roots and analytical frameworks. In J. van der Linden & P. Renshaw (Eds.), *Dialogic learning: Shifting perspectives to learning, instruction and teaching* (pp. 1–17). Dordrecht: Kluwer Academic.

Rothschild Ewald, H. (1993). Waiting for answerability: Bakhtin and composition studies. *College Composition and Communication, 44*(3), 331–348.

Saljo, R. (2003). Notes on classroom practices. In J. van der Linden & P. Renshaw (Eds.), *Dialogic learning: Shifting perspectives to learning, instruction and teaching* (pp. 251–261). Dordrecht: Kluwer Academic.

Sidorkin, A. M. (1999). *Beyond discourse: Education, the self and dialogue.* Albany: State University of New York Press.

Skukauskaite, A., & Green, J. (2004). A conversation with Bakhtin: On inquiry and dialogic thinking. *Journal of Russian and East European Psychology, 42*(6), 59–75.

Wegerif, R. (2007). *Dialogic education and technology: Expanding the space of learning.* New York, NY: Springer.

3

DIALOGIC PEDAGOGY IN THE EARLY YEARS

Having now gained an understanding of Bakhtinian dialogism and its relationship to dialogic pedagogy we are, at last, in a position to ask, "What is the relevance of dialogic pedagogy for the early years?" If you accept its significance, you might then join me in asking, "So what does (or could) dialogic pedagogy 'look like' in the early years?" This chapter will explore the current possibilities for these questions, based on known pedagogical practices employed in the early years to date, and the potential for further developments. Consideration will be given to Bakhtin's interpretation of pedagogy as an answerable act that is accountable to the learner and which therefore impacts all who are involved. The role of the teacher will be explored from this standpoint across a number of contexts in early years settings and you will be invited to watch some footage to bring the ideas to life.

Pedagogy and the early years

In the early years pedagogy is still a contentious concept. The legacy of pedagogy as a process of learning and teaching originating in early Greek history suggests that a teacher's role, as pedagogue, is to bring the learner into a state of enlightenment (Farquhar & White, 2014). Such a view presupposes that the teacher, as expert, possesses valued knowledge that the learner is supposed to receive. While this may not necessarily have been the overall intention of Plato's thinking, there is no doubt that this is how it has been interpreted over the years. Many formal schooling processes have been developed based on the premise that learners should be exposed to knowledgeable adults who will 'teach' them by providing the valued information they are deemed to need in order to be successful in later life. The content of that knowledge is typically decided by the government or state and forms the basis of the curriculum.

But in the early years there has always been a strong suggestion that very young children do not need to be 'taught' in formal, transmissive ways. Based on the heavy influence of theorists such as Piaget, Vygotksy, Bruner and Bronfenbrenner in the West last century, early years pedagogy today is typically underpinned by constructivist, sociocultural and ecological theories. These suggest that children learn best when learning is derived from their own experience, has personal meaning and is developmentally responsive. In other words learning takes place in meaningful contexts of relevance to the learners themselves. A great emphasis has been given to care and education (or 'educare') which positions learning within a circle of caring relationships. Thanks to Loris Malaguzzi, founder of Reggio Emilia, and many others there is now a strong push for associated 'relational pedagogies' that emphasise mutual relationships between young children, their families and teachers. Such an approach relies heavily on teachers understanding children's interests and prior experiences by listening and watching them closely, interpreting their multiple languages and talking with their families. Teachers' personal views about children, learning and society are also implicated as part of a relational pedagogy (Brownlee & Berthelsson, 2007). They form the basis of many early years curricula today.

Check out *Reggio Emilia* in Italy (as explained by Smidt, 2013), *Te Whāriki* (Ministry of Education, 1996) in New Zealand, the Australian *Early Years Framework* (Australian Government Department of Education, Employment & Workplace, 2009) and, to a lesser extent but nonetheless evident, the United Kingdom *Early Years Framework* (Department for Education, 2012) and the Swedish *Early Childhood Education and Care* (Taguma, Litjens, & Makowiecki, 2013) to see manifestations of these ideas in curricula. You will not see core subjects such as English, Mathematics and Science listed alongside desirable outcomes. Instead you will discover principles that privilege relationships with people, ideas and concepts (what Te Whāriki describes as "people, places and things") or "the provision of instructive learning play environments and routines" (Siraj-Blatchford, Sylva, Muttock, Gilden & Bell, 2002, p. 38). As frameworks, these curricula documents reveal much about what is (and by their absence, what is not) valued in early years education.

These curricula, as much as they can avoid it within an era of accountability, do not prescribe how to teach nor do they directly suggest how to learn; instead they invite teachers to consider ways that they can positively contribute to children's early years experience in its broadest sense. Here ideas such as 'belonging', 'becoming', or 'exploration' replace traditional subject boundaries to suggest that early years experience should be a time of wonderment – across all domains. Early years teachers are now beginning to talk about the importance of 'immanence' as a legitimate aspect of their pedagogy in accordance with these perspectives (see for example, Lenz-Taguchi, 2010).

Despite a much greater tolerance for freedom of thought and engagement in the early years than other educational sectors, there are also increasingly neo-liberal demands on twenty-first-century early years teachers to justify their 'educative' practice based on rationalist terms (often inappropriately borrowed from other educational domains). More recently, and in reaction to this educational 'push down' for accountability, increased attention has been given to alternative ways of thinking about learning and its relationship to human experience, especially for the young child. Not only do these different ways of viewing the experience invite resistance to the kinds of certainties rationalist approaches demand, but they also move far away from exclusive psychological or developmental domains that claim to know what children are thinking. Increased consideration is now being given to alternative ways of thinking critically about these important issues through a series of structuralist–poststructuralist 'turns' that now position early years pedagogy as "a complex, contested and contestable domain" (Farquhar & White, 2014, p. 10). Bakhtin's philosophical contributions have an important role to play in this space – not only is there an alignment to the flux of uncertainty that underpins all relationships, but from a pedagogical standpoint dialogism invites a careful examination of the nature of dialogues that take place, their interrelatedness and orientations. In a dialogic emphasis, there is always an 'other', even when that other may not be visibly present.

A dialogic challenge

Bakhtin's view of meaning-making as a *living event* of *dialogue* that takes place *between people* calls into question the authoritative pedagogical tenets of leading theories in the field. Dialogism challenges emerging trends towards a pedagogical role that is oriented towards the novice learner in opposition to the expert teacher or the teacher who sits back and 'allows' learning to occur. Neo-Bakhtinian scholar Rupert Wegerif (2013) suggests that Vygotsky's assumptions about the individual as an isolated, albeit socially constructed, entity acting upon (and acted upon) in the world are now challenged by the idea that individuals cannot exist outside of relationships. In a similar theme, Karin Junefelt (2007) has persuasively argued that Vygotksy's notion of private speech is flawed when viewed dialogically because it fails to appreciate the presence of unseen others in dialogue. Developmental strongholds that have imposed limitations on the way infant subjectivity is perceived as inattentive to other in the first few months of life, based on the observations of Jean Piaget and others, are now challenged by Vasudevi Reddy (2008) with the inspiration of Bakhtin's dialogic emphasis on self–other relationships:

> If the infant did not *feel* the other's attention to herself, she would have little more than academic curiosity as a motive to explore the other's attention in the world. It is this affective awareness of others' attention to *the self* that

allows infants to develop a broader and eventually conceptual awareness of others' attention.

(p. 116)

The increase in neurological scientific inquiry, revealing the idea that very young children are far more socially attuned at a much earlier age than was previously thought, has brought many of Bakhtin's ideas into further alignment. From this perspective the brain is not merely enhanced by social encounter but synapses are actually ignited through such experience. This idea is closely aligned to Bakhtin's friend Voloshinov's depiction of meaning (*znachenie*), which he likens to an electric circuit that ignites through connection. I interpret this as a 'spark' of meaning that takes place in meaningful encounters between children and adults who take the time to try to understand them (White, 2011b, p. 42). From a dialogic standpoint we are less interested in what is happening in the individual brain (as is typically the case in contemporary neurological studies) but in the 'ignitions' that are taking place between people and their whole bodies in a much broader sense. Instead of a resource or programme acting as a catalyst for learning, it is in the relationships between people that meaning is ignited (or, conversely, remains unkindled).

These ideas represent a real challenge to early years teachers who believe that their role is to apply theories that generate certainty about all children and their capacities and transmit knowledge accordingly. Taken together, these new understandings remind us that we can no longer assume that all infants, toddlers and young children draw from the same trajectory or source. Nor can we view these young people as entities isolated from the world around them, removing ourselves from the process to take on the role of impartial observers, facilitators of the environment or distributors of knowledge. Our relationships lie at the centre of pedagogy and form the basis of ontological engagement about what is meaningful rather than what is 'true'. Hence, from a dialogic standpoint, those same questions asked of classroom teachers in chapter 2 also apply to the early years where teachers can examine their practice in terms of what it means for the child.

1. How will this child's participation in this dialogue affect his or her life?[1]

When we think about dialogue in a broad manner that includes the body and its social orientation, as Bakhtin suggests in his earliest works, we can conceive of multiple, diverse dialogues that take place constantly in the early years setting. Even when children do not appear to be actively involved in a conversation they are still part of the dialogue – watching, listening or perhaps simply experiencing the flow of events. However, when a child experiences rejection from a dialogue they learn that an aspect of him or herself is not valued. The same applies when they are ignored, trivialised, misinterpreted, overlooked or perhaps even 'professionalised' by well-meaning teachers who claim to know best. Conversely, when they are welcomed into the dialogue on their own terms they experience a sense of acceptance within the setting that they are likely to take with them to other parts of their lives, including their future. This means that everything teachers do (or don't do) is part of that dialogue and is influenced by ideologies. With this understanding we recognise that children in early years settings are influenced by the presence or nonpresence of others in profound ways. How a teacher acts, speaks, enunciates, intonates, sounds, moves, behaves and orients himself or herself plays a big part in the becoming of each child. These acts will be explored, as loving encounter, through play, in humour and with others (adults and peers) in the chapters that follow.

2. What is meaningful to this child at this moment? How will I find out?

Early years teachers are usually particularly vigilant about the kinds of reciprocal relationships that convey the message that a child is valued and perhaps even loved (a concept we will discuss in the next chapter). This means that teachers need to have sufficient understanding of the child and their world(s) to be able to attempt to interpret what is being conveyed and respond in ways that convey genuine interest. Teachers may also initiate ideas and insights on the basis of the cues offered by the child, as 'points of wonder' (Berlyand, 2009). Often these are highly individual: one topic of inquiry will mean different things to each child because their response will be based on what is personally significant rather than what is important to the teacher, or other children for that matter. This calls into question the idea that a collective centre 'project' or curriculum will unquestionably respond to every child or to their internally persuasive discourses. Effective pedagogy in a dialogic sense relies upon teachers taking time to know this child, this family and their priorities – recognising the plurality of perspectives each child brings to the experience and its significance in a specific time and space.

3. What knowledge matters, and to whom?

If we accept the idea that curriculum is less concerned with topics, subjects or facts to be learnt, we are released to consider the idea that knowledge is not an end point but a process. When a child offers a 'working theory' that, for example, death is not a permanent state (as was examined by two 4 year olds in a 2005 study by Annica Lofdahl), we are not concerned with correcting their response according to our assumption. By discussing this idea with the child and finding out their point of view, perhaps then sourcing texts or surfing the net together to find out more, it is actually possible that new or modified theories can be generated based on the inspiration of the child. In a dialogic sense the adult is not necessarily 'right' and neither, for that matter, is the textbook. Being right or wrong is not the point in a dialogic learning experience. Thinking deeply and creatively about issues and problems of significance in a child's life through dialogue is.

In a 2013 study by Kelly & White, a group of teachers took this idea very seriously. During their outings with children teachers became increasingly aware of the potential in their pedagogy to provide answers rather than provoke questions. The perceived potential to 'hijack' their students' learning by disrupting the children's own theories presented them with a similar pedagogical dilemmas to that encountered by classroom teachers (as discussed in chapter 2). The following dialogue, which took place following the discovery of olives lying on the ground under an olive tree, reveals their concerns:

Child: They're beans.
Teacher: Beans on an olive tree?
          [Teacher turns to talk to her colleague nearby] Do you think? . . . Am I hijacking?
Child: Those are olives. They have to be ripe to eat. The purple ones are.
Teacher: Look what's inside!
Child: It's the juicy stuff!
Teacher: Feel it! Smell it!
Child: Look it has a bean inside it!

(Kelly & White, 2013, p. 63)

Did the teacher try to manipulate this child into adopting her 'superior' understanding of identifying the olive correctly? Or did the child strategically manoeuvre the dialogue towards a shared resolution in order to satisfy both (1) her teacher's need to identify an olive and (2) her own need to justify her claim that it is a bean? Either way there is dexterity in this dialogue that surpasses mere transmission of knowledge – in fact, one is left to ask, "Who is the learner?" Opportunities for extended, rich, reciprocal dialogue on ideas of personal concern are essential in dialogic pedagogy. For young children emphasis is placed on imagination and speculation, rather than privileging logic and 'truth'. As Alexander Lobok explains:

> In a broad sense, we professional educators are prepared – sometimes with unaccustomed ease – to snuff out the world of children's expectations for the sake of being able to create, in the child, the ability to make logical constructions. On the other hand, we always have "didactic goals and objectives," with which we can account for ourselves in front of our auditing superiors. But does the child need our "didactic goals and objectives"?

(Lobok, 2012, p. 105)

Bringing dialogism to bear in the early years

Although Bakhtin's work signals a revision of learning as creative dialogue, his contributions have not been fully realised in the early years. Yet when we consider all that is now understood to comprise contemporary early years pedagogy, there are many relevant concepts to consider. Bringing dialogic pedagogy to bear on the early years offers a revisioned means of trying (not necessarily succeeding) to understand our youngest in the complex early years setting we now share with them as an important part of daily experience. Moreover, dialogism as a principle reminds us that learning is rooted in experience not just theories or (however helpful they might be) early years curriculum guidelines.

Alexander Sidorkin (2014) suggests that interpreting meaning on behalf of children by romanticising the dialogue (that is, presuming to speak on their behalf about what is being learnt or ascribing significance to language based on adult assumptions of meaning) presents a problem from a dialogic standpoint. From a Bakhtinian perspective, if we are serious about this relationship, we must begin to see each child as a person in their own right not just as a member of a family, a developmentally 'known' human being or member of the early years setting. There is a necessary 'aesthetic struggle' in our relationship that does not allow for any final conclusion to be drawn about a child as a person in the world. In a dialogic space such as this teachers and children are in constant action and reaction, which transforms potentialities into real life events of authorship that exceed any imposed domain a curriculum might offer, though of course a curriculum is undoubtedly an feature of the chronotope through which meaning-making takes place.

This emphasis on the value of a person, their personality, their contribution and their orientation in the world in relation to others forms the basis for dialogic pedagogy in the early years. From a dialogic standpoint we are less concerned with the isolated child or even the child as a member of a community of practice. Our emphasis is on his or her potential impact on others, and our impact on him or her, as interlocutors. Though infants cannot necessarily talk in the same language as adults who share their world, even the very newest baby can shape the social experience. The question of when and how this infant becomes a person in his own right takes on an increased significance in a dialogic world, a question shared by many psychologists today.

Understanding the depth of this kind of relationship is really important for early years teachers who are given the challenging task of trying to understand the children they work with as nonfamilial dialogic partners who are called into this intimacy. Here we are reminded that each child is a member of his or her family but they are also interlocutors within and beyond this family. Just as children will act on and in the early years context, a lot of information from previous chronotopes at home and across the various social domains they locate will play an important part in this space also. Each child is already a personality in their own right with their own unique ways of communicating that will alter through every experience. Children also receive significant messages through the volitional tones in our language (spoken and unspoken) concerning how they (and their families) are valued and the significance of words as well as their meanings in each space. Moreover, and of particular significance from a dialogic standpoint, children are profoundly shaping those around them – engaging in a complex exchange of growing, moving and shifting subjectivities that hold potential to alter those meanings. These messages convey meanings for children to interpret about their value and how they might orient themselves in this revised world beyond the home – in order to be seen and heard. This is important learning.

As early years teachers it would therefore seem important to try to understand something of the chronotopes each infant, toddler or young child brings to the early years experience that will influence their styles of communication, sense of agency and personality. The ability or inability of the teacher to see, and perhaps celebrate, this child as an individual beyond their own experience can be challenging to say the least, but it is the most important threshold the early years teacher encounters. While, as a well-meaning teacher, I might attempt to read this optic through observations, records, dialogue with family, reading texts on child development and so on, it is most important that I recognise each child's capacity and potential to "amaze, challenge and perhaps even demolish preconceived ideas" (White, 2011a, p. 82). This means I need to give priority to the relationship that we share – which is unique to any other and that changes over time. I need to dialogically engage with each child through the people who are part of their world – past, present and future. Trying to understand individual children rather than children as known developmental objects for intervention means that I may need to challenge the texts that inform the profession. I may need to suspend some of the certainty they offer concerning child development and learning on the basis of my lived experience with this child, in this place, in this time. In this dialogic space there is a need to suspend authoritative truths to engage creatively and openly within people in the living event with all its potential.

Dialogic pedagogy in the early years setting

When we talk about early years settings we are spanning a large age group of children from birth right through to middle school (approximately 8 years of age). The way dialogic pedagogy 'looks' for this wide range is obviously going to differ across ages. There are undeniable differences – infants rely a lot more on their bodies and sounds than they can on words in the first instance, for example. However, there is no sense of inferiority or developmental deficit in suggesting younger children summon different approaches in their dialogue. I remain unconvinced that a baby of 4 hours old has any less to contribute in dialogic exchange than an 8 year old: that baby simply has a different way of participating that may evade our understanding.

What dialogic approaches allow us to understand in communication with very young children is that the sounds, movements and words that are used always have the potential to mean something, that this meaning is always shaped by the experience and that, in accordance with this principle, meaning is totally influenced by the presence (virtual or real) of others in the event of in-between-ness. A dialogic interrogation of the following scenario between a teacher and group of 4 year olds completing puzzles highlights and, to some extent problematises, the central engagement of the teacher as dialogic partner in such space (see the 'Puzzling' video footage).

FIGURE 3.1 Puzzling

Three children are sitting on the floor near their teacher, Jayde. Each has a puzzle in front of them and Jayde is helping 4-year-old Selina to finish hers. Jayde asks: "Can you carry on from there?" Clayton leans forward to help but Selina puts her hand over the puzzle. Jayde intervenes: "Remember where that pattern has to go, see that pattern matches?" Zen calls out from behind, "I done it," to which Jayde replies, "Good job, Zen – you didn't even need help. You did it all on your own. Good job." All three children now look at Zen's puzzle. "And me, and me," says Clayton. Jayde leans towards Clayton and begins to sort out the pieces with him. Selina tries to fit the pieces. "This is hard work," she says. The teacher turns back to Selina and shows her how to match the pieces through an extended narrative. Zen and Clayton abandon their own puzzles and watch. When a piece cannot be found Clayton holds it out – "I know where it goes" – and leans forward to insert the puzzle piece. Jayde says: "Could Selina put the last piece in her puzzle?" Clayton continues to try and the teacher takes it from him: "Stop, Selina's doing it please." At this moment Selina inserts the last puzzle piece and the teacher claps and says, "Yay."

What this vignette cannot portray, but which is evident in the video, is the body language of the children as they consistently seek their teacher's engagement. Dialogically speaking there appears to be a strong physical orientation by the children to become involved in dialogue with their teacher. Their attention appears to be drawn towards the priority given by the teacher – in this case the completion of Selina's puzzle – and the teacher is sending very strong messages about this in her use of language (including tonation), the positioning of her body and the focus of her attention. We can start to see the complex task of the teacher in trying to engage effectively with each child and his or her priorities (as interpreted by the teacher) while recognising the tensions that arise in such encounters.

Of course we, as outsiders, cannot know the meaning (what Bakhtin describes as the 'content') of these acts for each person – the only evaluation we can make is to impose form based on the images and sounds we have at our disposal. We can, however, see the complexity of the encounter, the orientation of each interlocutor, and guess at the kinds of ideologies that are (or might be) at play for this teacher and the children. Our outsidedness allows us to contribute our own visual surplus to the event in its aftermath.

Our necessary outsidedness (*vnenakhodimost*) position does not allow us to make any further judgements than this. This outsidedness is also limiting for the teacher, who is simultaneously 'in' the pedagogical event that requires her to make pedagogical judgments that far exceed what can be known. Her analysis reveals some deeply confronting issues arising from this encounter:

> Watching Zen sit down and show such determination and perseverance to complete the puzzle displayed development and growth in him that I had not observed before, which is why I felt the need to verbalise what a great job he did . . . By saying, "you didn't even need help," may have made Selina feel bad that she was asking for help, when in fact what I try and foster in our children every day is that it is OK to ask for help and for others to support and do things with you. So the underlying message in this statement was not meant to make Selina feel bad but rather to congratulate Zen. I could sense that Selina felt a little disappointed (possibly by my words or by the frustration with the puzzle that was building up) and so when Clayton placed the last piece of the puzzle in that Selina had worked so hard to do up until that point, I admit I felt a little 'over protective' of Selina and wanted HER to complete the puzzle and earn the rewards of her hard work. However I feel the reaction was too quick as taking the puzzle piece out and giving it to Selina to replace achieved nothing . . .
>
> *(Jayde, Reflective notes, May 2014)*

The living nature of language means that dialogue is always an event in the moment of its enactment, not in its aftermath. While Jayde is able to reflect on the event by considering what she could or should have done differently, at the end of the day she is still called upon to act thoughtfully moment by moment in a curriculum that is characterised by relationships with others rather than set lesson plans or pedagogical goals that are determined outside of the encounter. When she laments that she "achieved nothing," Jayde reveals a tension she faces. In suggesting an outcome focus to her pedagogical engagement – one of assisting Selina to completion – her attention is drawn away from the relationships with others that she sees as central to her role. Yet it seems impossible for Jayde to resist such an outcome orientation. Perhaps this is due to her desire to demonstrate 'learning' in a traditional sense even though she appears to be personally oriented towards a very different agenda.

How do teachers reconcile these different agendas in early years dialogues? John Shotter (2012) suggests that this is very challenging work indeed, requiring professionals to come to the experience of dialogue uncertain of how it will play out but nevertheless equipped to cope with a variety of strategies and resources based on judgements in the moment that are informed by what has gone before:

> Our ability to say explicitly, "This is an X (but not a Y)," requires our already having come to know, *implicitly in our bodily activities*, what X-ness and Y-ness is; and this capacity to orient towards the "what-ness of things" in our surroundings and in the same manner as those around us, and to *judge* that this is indeed an X and not a Y, is something we acquire in the course of our everyday spontaneous involvements with those others.
>
> *(p. 149)*

Again, John is not advocating for a specific method but rather the exercise of what he calls "poised resourcefulness" in the form of a sequence of judgements that rely on an awareness of ourselves and our responsiveness to others. As Jayde highlights earlier, this does not always lead to a perfect solution for all – indeed it may require a suspension of solutions – requiring her to examine (perhaps challenge) some of the values that underpin her pedagogical acts. There might be an opportunity to contemplate the overarching ideology of the pedagogical approach that is privileged by the setting or the profession. The event and all it generates is of great interest to us in consideration of dialogic principles and, in accordance with these, invites a more critical response than is typically contemplated in early years practice. As Bakhtin reminds us, language betrays our ideologies and we are all implicated accordingly.

Contexts for learning

Now that we have established the idea that early years pedagogy is characterised by (1) a broad view of language; (2) the strategic orientation of language; (3) the value positioning of teacher; and (4) responsive relationships, there is a great deal to consider across these contexts. In a more structured setting, for example, you might see the teacher leading groups of children in activities (such as group or mat time) with more formal learning processes foregrounded. Here a consideration of dialogic acts might be more aligned to the classroom pedagogies discussed in the previous chapter. The teacher is likely to be 'out front' with groups of children or in very intensive one-on-one teaching situations where questioning (or perhaps even inter-rogation) is utilised as a pedagogical tool.

However, there are other approaches in the early years for us to contemplate. Often play is at the centre of the curriculum or at least a considerable component of it. Here the teacher may not be active in the dialogue at all and certainly not dominating it if so. Similar practices might be evident in heuristic learning where the role of the teacher is much less prominent – though nonetheless integral to the experience. Questioning is less of a priority in these spaces than listening, watching or 'being present' (a point we will return to shortly). Perhaps the teacher is observing, on the periphery of the experience or even elsewhere in the environment. Perhaps there is a combination of all of the above. Does this mean that they are engaged in dialogic pedagogy or not?

Loving contemplation as pedagogy

The kind of dialogue that dialogic pedagogy promotes in the early years is, I think, beautifully captured in the concept of loving contemplation. Paul Sullivan and John McCarthy (2003) describe this concept as a serious act of lovingly lingering with another. It is an imbued, ethical and aesthetic encounter that posits agency as embodied and experienced. By this they mean that agency is not something that is granted or given to someone else but that arises out of encounter – it already exists, in other words. This idea goes well beyond the Buddhist notion of 'being present' which has gained popularity in literature about early years pedagogy (see for example, Duhn, 2011). Where 'being present' is a psychological state in which the individual sets out to create a shared physical and emotional space, 'lingering lovingly' demands a more active, reciprocal engagement and answerability. There is a sense of emotional commitment to want to learn more about this other person and their interests and to be prepared to make the effort in order to find out more, adjusting one's practice in response.

To linger lovingly recognises that there is some emotional investment by the teacher too. When teachers slow down their pace, pause and openly engage with learners in this manner, a great deal of effort is needed on their part. Such effort is not always visible to others but it is oriented to the teacher's pedagogical decision-making and associated location based on this relationship. Rachel, an infant teacher, explains her subtle and purposeful engagement during play:

> And sometimes it's not even about the verbal communication, it's – I'm there and I'm watching what she's doing with the scarves and it's OK not to talk all the time. Like I'm there and she knows I'm there.
>
> *(Teacher interview in White, Peter, & Redder, 2014)*

The route to such understanding is through Bakhtin's attention to utterance. Remember that utterance, from a dialogic standpoint, is concerned not with just one person's voice, a word or set of words but rather with answerable language. This means that utterance only exists when it is answered – by being noticed and responded to in the social event. In this sense listening is not enough: teachers must implicate themselves in the dialogue, taking responsibility for what they see and hear and the way it is interpreted. Bakhtin explains that unless this responsibility is understood the author is merely a mirror image of the child who replicated him or her: "He cannot be an-other or other for the author, he cannot have any surplus that is determined by this otherness" (Bakhtin, 1986, p. 165).

It is important to remember that, for Bakhtin, such attempts are not a route to absolute certainty – because that would mean the child was finalised with nothing left to offer because they are already fully known. It is the effort that is of central importance here, and the moments of engagement that generate wonder. Lingering lovingly implies that there is value in the effort of trying. The reciprocal exchange that transpires in this event is what sets this moment apart from any other. It is shared between teacher and student(s) and we can recognise its uniqueness in this respect. Dialogic pedagogy is thus characterised by the uniqueness of the event itself rather than some predetermined goal or outcome.

Here we can pause for a moment to recap several very important provocations for the early years:

1   Each child is an individual personality in his or her own right and has the potential to contribute in ways that go beyond adult-led orientations.
2   A child is influenced by their family, culture and physical context but not defined by them.
3   A child may or may not reveal something of themselves in any moment. What they reveal can alter in the next moment and that is OK.
4   What a child reveals to one person at one point in time may be a completely different aspect of their personality than what they reveal to another person at another (or even the same) point in time.
5   How a child presents him or herself in any event, and how this is received, is totally connected to the time, space and value given to the act and its composition.
6   Lingering lovingly to richly contemplate another is much more important than rampant or even sustained questioning.

Aside from the tangible benefits of getting to know someone as a fellow human being, the effort of trying to know young children – while accepting the necessary mystery of their experience – is a central means of ethically under-standing what might be important for this 'other' person. If we agree that learning takes place in moments of significance rather than simply because knowledge is offered, it is vital for teachers to appreciate what is meaningful for the children they teach.

But it is easier said than done. As with all relationships, teachers do not get along or 'gel' with every child they work with. Nor, if we are honest, can we always appreciate the values held by other families or cultures who enter into the early years setting. This is especially true for teachers who have lived and worked in a dominant culture all of their lives and for whom the dominance of the reigning chronotope is seldom questioned or challenged. Yet, strange as it may seem, it is these difficult moments – where tensions, differences and perhaps even disagree-ments take place – that provide "the impetus for individual agency in the form of the creative stylization of speech genres" (Cresswell & Teucher, 2011, p. 117). In a dialogic sense, then, difference is highly valued. It is no longer a problem if the teacher draws from different experiences or genres. In fact it is very important to the ideological becoming of the child from a Bakhtinian perspective. Differences are also likely to exist across different contexts for learning in the early years. As Vladimir Zinchenko (in press) reminds us, it is in these "zones of indeterminacy" that dialogue has space to thrive:

> Such gaps in the continuing experience provide a place for creativity, for cre-ative comprehension and, it goes without saying, for delusion and error. This leads to unfinalizability of dialogue . . .

As we shall see in the chapters that follow, many early years studies employing dialogic methodologies emphasise the dynamic peer interactions that also take place in early years settings – at meal times, in routine events and in playful encounters. The role of pedagogy is much more subtle here, in part due to the very different chronotopes that are known to exist for children in most early years settings. Think of the number of contexts children draw from and their very different ways of com-municating in each of these. As the world expands due to the internet and other dynamic communication genres, the experience of the child is likely to become increasingly sophisticated.

Each of these contexts has its own complex set of genres that set the scene for the way this child will interact. For example, the family home may include a television set which provides a rich source of information to the child beyond their immedi-ate environment, information they will more than likely bring to the centre. How often have you seen children act out favourite TV shows with their peers? Many children now communicate with grandparents through software programs such as Skype which rely heavily on turn-taking – have you ever tried to hold a group conference on Skype where no one waited their turn? Often in these chronotopic encounters the rules are quite different and have to be negotiated. Thresholds, as windows into a different way of understanding, are created as more worlds are encountered. They are very important sites for learning since it is only when we encounter other ways of engaging with the world that we have the opportunity to recognise ourselves in relation to others, according to Bakhtin. This does not mean that we transform ourselves in response, but it is an opportunity for *transgradience* – a way of 'seeing' more through engagement with others.

Bakhtin suggests that culture is revealed in these threshold experiences – providing a means of recognising the essential 'otherness' of the different experiences each person brings. As each chronotope meets it creates necessary miscommunication, uncertainty and/or surprise that, according to Bakhtin, is central to learning. You can see how much potential there is for threshold encounters in the early years as children move between very different worlds – bringing them to bear on their experience in the centre. Children's questions and curiosities about what is happening are a very important part of these threshold experiences. As Bakhtin explains:

> Without one's own questions one cannot creatively understand anything other or foreign . . . Such a dialogic encounter of two cultures does not result in merging or mixing. Each has its own unity and open totality, but they are mutually enriched.
>
> *(Bakhtin, 1986, p. 7)*

One of the insights generated in my studies has been the understanding that when threshold encounters occur they are not always revealed in an immediate response to an event. Sometimes they appear, often in a different guise, hours, perhaps even days or weeks later. The vigilant teacher can appreciate these more with experience of the child, their personality and in dialogue with others over time. In the following vignette Lola has brought the game of peek-a-boo to the early years setting from home. Luckily this key teacher has ample background information and is making the effort of trying to understand what is happening in order for this new genre to be valued within the centre too.

Teacher Lynette has been talking to Rachel (Lola's key teacher) about her learning, as they do every day. Rachel shared Lola's interest in the game of peek-a-boo, explaining that Lola had been playing this game at home with her mother. Later that morning Lynette is sitting on a chair feeding Harrison his bottle. She looks over at Lola, who peers at her through the arch created in a basket handle. Lola quietly says, "Boo." Lynette, recognising Lola's invitation, responds with a "boo" and a game ensues.

FIGURE 3.2 A game of peek-a-boo

Yet there are plenty of moments in the early years experience where genres and their chronotopic origins are not noticed, recognised or valued at all. Even the most well-meaning teacher can easily misunderstand despite all his or her efforts. In an earlier study I undertook with a toddler and his teacher, an example of the shifting meanings of language forms was evident when 18-month-old Jayden raised his hand in a fist (White, 2009). The teacher interpreted this action as the toddler trying to convey his masculinity, responding by saying, "He-man," and showing her muscle. It was only much later, when speaking to Jayden's mother, that we learnt his family had been watching a favourite Jim Carey movie, *Liar Liar* – where the father is tricking his ex-wife on the phone and signals to his son a shared sense of achievement by raising his hand into a fist. Once the teacher realised this revised meaning she was able to deploy this movement to convey moments of shared delight with the toddler – such as when he built a tower of blocks up high or caught a ball. The shared genre was only then able to be appreciated, to its fuller extent, within the centre dialogue too. As its interpretation altered with use in the early years setting the fist came to mean a number of different things depending on who employed it, such is the dialogic nature of language.

Taking into consideration Bakhtin's idea of the chronotopic threshold helps to explain why a young child might use a particular genre, as in the case of Jayden and his engagement with favourite family movies at home. It helps to explain, too, why a teacher may find language impenetrable or, conversely, be amazed by the same language that a parent may see as very ordinary and commonplace. For example, when I asked Zoe's mother what she could see that was potentially significant about Zoe's language acts, she repeatedly said that she couldn't see anything at all. We could postulate that this mother felt so close to her child that there was nothing Zoe could offer that was any different to what she, the mother, already knew about her, highlighting Bakhtin's idea of extreme intimacy in authorship, which he describes as ultimate consummation if taken to the extreme. Yet if families are given opportunities to engage in dialogues about what teachers do or do not see (and vice versa) there are opportunities to appreciate different aspects of the child. At the same time, a sense of mystery, speculation and surprise is important in fully appreciating another without trying to know them through and through.

Implicating teachers

Of course it is not only children and families that bring rich insights to the early years context. Drawing from different experiences, contexts and interpretative orientations, teachers bring their own internally persuasive discourses to and from the setting. Early years teachers have had the privilege of spending many years studying the work of experts and learning the professional (authoritative) discourses that provide a range of ways to theorise practice. These contributions are by no means superior, but the difference generated out of any interpretation (formal or informal) is a source of visual surplus. While the potential for conflicting or competing understanding is enormous, with it comes the opportunity to offer new ways of seeing the young child within the world. For Bakhtin this is not a choice but a moral imperative.

From a dialogic stance, then, it is not necessary for teachers to agree with everyone, but it is important for them to engage in dialogues about their differences and to resist the urge to be the author of everything – allowing each personality to speak for himself or herself. Unless teachers are vigilant about their interactions and open to diversity as an opportunity for growth, the children, and families, who need it most may not benefit from the kinds of relationships that will support their learning – that is, those that draw on their own priorities, value them as individuals and invite a response. Worse still, other children will pick up on the social cues offered by teachers and may orient their relationships accordingly. The child who might potentially benefit from teacher engagement is not only denied this relationship but is now treated negatively by their peers, thus further perpetuating their social isolation. In the following scenario you can see a vivid example of this as a teacher reprimands a child in negative tones. Zoe is watching carefully. Watch her response several minutes later as she relates to this peer (see the 'Judgement day' footage).

FIGURE 3.3 Judgement day

Zoe watches 4-year-old Wayne . . . throw blocks across the room. Teacher A . . . enters the scene and speaks to Wayne in harsh tones, telling him that he must "STOP throwing the blocks." Her body language seems angry and is characterized by a frown, a wave of her finger, and severe tone of voice. Teacher A leaves. Zoe approaches Wayne and takes one of the blocks from his pile. Wayne turns to Zoe and says, "NO." Zoe looks across the room to Teacher A, who is now occupied elsewhere, picks up a block, and hits Wayne on the head. Her arm is used in full force and she repeats, "NO," in the same tone as Teacher A has used. Wayne cries and hits her back. Teacher B enters the scene and removes the block from Wayne, explaining, "We don't hit. We don't hit smaller children," and asks Wayne to say sorry, which he does. Teacher B leaves. Zoe turns to a second boy, then repeats the action, using the same tones, saying, "NO" and hitting him with the block. Teacher B returns and repeats the phrase, "We don't hit."

(White, 2013, p. 70)

Did you notice the way Zoe used her body in a similar volitional tone to that of the teacher? While we cannot know for sure, I have pondered the thought that

Zoe may be acting in response to what she has observed, which may resonate with other experiences she has participated in or observed from elsewhere that we don't have access to. In any case it now appears to be a genre that she adapts to convey disapproval toward this 'naughty' boy. Her observations and experiences are likely to have taught her a great deal about this relationship, this child, this teacher and herself. Vivian Gussin Paley (1998) has described encounters such as this as a painful experience for children in a centre who have watched carefully the practice of their teacher. One child's shame can most certainly become another child's pain in the dialogic world that makes up the early years setting. This pain, or shame, is as much a source of learning as any other experience. In exploring this footage, I describe the teacher as an "emotional compass" (White, 2013, p. 74) for the child. Learning of this nature is just as much a part of the curriculum as any form of activity teachers might provide.

However we package it, teachers are seriously implicated through the kinds of relationships they forge with young children. To a large extent these relationships are influenced by the teacher's ability to see and hear the voices of children and those who matter to them (present and absent) in early years settings. Such is the focus of early years pedagogy. It is often very subtle but nonetheless central to what we do as an answerable deed. See if you can see this kind of nuanced subtlety in the dialogue that follows (see 'Block play' in the video companion).

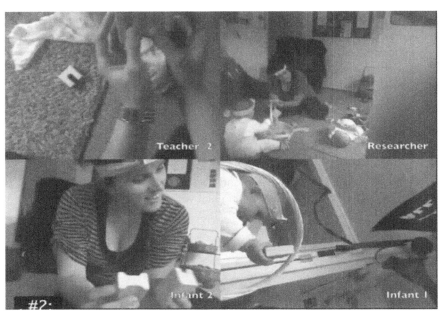

FIGURE 3.4 Block play

Rachel, the teacher, is sitting on the floor with Lola and Harrison on either side. She places a basket of small wooden blocks in front of Lola who says, "Ahhh." Rachel replies with a smile and mimics the sound. Harrison is watching Rachel. Lola pats the basket and says, "Heeeey yeah," to which Rachel replies, "Yeah?" Lola picks up two blocks immediately followed by Rachel, who also picks up two blocks and taps them together several times. "I wonder what noise they make when you bang them together?" Lola drops her blocks and reaches out to Rachel. "Ho ho, you want these ones?" Rachel passes Lola the blocks and she commences banging them together. Rachel picks up another two differently shaped blocks: "Look, these other ones do it too." Lola continues banging. "That's it," says Rachel. Lola puts her blocks back in the basket and holds her hand out to Rachel. "Oh, you want these ones?" Rachel passes Lola the blocks: "Bang them together and make some noise?" "Ahhhh," says Lola, a sound that Rachel repeats. Turning to Harrison, Rachel bangs the blocks together and then passes two blocks to him. Lola, who has retrieved another set of blocks, farts. Rachel looks back at Lola, laughs and says, "OOpp."

What is evident in this event is the constant cueing of the teacher to the infants – a strategy that is considered to be highly desirable in many Western pedagogies (White, Peter, & Redder, 2015). While she initiates the experience by offering the game of blocks, her responses are built upon the orientations of the infants. When Lola reaches out her hand Rachel interprets this to mean "I want that" and responds by offering the block. Rachel builds on her interpretations of Lola's interest in the sounds of different blocks by offering her a variety of options, accompanied by a provocation "I wonder . . .?" which Lola picks up on. The visual aspects of this event – the smiling face and open body language offered by Rachel – are also worthy of our attention. Accompanied by mimicking sounds that then extend on the experience by adding more complex sentence structuring, building on what has been offered, there is definitely a very rich exchange going on here.

But that's not all that is happening. Lola is also engaging in a kind of turn-taking 'conversational' genre that she can adapt for other contexts as a source of orienting herself socially. She is learning the origins of a specific genre of block play that is comprised of construction and sharing of ideas through the use of wooden artefacts that are exchanged and built up. She appears to understand that she can play a role in shaping the environment and that she is seen, heard and valued – evident by her teacher's response. Through the teacher's constant vigilance regarding the additional presence of 4-month-old Harrison, Lola may also be learning that she is part of a peer group that her teacher also cares about, evident in the teacher's consistent daily exchanges with the children.

Although it may seem as if Lola and Rachel are communicating with ease, this is by no means a chance encounter. Rachel is Lola's 'key teacher', meaning that she spends a lot of her time with Lola and, as Rachel explained in our discussions, takes every opportunity to linger lovingly in order to understand her interests and priorities. Rachel has deliberately set out to understand Lola and her means of communication through a variety of strategies – some of which we have just seen. This had occurred over a long period of time and was described by Rachel as her pedagogical imperative. These two appear to know each other very well yet Rachel is prepared to be amazed by Lola at any moment.

Even this is not enough to generate a rationale for the meaningful encounter we have witnessed, however. There are other, unseen, participants in this dialogue: for starters, the other teachers who are supporting Rachel to sustain this conversation by fulfilling a myriad of other duties in the background such as answering the phone, wiping the table or writing notices. Working as a team these 'buddy' teachers rely on one another to support interactions of this nature through sharing information, acting as a sounding board for ideas and stepping in when needed, as well as allowing time and space. The same is true for Lola's family, who play an enormous role in supporting these kinds of interactions. Lola brings an expectation that she will be seen and heard in dialogue – perhaps something she has already experienced at home. Her family take the time each day to share events and experiences in ways that provide important clues to Lola's language. Rachel values these relationships as part of the pedagogical experience.

The centre itself is implicated too. Rachel is able to spend time with Lola because she is not bound to rigid rosters that preclude her from being immediately responsive. She is able to access time and space to think about her practice through professional development and noncontact time where she reads literature about infants and their learning. The centre's ratio of adult to infant is 1:3 – considerably better than that endorsed by the state in regulations. Rachel's work is recognised by centre management[2] as 'professional' and, by association, valued through a salary that reflects her skill and expertise. The curriculum framework that she works with is well understood as a framework rather than a set of rules and Rachel understands that she can approach her practice in a flexible, open-ended manner. Taken together all these elements make up an early years pedagogical chronotope that is able to see and respond to infant voice – a polyphony of multiple perspectives that create a dialogic chorus of voices in concert with one another.

The dialogic nature of 'voice(s)'

In dialogic thinking voice is a plural construct. As we have seen, a selection of voices, conveyed as genres that are made up of both language forms and their meanings, are deployed in dialogue according to their perceived significance to the speakers and their interlocutors. While all forms of language have the potential to contribute to meaning-making, it is the *strategic orientation* of voice that a dialogic approach pays attention to. How it is employed and the response it receives – both in the moment and over time – is what takes precedence here.

Thinking back to Rachel, Lola, Harrison and the blocks, can you remember how Rachel and Lola built on one another's dialogue throughout the exchange – first imitating and then expanding on sounds and actions as they became available to each other? We do not know for sure if Lola was employing voices from home here – we would have to ask her parents about that and even then we couldn't be sure – but we can see the organic properties of language that is living and active in this dialogic exchange. Lola is also taking turns, trying out combinations and selecting different objects from the basket in ways that she later developed in play without Rachel. We do not know what Harrison, lying on the floor and watching this exchange, is thinking, but we do know he is much more than a passive observer – he is very much a part of this dialogue too. Even though the camera cannot portray the fullest extent of his engagement, we cannot dismiss his presence in the dialogic space.

The role of the teacher

Dialogic pedagogy in the early years therefore shifts the emphasis of the teacher from facilitator of an external curriculum, activities or projects to one of partner, co-learner, investigator and provocateur. Early years teacher interactions are now much less 'didactic' than might be seen in settings where teachers are rampantly questioning or actively 'leading' learning. Much of the early years literature now concurs that a 'high-quality' early years setting is characterised by practices that support children's engagement with a variety of personally meaningful experiences that are comprised of rich dialogues with infants, toddlers and young children, their parents and wider community. Dialogic pedagogy asserts this principle in action but makes a great deal of trouble for any simplistic or formulaic approach.

What is of special interest here, from a Bakhtinian standpoint, is the significance of the teacher's presence *even when he or she is not directly involved in the experience*. Po Chi Tam's 2012 study of 3–4-year-old children in a Hong Kong kindergarten highlights this point. She found that the topic of children's interactions was strategically oriented towards – and away from – the teacher's agenda depending on the teacher's location. If she was within earshot, the dialogues differed markedly from when she was perceived to be at a distance. This same phenomenon was evident in a number of studies of children's humour, which we will explore in chapter 4, highlighting the fact that teachers make a profound difference to the nature of experience in early years settings even when they don't realise it or reside on the periphery of the event.

Of course teachers often recognise this. One of the teachers in my PhD study (White, 2009) pointed out her frustration at being placed on a roster that precluded her from locating herself in the same physical space as the children she wanted to develop relationships with. Her duties often took her away from the experiences that she perceived would generate important insights that could provide a means of deepening the dialogue:

. . . being inside, I felt like I wasn't doing my job [laughs] . . . every now and then I found myself glancing outside to see what he was doing . . . I kept thinking "Oh what am I missing, what am I missing?" . . . I should have been out there.

(Teacher interview in White, 2009, p. 186)

While many early years settings have developed other ways of ensuring teachers have every opportunity to consistently engage in meaningful dialogue with children, there are always going to be other duties that must be performed and routines to participate in. The extent to which those duties can also be considered part of the dialogic experience is a topic well worth consideration. We will do this in the next chapter when we look at routines. For now it is enough to know that such encounters are no less dialogic than any other.

Research on dialogic pedagogy in the early years

So far we have considered the potential of dialogic pedagogy for the early years as a primary means of engaging with the infant, toddler and young child and their many, multiple and competing voices. As such we have looked at the role of the teacher and some of the challenges and opportunities they face from a dialogic standpoint. These range from not being able to see or understand, misinterpreting and speaking on behalf of the child rather than with them to seeing more and learning about oneself and the child through the process. Whether these events are positive or negative does not preclude them from playing a central role in children's learning – for better or for worse. As such, it is important for teachers to understand what is happening in the various dialogues that take place in the early years setting and the potential impact of their actions on learners.

1) Dialogue as reciprocal spoken word

A small number of researchers have set out to capture the explicit nature of language in the early years. These studies emphasise spoken word as a central source of dialogue in the early years. For instance, Helena Rasku-Puttonen, Marja-Kristiina Lerkkanen, Anna-Maija Poikkeus and Martti Siekkinen (2012) explored dialogues of 6 year olds in Finnish preschools. They looked at episodes, patterns and functions of teacher–child exchange in what they describe as developmentally appropriate settings that cater for both "adult-guided and child-guided experiences and practices" (p. 140). Videoing classroom exchange including sentence, single word and nonverbal language, researchers sought to understand the lived experience of dialogue. They found that children's interactions ranged from brief, initiation-response type exchanges to lengthy and diverse contributions on the part of the children in response to their teachers. Interestingly what appeared to distinguish the two types of response was the attentiveness of the teacher to the children's points of view. In those interactions where children initiated dialogue,

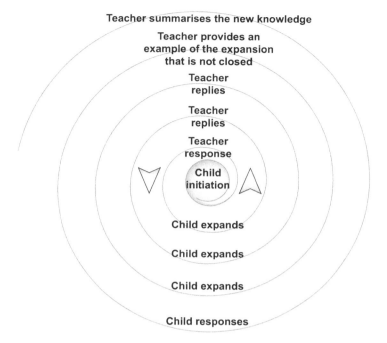

FIGURE 3.5 Expanding dialogues.
Source: Adapted from Rasku-Puttonen et al. (2012, p. 146).

the teacher's role was to sensitively prompt them to share their ideas by allowing ample space in expanded discussion. In other words, the more expansive the dialogue, the more it was considered to represent forms of dialogue that would contribute to learning. According to these researchers the role of the teacher is thus oriented towards immediate and sustained responsiveness, asking open-ended questions, probing and building on children's interests as a kind of pattern, as the following model suggests.

This idea is closely aligned to the findings of the EPPE[3] project that suggest sustained, shared thinking like this is critical for the types of problem-solving behaviours that are likely to enhance learning in young children. From a dialogic standpoint, however, there may be a problem with the summarising conclusion mapped out for the teacher. This is because the summary could be interpreted as finalising, or closing off, the event. In some cases, from a dialogic standpoint, such a finale can lead to the shutting down of dialogue.

In the following vignette, early years teacher Jayde attempts to sustain a dialogue with 4-year-old Cory based on his experience of snowboarding. As you watch the video (see 'Interrogations' in the video companion) it may be helpful to map out the dialogue in terms of initiations, responses, expansions and summary:

FIGURE 3.6 Interrogations

Cory is engaged in block play sitting on the floor beside his teacher, Jayde. Provoked by the triangular blocks, Cory explains to Jayde his understanding of slalom skiing down a ramp. "How do you do that?" asks Jayde. Cory pulls his legs up and pushes one down. "Like that, and then they go down it." "Very cool," replies Jayde. "And does that stop you from falling off?" "Yep," answers Cory. "What a good invention," says Jayde. "Yeah, it's like snowboards," responds Cory. "Like snowboards?" "Yeah, I saw it on TV." "You saw the snowboards on TV?" asks Jayde. "I saw it with Daddy," Cory answers. "And what were the people on the snowboards doing?" "They had some trucks and they do crashes," says Cory. "Did they do some crashes? Ouch!" says Jayde. "Yeah." "Do you think it would have hurt them?" "No," says Cory. "Maybe they're used to it, eh?" Jayde says. "Yeah." "And what else did you see on TV?" "I saw, I saw flying things going in the air." Cory waves his arms in a large circle. "Flying things going in the air?" asks Jayde. "Yeah." "What sort of things?" "Ummm, skaters, skaters," Cory says. "Skaters? Going in the air?" "Yeah." "What were they doing in the air?" Cory explains: "So they can't go past the blue lines." "Oh, they can't go past the blue line. What happens if they go past the blue line?" probes Jayde. "They fall down into the [unclear but sounds like rain cloud]," says Cory, putting his fingers into the shape of a square. "Ohhhhh. Have you ever gone skiing?" Jayde asks.

"Yeah," replies Cory matter-of-factly. "Have you? You've gone on the snow?" Cory becomes more animated: "I saw, I saw me on TV." "Ohhh, you saw you on TV? What were you doing?" "Ummm, I was doing some robots." "Ohhh how cool, where did you go there?" Cory pauses. "Ummm, to learn how I can do it." There is a pause. "Hmmm, so you do practising with your snowboards and your skateboarding?" summarises Jayde. "Yeah," says Cory. "Wow, Cory! You're pretty talented!" "Yeah." "Must be lots of fun?" Jayde suggests. "Yeah." "And Mummy and Daddy – do they snowboard as well?" "Yep," says Cory. "Very cool."

What did you think?

Many early years scholars advocate for the use of questioning, a method Jayde has dutifully followed here. However, despite her considerable efforts the dialogue loses its thread of meaning in places when she probes into topics that orient more to her interest (or lack of understanding) than to Cory's. As such an expansion of the dialogue is closed off. For instance, Cory's focus on the process of skiing down a ramp to stop falling is interrupted by Jayde's questioning emphasis on safety. Though Cory attempts to get back to this orientation, in his description of falling, flying and the blue line, he is redirected to an emphasis on the social nature of the event. It is at this point that the dialogue dies out because the teacher has summarised the event once and for all as "very cool." Note Cory's body language when these redirections or conclusions take place and the animated difference when authentic response is evident – the body betrays the significance of the dialogue even if we are not attuned to its content. In a curriculum that is underpinned by learning relationships these dialogues deserve our urgent and detailed attention.

I should pause here to say that, from a dialogic standpoint, dialogue of this nature is only one genre that takes place here. Despite a great deal of espoused certainty in current policy documents we cannot say for sure what kinds of dialogue comprise the most important learning. Indeed, as you will discover as you read on, Bakhtin has some serious challenges to this singular approach to dialogue, orienting more towards the subtle complexities of language as utterance – in terms of what gets noticed, when, why and by whom. How the language plays out as an event-of-being, rather than what outcomes it yields, is much more pertinent to Bakhtin's entreaty. Learning takes place in many unpredictable and interesting ways that go beyond one-off extended teacher–child exchanges in such encounters.

Elin Odegaard (2007) in Norway took this broader approach in her investigation of teacher-child dialogue by studying co-narratives between 1–3-year-old children and their teachers during mealtimes. She was also able to identify patterns in teacher–child exchanges with an emphasis on the way teachers took children's ideas into account, versus their own agenda. This is a particularly important idea in dialogic pedagogy – the extent to which the voices are silenced or privileged (remember Olga Dysthe's research from the previous chapter?). Elin discovered that narratives where teachers took the specific language styles of children seriously generated more genuinely interactive dialogues than those that were driven by teacher priorities alone. This meant that they were characterised by a balance between children and adult agendas and contributions – creating space for alternative contributions, including those that may initially seem puzzling to adults. Taking into perspective the individual style of each child seemed to make a great difference to their engagement and required teachers to negotiate their way through dialogue rather than impose a set agenda. This was the case for all age groups studied.

Hiroaki Ishiguro (2010) also studied children's dialogues at meal times, but this time in a Japanese nursery school caring for infants up to age 6. He analysed the genres that were employed by children and teachers as they ate their lunch. He found two competing agenda at play during these events. The first, the teacher's agenda, emphasised 'good' eating behaviours using methods such as stimulation, guidance, and suggestion, while the second, the children's agenda, oriented towards playfulness and social contact using genres characterised by jokes or teasing. Ishiguro concludes that children are not merely appropriating language as it is offered to them directly but that they appear to be creatively engaging with different language forms that are specific to their experience. We will discuss some of the wider implications of this type of language play in chapter 6; suffice to say that voices are not necessarily shut down in these contexts but rather go 'underground'. In this location they might not be 'seen' by adults but they most certainly exist, as we will soon discover in the chapters that follow.

While there are now several studies that have explored 3–5-year-old children's dialogue employing Bakhtin's ideas on dialogism, specific studies of dialogic interactions with infants and toddlers are few and far between. At the time of writing there are only two studies I am aware of, outside my own, where this age group has received specific dialogic attention. The first, by Karin Junefelt in Sweden, takes place in the home of a 22-month-old sight-impaired toddler. Video of his interactions with his mother highlights the significance of nonverbal language to these early dialogues:

Mother: *Ska vi forst sjumga sma grodorna?* (shall we first sing little frogs?)
Child: (Jumping rhythmically)
Mother: (sings the song)
Child: (performs the gestures simultaneously with the song)
Child: (touches mothers arm, claps his hands) gr gr grna (phoneme for 'frogs')
Mother: Ja (yes). (she sings again).

(Junefelt, 2011, p. 163)

What is evident, and what Karin points out in her analysis, is the way this child was able to establish shared meaning using his body *even when he had no visual experience of it.* Her study goes on to show how nonverbal communication decreased with age and became increasingly coupled with spoken language over time. The use of language is revealed here as a complex, quite remarkable interplay between bodies, words and meaning – it is not an either/or as is commonly perceived. In dialogic terms, it represents a pedagogical strategy of shared meaning (intersubjectivity) and difference (a term Bakhtin describes as *alterity*) in a constant quest for authorship. This is an advancement on the notion of sustained, shared thinking that we looked at earlier because it suggests that thinking which is not shared is also of great significance. It represents an opportunity to present oneself as 'other' – to be otherwise – a very important dialogic principle indeed!

John Dore (1989) also set out to understand the verbal communication strategies between a toddler and her parents in a study of Emily at bedtime. By analysing genres used by Emily he explains the kinds of "feedback loops" (p. 234) that take place during her parents' attempts to get this toddler to go to sleep alone. Over a series of months Dore tracked the shifts in dialogue ranging from monologue to what he called "re-envoicement." He concludes that young children's genre use is both learnt and strategised within the context, over time and with consistent repetition. Dialogue is, again, revealed as highly strategic at this very early stage of life.

2) Dialogue, the body and beyond

Typically, as we have now established, studies of dialogue tend to privilege the spoken word rather than combinations of sounds and/or body movements. This seems odd since Bakhtin privileged the body in his earliest works and remained devoted to the idea of dynamic language forms his whole life. As Tim Lensmire (1997) suggests, Bakhtin was also concerned with un-uttered language – that which has not yet been spoken – as much as that which was more obvious. Of course this is almost impossible for us to capture in any certain manner.

As you will by now have realised, my own studies of very young children over the past few years have focused on an expanded view of utterance and the different genres employed by infants and toddlers in early years settings. On many occasions in my analysis of infant-teacher interactions I discovered the importance of language forms such as a smile or even the presence of silence in dialogue. Infant communication with teachers in early childhood settings was often characterised by seemingly 'second-party' interactions where the infant was not directly part of the dialogue but appeared to participate from a distance – sometimes as an observer, sometimes seeking eye contact. In such cases the patterns that were evident were less oriented to sustained shared dialogues than to the notion of 'lingering lovingly'. It was at these pedagogical moments that a sustained look, touch or even physical proximity played a critical role in the nature of dialogue, as we saw earlier in the game of blocks that took place between Lola, Rachel and Harrison. We will examine the significance of these subtle language forms in the next chapter – a silent yet potentially rich form of dialogue.

At other times there were significantly animated examples of dialogue where the infant or toddler played a central role in the strategic orientation of events. I was continually amazed by their skill in achieving the goals they had set for themselves. It was during these events that I became aware of the agentic capacity of young children to orient others towards or away from themselves. I view this strategic orientation as a

FIGURE 3.7 Baby rock

call for answerability. Perhaps the most poignant example of this is in an event that took place towards the end of our study between Zoe, her teacher and a doll where the body plays a vital role in meaning-making (see the video 'Baby rock').

What do you think Zoe was trying to do here?

As you watch the footage, try to look at it through dialogic eyes using the principles we have explained so far. Here you are analysing the language forms that are being used, their interpreted meaning by the teacher (genre) and her response (which makes up the utterance). What genres are being employed? By whom? What is Zoe's strategic orientation? Is her call for answerability responded to? If so, how does she achieve this? Notice how Zoe draws her teacher back to herself and the doll – even in the face of several obstacles. How does she do it? Did you notice that the doll looked a bit like the teacher – in fact I realised several days later that Zoe always employed *this* doll when she initiated play with *this* teacher. We will explore some of these questions further in the chapters that follow.

Accepting a broader view of language and its between-ness in the event, I quickly discovered that there were very few occasions where the teacher wasn't somehow implicated in the dialogic experience of the very young child. This was true whether or not the teacher was physically present. But what differed was the nature of the experience across different contexts. For instance, the teacher was very rarely involved in events that were characterised by what I called 'free-form' genres whereas they were keenly attuned to more formal 'learning experiences' such as group time, painting or story reading activities. The latter populated almost entirely the portfolio records in the setting which told stories of Zoe's learning. Yet in free-form genres there was also much to be celebrated. These often involved sophisticated levels of social movement in the peer group and were comprised of noises and running combinations such as "Whhhheeeeee" sounds as toddlers ran through the wind chasing a balloon or an onomatopoeic "OOOOOOOoooooo" as they rode a trike down a ramp. Gunvor Lokken (2000) has also written about these types of events in her study of Norwegian toddlers, describing acts such as 'wall licking' and 'curtain running' as often misunderstood or overlooked joyful exchanges between toddlers as a specific cultural group in an early years setting. Adults are seldom physically present in this genre or, if they are, may consider themselves to be obsolete. However, this is rarely the case as we will see in the chapters that follow. Whether the teacher is there or not, they play a significant part in the dialogues that take place in the early years setting.

Looking back, moving forward

So far we have established that dialogic pedagogy does have an important place in the early years. Given our increased contemporary emphasis on dialogue and interpretation at the centre of learning for young children, we have seen that dialogic pedagogy offers a means of not only interrogating practice by carefully examining dialogue as a central route to meaning-making but perhaps even altering the kinds of relationships we are able to develop with learners through a heightened awareness of our centrality to these. This is generated through increased insight that forms the basis of aesthetics and enhanced accountability through an understanding of ethics. I hope you have discovered that in dialogic pedagogy it is not enough to simply observe a child as a means of understanding them but that instead, through a reciprocal encounter of answerability, we can better appreciate the possibilities that we offer them and they us. It is a loving entreaty or deed. We end this chapter with the proposition that the early years teacher is not only the central pedagogical anchor in early years setting experience but that their responses and interactions may play a vital role in the 'ideological becoming' (*Bildungsroman*) of each child in these dialogic spaces of in-between-ness. This is a rare privilege indeed, but with it comes significant challenges we will explore further in the following chapters. Perhaps we can now more fully appreciate what Bakhtin means when he tells us "there is no alibi"!

Notes

1 These first two questions are borrowed from Eugene Matusov (2009), p. 8.
2 At the time of this study infant pedagogy was not valued nationally by the New Zealand government and the centre was upholding standards in spite of considerable funding restraints accordingly.
3 The Effective Preschool and Primary Education Project (2004) was developed in the United Kingdom by Kathy Sylva, Edward Melhuish, Pam Sammons, Iram Siraj-Blatchford and Brenda Taggart at the Institute of Education, University of London (http://www.ioe.ac.uk/research/153.html).

References

Australian Government Department of Education, Employment & Workplace. (2009). *Belonging, being and becoming: The Early Years Framework for Australia.* Retrieved from http://docs.education.gov.au/system/files/doc/other/belonging_being_and_becoming_the_early_years_learning_framework_for_australia.pdf

Bakhtin, M. M. (1986). *Speech genres and other late essays* (C. Emerson & M. Holquist, Eds.; V. W. McGee, Trans.). Austin: University of Texas Press.

Berlyand, I. (2009). Puzzles of the number and dialogue in the early grades of the School of the Dialogue of Cultures. *Journal of Russian and East European Psychology, 47*(1), 61–95.

Brownlee, J., & Berthelsson, D. (2007). Personal epistemology and relational pedagogy in early childhood teacher education programmes. *Early Years: An International Journal, 26*(1), 17–29.

Cresswell, J., & Teucher, U. (2011). The body in language: M. M. Bakhtin on ontogenetic development. *New Ideas in Psychology, 29*(2), 106–118.

Department for Education. (2012). *Statutory framework for the early years foundation stage: Setting the standards for learning, development and care for children from birth to five.* Retrieved from http://www.education.gov.uk

Dore, J. (1989). Monologue as reinforcement of dialogue. In K. Nielson (Ed.), *Narratives in the crib* (pp. 231–259). Cambridge, MA: Harvard University Press.

Duhn, I. (2011). Being a community: A relationship-focused pedagogy for infants and toddlers. *The First Years: Ngā Tau Tuatahi New Zealand Journal of Infant and Toddler Education, 13*(2), 24–28.

Farquhar, S., & White, E. J. (2014). Philosophy and pedagogy of early childhood. *Educational Philosophy and Theory, 46*(8), 821–832.

Ishiguro, H. (2010). Speech genres using during lunchtime: Conversations with children. In K. Junefelt & P. Nordin (Eds.), *Proceedings from the Second International Interdisciplinary Conference on Perspectives and Limits of Dialogism in Mikhail Bakhtin* (pp. 55–59). Stockholm: Stockholm University.

Junefelt, K. (2007). *Rethinking egocentric speech: Towards a new hypothesis.* New York, NY: Nova Science.

Junefelt, K. (2011). Early dialogues as a teaching device from a Bakhtinian perspective. In E. J. White & M. A. Peters (Eds.), *Bakhtinian pedagogy: Opportunities and challenges for research, policy and practice in education across the globe* (pp. 159–178). New York, NY: Peter Lang.

Kelly, J., & White, E. J. (with Dekker, M., Donald, J., Hart, K., McKay, F., McMillan, L., Mitchell-King, A., & Wright, G.). (2013). *The Ngahere Project: Teaching and learning possibilities in nature settings.* Hamilton, New Zealand: Wilf Malcolm Institute of Educational Research.

Lensmire, T. J. (1997). The teacher as Dostoevskian novelist. *Research in the Teaching of English, 31*(3), 367–392.

Lenz-Taguchi, L. H. (2010). *Going beyond the theory/practice divide in early childhood education: Introducing an intra-active pedagogy.* New York, NY: Routledge.

Lobok, A. (2012). Preschool education bullied: An experiment in establishing a dialogue with a kindergarten educator. *Journal of Russian and East European Psychology, 50*(6), 92–114.

Lofdahl, A. (2005). 'The funeral': A study of children's shared meaning-making and its developmental significance. Early Years: An International Research Journal, 25(1), 5–16.

Lokken, G. (2000). *Toddler peer culture: The social style of one and two year old body-subjects in everyday interaction.* Trondheim, Norway: Trondheim University.

Matusov, E. (2009). Guest editor's introduction to parts I and II. *Journal of Russian & East European Psychology, 47*(1), 3–19. doi:10.2753/RPO1061–0405470100

Ministry of Education. (1996). *Te Whāriki: He Whāriki Mātauranga mō ngā Mokopuna o Aotearoa; Early childhood curriculum.* Wellington, New Zealand: Learning Media.

Odegaard, E. (2007). What's up on the teachers' agenda? A study of didactic projects and cultural values in mealtime conversations with very young children. *International Journal of Early Childhood, 39*(2), 45–64.

Paley, V. (1998). *Wally's stories.* Cambridge, MA: Harvard University Press.

Rasku-Puttonen, H., Lerkkanen, M., Poikkeus, A., & Siekkinen, M. (2012). Dialogical patterns of interaction in pre-school classrooms. *International Journal of Educational Research, 53,* 138–149.

Reddy, V. (2008). *How infants know minds.* Cambridge, MA: Harvard University Press.

Shotter, J. (2012). Agentive spaces, the 'background', and other not well articulated influences in shaping our lives. *Journal of Theory of Social Behaviour, 43(*2), 133–154.

Sidorkin, A. (2014, January). *The limits of dialogue.* Presentation to the Fourth International Interdisciplinary Conference on the Perspectives and Limits of Dialogism in Mikhail Bakhtin: Dialogue at the boundaries, Hopuhopu, New Zealand.

Siraj-Blatchford, I., Sylva, K., Muttock, S., Gilden, R., & Bell, D. (2002). *Researching effective pedagogy in the early years* (Research report No. 356). London: HMSO.

Smidt, S. (2013). *Introducing Malaguzzi: Exploring the life and work of Reggio Emilia's founding father.* Abingdon: Routledge.

Sullivan, P., & McCarthy, J. (2003). Towards a dialogical perspective on agency. *Journal for the Theory of Social Behaviour, 34*(3), 291–309.

Taguma, M., Litjens, I., & Makowiecki, K. (2013). *Quality matters in early childhood education and care: Sweden 2013.* Paris: OECD. Retrieved from http://www.oecd.org/edu/school/SWEDEN%20policy%20profile%20-%20published%2005–02–2013.pdf

Tam, P. C. (2012). Children's bricolage under the gaze of teachers in sociodramatic play. *Childhood, 20*(2), 244–259.

Wegerif, R. (2013). *Dialogic: Education for the internet age.* Abingdon: Routledge.

White, E. J. (2009). *Assessment in New Zealand early childhood education: A Bakhtinian analysis of toddler metaphoricity* (Unpublished doctoral thesis, Monash University, Melbourne, Australia).

White, E. J. (2011a). Response to the School of Dialogue of Cultures as a dialogic pedagogy. *Journal of Russian and East European Psychology, 49*(2), 79–84.

White, J. (2011b). A spark of meaning. *The First Years: Ngā Tau Tuatahi New Zealand Journal of Infant and Toddler Education, 13*(2), 37–42.

White, E. J. (2013). Cry, baby, cry: A dialogic response to emotion. *Mind, Culture, and Activity, 20*(1), 62–78.

White, E. J., Peter, M., & Redder, B. (2015). Infant and teacher dialogue in education and care: A pedagogical imperative. *Early Childhood Research Quarterly, 30,* 160–173.

Zinchenko, V. (in press). The unlimited nature of Bakhtin dialogism. *Knowledge Cultures.*

4

TEACHING WITH LOVE

Bringing together the idea of teaching and love is a very contested issue in education. Many educationalists struggle with the concept that teachers might actually
love their students. And, of course, love brings with it many personal and ideological experiences that shape its meaning and manifestation. Yet from a Bakhtinian
perspective love, as a dialogic act or deed, is exactly what is required. In Bakhtin's
conception of love we are not talking about romance or some sort of obsession but
rather an answerable, aesthetic act or deed that gives value to another. Bakhtin's
approach to love binds together notions of humility, transformation and subjectivity
within an attitudinal tenet of respect. It is an authorial gift to 'other' that lies at its
centre, rather than some romantic aspiration.

When love is conceptualised within the dialogic relationship it is represented
as a kind of axiology or value. It only becomes legitimate when responded to by
another, in the relationship itself. However, with it come many dangers because
loving relationships that are not genuine can be manipulative, particularly in the
hands of an unethical 'other'. In this chapter you are invited to consider the idea
that when a teacher enters into a relationship they are giving value – whether or
not they realise this. This, for Bakhtin, is an act of (aesthetic) love when it is done
in a way that responds to the person as a unique individual with much potential.
In such a consideration emphasis is given to two extremes that should be avoided.
The first, to mould the child into an image of the self (a 'mini-me', if you like)
or a desirable outcome (in a way Paulo Freire might suggest); and the second to
adopt an impartial stance that professes to have no evaluative opinion (i.e. the
unknowable other that poststructuralism purports). If neither extreme is advised,
what is the adult to do within intimate relationships that characterise early years
pedagogy (even if they are not always acknowledged)? It is here where Bakhtin's
Janus-like attention to language and its meaning takes centre stage – reminding

us to recognise and embrace the impact we have on others as creative potential. By now you will appreciate that this is a very important agenda for the early years.

Why love?

> Love is a teacher, but one must know how to acquire it, for it is difficult to acquire, it is dearly bought, by long work over a long time, for one ought to love not for a chance moment but for all time.
>
> *(Dostoevsky, 1879–1880/1991, p. 319)*

Discussions of 'pedagogy' in the same sentence as 'love' are rare to educational discourse. Although fields such as religion and philosophy discuss love as an attitude that includes "kindness and empathy, intimacy and bonding, sacrifice and forgiveness, and community and acceptance" (Loreman, 2011, p. 106), few have ventured into this domain in education. Other approaches to love in educational theory are located within a strand of thought loosely described as 'critical pedagogy'. In this domain pedagogy is constructed as an emancipatory practice that takes place within sociocultural contexts and draws on the ideas of Marx, Freire, Dewey and others to explore notions of power within the classroom (Ryoo, Crawford, Moreno, & McLaren, 2009). Drawing from the Frankfurt School, Freire (1997) emphasised the importance of a teacher's love for students as central to a process of transformation. Marx's revolutionary and materialist theories invoke a call to arms for teachers who are serious about change to enable critical resistance through emotion. From this standpoint, pedagogy is an intervention that will bring about societal change.

For Bakhtin, however, love is conceptualised within the dialogic relationship that is represented as both admiration (1986) and faithfulness (1993). As Deborah Haynes (1995) explains: "Love, for Bakhtin, is only possible in relation to an other" (p. 181). Aesthetic love is therefore "a meeting of two consciousnesses which are in principle distinct from one another" where the consciousness of one is "localized, embodied and lovingly consummated" by the other as a deed of care (Bakhtin, 1990, p. 89). Central to this notion is the tenet that one should not attempt to mould the other into an image of the self or a desirable outcome, yet neither should one adopt an impartial 'acceptance' stance that professes to have no evaluative opinion (the unknowable other). Instead aesthetic love recognises the objective role of the author in appreciating the "unique answerable consciousness" of the other based on their "unique place in the given context of the ongoing event" (Bakhtin, 1993, p. 30) while simultaneously recognising the impact of one's own standpoint on any evaluation. Within this entreaty resides a strong ethical responsibility:

> I love him as another, and not as myself. The other's love of me sounds emotionally in an entirely different way to me – in my own personal

context – than the same love of me sounds to him, and it obligates him and me to entirely different things.

(Bakhtin, 1993, p. 46)

Any consideration of dialogic pedagogy in the early years should not, in my view, overlook the significance of love from this standpoint. In contrast to most scholarly texts on pedagogy, almost all of the content of Bakhtin's earliest work is populated with images of love or, more especially, entreaties towards loving encounter through "discovering the aesthetic moment in co-experiencing" (Brandist, as cited in Wyman, 2008, p. 59). Bakhtin suggests that love, in this regard, is the *only* way individuals can see themselves to their fullest extent – as valued persons in their own right who can uniquely influence others (Bakhtin, 1990). The capacity to see oneself as capable of influence lies at the heart of human agency (Wyman, 2008).

Caryl Emerson (1995) describes Bakhtin's theory of love as a concept arising out of his ideas about answerability. Remember that answerability is concerned with the moral dimensions of authorship in relationship and the responsibility we have towards 'other'. According to this view, she suggests, there can be no *directive* for us to love others as ourselves (as in the Christian sense) since, according to this view, we would consume the other if we did so. Instead, "we should love our neighbor as our neighbor" (p. 112) in order to keep our authorship of other separate to ourself. In this way love creates a boundary between one and the other that enables a fuller appreciation of aesthetic difference:

The words of a loving human are the first and most authoritative words about him; they are the words that for the first time determine his personality from outside, the words that come to meet his indistinct inner sensation of himself, giving it a form and a name which, for the first time, he finds himself and becomes aware of himself as a something.

(Bakhtin, 1990, p. 50)

In this way Bakhtin asks us to "linger intently" (p. 64) with other in order to develop a deeper appreciation – an important agenda for any teacher enshrined in the concept of lingering lovingly. Kenneth Gergen (1999) suggests that teachers are constantly immersed in multiple emotional flows and legitimacies that they bring to the pedagogical experience. However, he reminds us that students also arrive with the same multiple immersions and that both teacher and learner are part of a wider world. These complex emotion-response relations require teachers to be open to the multiple, constantly changing nature of learning, and to value the many voices that are brought to play in any pedagogical moment. Such an approach also calls upon the teacher to be aware of her own emotional responses and to spend time getting to know her students. Thus when a dialogic view of love is brought to bear on pedagogy it is possible to return to seeing love as a kind of aesthetic appreciation that maintains an openness to other – their influence on ourselves and vice versa. It is deeply emotional work.

Axiology

Remember in chapter 2 you were introduced to this idea of axiology in relation to answerability and chronotope? You may recall that axiology was described as the value foundation of any judgement. It determines both the ethical and aesthetic dimensions of evaluations – both in the moment and outside of the moment. We have access to those judgements by others when we are attuned to the responses they offer us. In turn we respond to those judgements by attempting to either match them or oppose them – depending on our intentions.

The significance of value in the dialogic relationship is particularly important in the early years (although, of course, it is important for our whole lives too). Positive relationships in early experience are now understood – by psychologists and neurologists alike – to be instrumental to brain development, cognitive functioning and emotional well-being. Although Bakhtin never claimed to be a psychologist or to study infancy, and he did not have access to neurological or child development theories, he did make some very targeted statements about infancy that were ahead of popular thinking at that time. Here is one of his most famous ones:

> The plastic value of my outer body has been as it were sculpted for me by the manifold acts of other people in relation to me, acts performed intermittently throughout my life: acts of concern for me, acts of love, acts that recognize my value. In fact, as soon as a human being begins to experience himself from within, he at once meets with acts of recognition and love that come to him from the outside – from his mother, from others who are close to him. The child receives all initial determinations of himself and of his body from his mother's lips and from the lips of those close to him . . . they are the words that for the first time determine his personality *from outside*, the words that *come to meet* his indistinct inner sensation of himself, giving it a form and a name in which, for the first time, he finds himself and becomes aware of himself as a *something* . . . The child begins to see himself for the first time as if through his mother's eyes, and begins to speak about himself in his mother's emotional–volitional tones.
>
> *(Bakhtin, 1990, pp. 49–50)*

In this seminal quote Bakhtin suggests that infants are, in the first instance, shaped through the recognition of others. But this is not merely a case of imitation or assimilation – far from it. First words are received as a *value-laden authorial gift*. In other writing Bakhtin (1990) uses the example of a mother describing her infant's toes as "footsie-tootsies" (p. 50) in an affectionate tone *that is central to its received meaning*. The words that are used and the tone of their use by others play an important part in how we come to see ourselves. In the following event 18-month-old Zoe lingers in front of the mirror to look at herself admiringly, giving clues to the way she has heard herself described by others (see the video 'Zoe's toes').

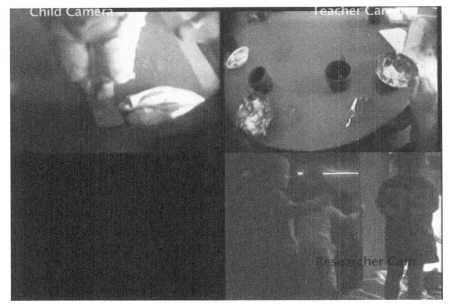

FIGURE 4.1 Zoe's toes

There is a mirror in the block area that Zoe returns to frequently. Though the camera lens is not particularly clear, and the mirror is already distorted, you can just see that Zoe is peering closely at herself. She repeats softly, "Zoe's toes," in lyrical tones.

While we cannot know the significance of this event for Zoe, it does seem clear that she is exploring aspects of her body through this image. Bakhtin (1990) describes the impact of a mirror as a projection of the self "into a peculiarly indeterminate possible other, with whose help we then try to find an axiological position in relation to ourselves" (pp. 32–33). Taken from this perspective perhaps Zoe's lingering interest in her image may be a type of affirmation – an outward manifestation of the loving bestowals she has received from others into her life that will contribute to her developing personality in the world. We can merely speculate here but, I suggest, should not dismiss this significant possibility in the life of a very young child and the associated implications for adults.

In her study of the visually impaired child Karin Junefelt (2011) found that the mother's use of exaggerated intonation patterns in dialogue with her son "made the infant 'come alive', become responsive" (p. 171). Karin suggests that such intonation plays a significant role in language development. Selective intonation is crucial for learning because it orients us towards or away from certain types of thinking and acting, as Bakhtin explains:

> Actual act-performing thinking is an *emotional-volitional thinking, a thinking that intonates, and this intonation permeates in an essential manner all moments of a thought's content.* The emotional-volitional tone *circumfuses that whole content/ sense of a thought in the actually performed act and relates it to the once-occurrent Being-as-event.*
>
> *(Bakhtin, 1993, p. 34)*

Bakhtin's attention to the 'seeing eye' that he borrows from Goethe is very important in understanding of this emotional-volitional exchange: "In aesthetic seeing you love a human being not because he is good, rather a human being is good because you love him" (Bakhtin, 1993, p. 62). 'Seeing' the infant, toddler or young child as an aesthetic act of authorship calls for a special kind of attunement (*ver'nost*) that surpasses mere observation. It requires us to linger intently to try to understand the individual outside of ourselves while we are, of necessity, in an intimate space. It sets a tone for the way we understand that others want to be with us or come to understand us better. There are many ways that this tone can be established beyond words. These include a lingering gaze or smile as well as the more obvious verbal cues such as speech tone or rhyming language. You will recall Bakhtin's example of a mother describing her infant's 'footsie-tootsies' to make the same point.

Karin Junefelt (2011) explains that eye-to-eye contact is a primary means of conveying affection, approval, and establishing intersubjectivity for young children. It is also a means of conveying disapproval. For Lynnette, Harrison's teacher in my studies, the gaze was identified as a significant pedagogical act. From her perspective the lingering gaze held a great deal of meaning – "that signified the trust that he has in me, the trust to know him, to respond to him and to care for him" (Lynnette in White & Mika, 2013, p. 102). Similarly the smile is also identified as a significant source of reciprocal communication. Junefelt (2011) explains that "smiles are regarded to be the outmost expression of positive affect in mother-child interactions" (p. 170). While such interpretation may be culturally determined (a point we will discuss more in chapter 5), what is important here is the significance of even the most subtle language form and its use within the relationship through which it will be interpreted. The same is true for the gaze (White, Redder & Peter, in press). Teachers cannot always see themselves during interactions with children but these nonverbal language forms, coupled with verbal tonations, play an important role in establishing an atmosphere that supports meaningful dialogue. This is what Bakhtin means when he uses the term 'circumfusion'.

The following scene takes place early in the relationship between Alicia and Zoe. Zoe appears to be trying very hard to get to know Alicia, and Alicia is responding in kind. Note the volitional tones that are evident in Alicia's use of voice, touch, smile and close watch or gaze (see 'The mole' video).

FIGURE 4.2 The mole

Zoe has raised her arms for her teacher to pick her up, which she does. They look closely at each other and then Zoe leans forward to pull Alicia's top down: "Nipple." Alicia adjusts her top and turns to look outwards, saying, "Wheeee." Zoe is looking closely at Alicia and says, "Milk." Alicia laughs nervously and repeats, "Milk." "Milk," says Zoe and continues to look closely at Alicia, who laughs again. "Milk . . . Oh one day there might be milk in there, one day." Zoe repeats softly, "Milk." "Oh," exclaims Alicia, looking closely at Zoe. "Milk. Do you like milk?" Alicia looks outwards again and waves, "Bye, H," to a child riding a bike nearby. "Byyyeeee," she repeats and together they watch the child on his bike and wave. "H is going for a drive . . . in his car," explains Alicia. "Bye bye, H, byyeeee." They wave together. Alicia turns to look at Zoe, saying, "Oh!" as Zoe touches Alicia's hat and places her hand in her mouth. Alicia repeats the word: "Hat, hat." Zoe then points to Alicia's face below her mouth. Alicia says, "Mooouuuthhh." Zoe points to her teacher's nose and eye then mouth, to which Alicia replies, "Nose, nose, . . . eye . . . mooouuutthh." Zoe now points beside Alicia's mouth. "Oh! That's my mole!" Alicia touches her own face. "Mmmmmmm," responds Zoe and peers intently at the mole. "Mole," Alicia repeats. Zoe points to the other side of Alicia's face. "Oh, I don't know if I have one on that side. Maybe a little one . . . Mooolllle." Zoe now touches an earring on Alicia's ear lobe. "Ear, ear," says Alicia. Zoe returns to touch the mole. "Mole," says Alicia. "Mole," says Zoe as she continues to touch Alicia's face. "What's that? Ah," exclaims Alicia with a smile. Zoe touches Alicia's earring on the other ear then returns to point at the mole again, saying, "Mole." Alicia replies, "Mole." Zoe touches Alicia's mouth and says, "Mouth." Alicia asks, "What's that?" as she touches her own cheek then rubs Zoe's cheek. "Mouth. Cheek. Cheeeeeek." Zoe returns to the mole and says, "Mole," to which Alicia replies, "Mole."

(White, 2014, p. 62)

This dialogue held great significance to Alicia – and you can clearly see the effort she is going to in order to engage with Zoe in ways that seek to understand her and her priorities. She is not alone in this endeavour. You can see Zoe trying equally as hard to learn more about her teacher – through her body. Thinking about this event from a dialogic standpoint you can clearly see the two consciousnesses meeting as an encounter that is characterised by attunement on the part of both people. In chapter 7 we will return to this excerpt as Alicia revisits this experience in her assessment records – lending further support to the significance of this act as a loving entreaty.

'Learning' emotion

From a dialogic position emotion is not merely a biological phenomenon. It is also learnt in and through social exchange. As well as learning a language comprised of words and actions, you can see Bakhtin arguing here for much more in this conception. The infant or young child comes to see aspects of themselves as precious (or otherwise) through such encounters. Bakhtin suggests that, as a result, the infant develops a sense that they are valued through relationships of trust and engagement. As such the infant adopts the language – not merely as lexicon, trope or even intonation but in its embodied expression of meaning. They can then utilise words, sounds, actions *and their imbued meanings* to various genres. They recall this significance throughout their life and develop the capacity to orient towards and away from shared meaning on this basis. As Bakhtin explains:

> He intuits their inner lives as well as desires; he understands both the actual and the ought-to-be sense of the interrelationship between himself and these persons and objects – the truth [*pravda*] of the given state of affairs – and he understands the ought of his performed act, that is, not the abstract law of his act, but the actual, concrete ought conditioned by his unique place in the given context of the ongoing event. And all these moments, which make up the event in its totality, are present to him as something given and as something-to-be-achieved in a unitary light, in a unitary and unique answerable consciousness, and they are actualized in a unitary and unique answerable act.
>
> *(Bakhtin, 1993, p. 30)*

We can see this principle in action in early years settings. Some early years writers have described this relationship as a kind of dance (see for example, Raikes, 1993, and Trevarthen, 2009). Children bring these dialogues of significance to their experience – overtly or covertly. They may be evident in the way children explain an idea or react to an experience. They may also be unseen but nonetheless influence an event in more subtle ways. For example if a child has received certain emotionally laden meanings about themselves as a boy or a girl or as competent or needy they are likely to bring those meanings to their engagement with other children in the centre. Bakhtin's notion of *hidden dialogicality* is important here: it suggests that even if a speaker is not present – physically or otherwise – "deep traces left by these words have a determining influence on all present and visible words of the first speaker" (Bakhtin, 1984, p. 197). We will revisit this notion in chapter 6. As an early years teacher you may want to alter those meanings but it is unlikely that you will completely erase them. They have contributed to who this person is, as a personality that you will want to learn to appreciate if you are committed to this loving entreaty.

Remembering that, for Bakhtin, language only has meaning in its use, necessary adaptations take place when young children meet peers and adults who bring different meanings to the same language forms. In the footage that follows you will see a vivid example of Zoe trying very hard to work out meaning by carefully observing then replicating a crying act that takes place between her teacher and an older peer

FIGURE 4.3 Fake crying

(see the video 'Fake crying'). Once she works this out she is able to employ the language, as genre, in order to receive the outcome she seeks:

> Four-year-old Hone is digging in the sandpit alongside Zoe, who is making 'cakes' for the teacher. She brings each one to her teacher who pretends to eat it. Meanwhile, Hone hits his toe with the shovel and begins to cry quietly. The teacher puts her 'cake' down in the sand and invites him to have a cuddle with her. She comforts him by patting him on the back as he leans across her lap. Zoe puts her utensils down and squats down in the sand, peering intently at Hone's face. She spends a few minutes watching Hone's face as the crying subsides. Zoe stands up and positions herself directly in front of her teacher. Screwing up her face in the same manner as Hone has just presented, she makes the same quiet crying sound. "Oh," says the teacher. "Do you want a cuddle too?" Zoe receives a cuddle joyfully and resumes making 'cakes'.
>
> *(White, 2012, p. 73)*

This event highlights the point that the same language forms do not necessarily mean the same things in the same way for all people, but that there is a 'right' way to use them in specific contexts, with specific people. In my analysis I contemplated the idea that Zoe might be trying to work this 'right' way out in relation to her teacher in this video clip. In doing so, she is seeking to understand the genres at her disposal in dialogue with her teacher. Here it seems that Zoe has learnt that crying (that is, screwing up your face and making whimpering sounds) has the potential to generate affection. She deploys this approach to orient her teacher towards herself. In another context, or with another teacher, this approach may not be so successful, may perhaps even be counteractive. Zoe cannot assume that all teachers will respond in the same way. As much as the teacher has to try to learn about the child, this example clearly highlights the child's similar efforts. It highlights the important idea that children participate in a polyphonic world comprised of words, sounds and actions that need to be negotiated over time. As James Cresswell and Ulrich Teucher (2011) explain: "A child is first brought along in the river of commonality among caregivers. A lack of experience means that a child is initially shielded from the complex magnitude of the adult polyphonic world and the many genres that constitute it" (p. 115). In an early years setting we can see how the shield is lifted and children are thrown into such polyphony – often very early in life.

How emotions are treated, that is, their meanings in different relationships, not only differs from one person to the next but also alters across different cultural groups. In a study of infant–mother interactions (Demuth, Keller, & Yovsi, 2012), the authors compared the communicative genres of Cameroon mothers and German mothers with their infants. They found that the German mothers negotiated a great deal with infants, while the Cameroon mothers were more likely to facilitate compliance. For the latter, crying was discouraged with no explanation given to the child while for the German mothers crying was a source of investigation in order to find out what was wrong. These very different approaches highlight the cultural significance of language use and the socially emotionally imbued nature of dialogue. We might consider a loving encounter for these Cameroon mothers as an opportunity to teach socially acceptable behaviour; while for the German mothers we can infer that interpersonal communication is a high priority for the infants. Consider what might happen if a German teacher, with the same orientation as the German mothers, meets a Cameroon baby in an early years context? If the baby doesn't cry to convey a need, because they have received messages that this is unacceptable, and the German teacher is seeking such language cues as an indication of need, a serious miscommunication is likely. However we interpret this, Bakhtin tells us that we are answerable. This means there is a responsibility to try to understand the meaning of each and every language act from the point of view of the person themselves, without subsuming other on the basis of our own limited (but also expansive because we can offer our visual surplus) terms. This is not easy:

> I love him as another, and not myself. The other's love of me sounds emotionally in an entirely different way to me – in my own personal context – than the same love of me sounds to him, and it obligates him and me to entirely different things.
>
> *(Bakhtin, 1993, p. 46)*

What's love got to do with it?

So, in the words of Tina Turner, "What's love got to do with it?" Most of the early years literature refers to the obligation towards respect for young children and the use of affective tones as 'care' that are based on Nell Noddings 'ethic of care' (see for example, Dalli, 2002, 2006; Rockel, 2009; Semetsky, 2012). Seen in this way relationships act as the primary focus for pedagogy, positing care as an act of "motivational displacement" (Noddings, 2010, p. 391) whereby one is drawn to pedagogical concern for the learner based on the learner's priorities rather than one's own. Here the quest is less concerned to bring about change in the learner than it is with integrity and respect for the learner as unknowable 'other'. This tenet is also evident in writers who are concerned with 'otherness' (see for example, Butler, Foucault, Lacan, Levinas) and who, in accordance with this principle, advocate for the subjectivity of the learner within power relationships (Ryoo et al., 2009). From a Bakhtinian stance this ethic does not sufficiently take into consideration the two-way nature of the experience. When dialogue is conveyed as mutual acts of loving concern, such as when we know someone cares about us, the infant is able to establish a sense of self as accepted, valued and special. But when we also consider the idea that words are always half someone else's, as Bakhtin did, it becomes necessary to pay attention to the way language is conveyed as interpreted meaning.

Bakhtin suggests that through such acts infants come to speak of themselves in the same (nonliteral) tones – recognising that they are worthy of respect, affection and consideration and able to influence others. They can then apply this understanding to their whole lives – not only in language acquisition but also in the way they interact with others and act upon the world. Knowing that we are valued, loved and listened to provides opportunities for agency to thrive. Rupert Wegerif (2013) explains that this capacity to participate as a partner in dialogue is central to the developing consciousness:

> Participation through mirroring is a larger context that both *precedes* and *exceeds* the emergence of consciousness and also is never overcome or left behind by this emergence so it remains throughout intellectual activity as the ever-present context of self-consciousness and of directed self-conscious thought.
>
> *(p. 41, my emphasis)*

Clearly, then, it is not enough to *say* the words – there must be a constitutive relationship that makes them real. In this Bakhtin shares a concept with Vygotsky in utilising the Russian term *perezhivanie* (Roth, 2013). While for Vygotsky this term is employed to explain the dialectic between emotion and cognition as "refracted through the prism of the child's experience" (Vygotsky, 1994, p. 339) – one which might include individual actions or conditions and their impact on the self – Bakhtin's dialogic imperative orients *vzhivanie* as a process of prioritising human relationships over any other experience. In a Bakhtinian sense the child is not just receiving or jointly engaging but mutually influenced (and influencing) through the authorship of 'other'. Remember that, for Bakhtin, learning is not a phenomenon that takes place inside a person's head but in negotiated, perceived human relationships between people who are totally imbued with emotion and volition – with consequences for all. This means that ideas are 'lived into' rather than received.

For Bakhtin it is *through other* that consciousness is given form. Alexander Lobok (2014) explains that the related term *obrazovanie* – the idea of emergence or formation through meetings in the spaces that give rise to the creative spirit – illustrates how education is a mutual effort of trying to understand another consciousness without overlapping or consuming it. As he concludes: "Every person without exception has his/her absolutely unique experience with culture . . . as the most profound and significant result of the educational process" (Lobok, 2014, p. 1). As such, teachers can also pay close attention to the experience of learners as a pedagogical encounter that cannot be subordinated, reproduced, scaffolded or transmitted since it is a deeply personal value-laden event in the life of an individual.

In accordance with this idea Vladimir Zinchenko (2009) explains that consciousness is made up of both sense (that is, "the *rootedness* of individual consciousness in man's existence") and meaning ("the *connection* of this consciousness to social consciousness, to culture," p. 105, my emphasis). Both are essential for consciousness to thrive. Where one or other is denied to an individual Zinchenko explains that "a person loses his own self" (p. 108). Yet at the same time it is necessary for all parties to recognise their otherness:

> My abstracting [myself] from my own unique place in Being, my *as it were* disembodying of myself, is itself an answerable act or deed that is actualized from my own place, and all knowledge with a determinate content (the possible self-equivalent givenness of Being) that is obtained in this way must be *incarnated* by me, must be translated into the language of participative (unindifferent) thinking, must submit to the question of what obligation the given knowledge imposes upon me – the unique me – from my unique place. Thus *knowledge of* [*znanie*] the content of the object in itself becomes a knowledge of it for me – becomes a *cognition* [*uznanie*] that *answerably obligates me*.
>
> *(Bakhtin, 1993, p. 48)*

For meaning to flourish, its significance must be shared in a relationship that is genuinely responsive to the embodied experience of the child and that draws out dialogue in the language event rather than as some predefined script. Dialogue that is characterised as "a lovingly affirmed concrete actuality" (Bakhtin, 1993, p. 63) is what gives life to the event. Accordingly words that are outside of this relationship are unable to penetrate the learner. This may explain why young children are less likely to learn language from watching television or computer games as easily as they do in real-life relationships with people they know (see for example, Zack, Barr, Gerhardstein, Dickerson, & Meltzoff, 2009). Dialogues that are shared through face-to-face (or should I say whole body-to-body) meetings thus become an experience of between-ness that gives words, sounds, actions meaning in each moment-by-moment exchange. Through such relationships the child comes to see himself or herself as a dialogic partner, and can then apply this understanding to future relationships. As such the infant recognises himself or herself in relation to other selves. This is the foundation of personality, according to dialogic theory – the recognition of the self as connected to others while also retaining one's own personhood and, with it, one's agency.

The dialogic self

But what exactly does Bakhtin mean by this 'self' in relation to love? Many philosophers concern themselves with 'the self' – ranging from the universal 'I' (or 'we') to the isolated 'I'. As we have already established Bakhtin rejected both extremes, claiming the dialogic self as discoverable only through others. Susan Petrelli explains:

> It is in relation to the other, in the relation of other to other, *autrui*, including the self as other – a relation that cannot be reduced to the subject-object paradigm – that the self manifests itself in its absolute otherness, as other with respect to another.
>
> *(Petrelli, 2013, p. 4)*

You can see how any concept of the self, or 'I', as an isolated entity in the world ceases to exist in this dialogic approach:

> 'I' transcends the boundaries of the self and is more than an isolated entity that is encapsulated in itself. The extended 'I', as contextualised, is never alone but is always together with an actual, remembered, imagined, or anticipated other.
>
> *(Hermans, 2012, p. 9)*

Instead there is recognition of the individual as part of a social world – past, present and future; real and imagined. As Deborah Hicks explains, the 'self' is now made manifest through "relationships with otherness" (2000, p. 235). There are now multiple 'I' positions to consider, each with a different orientation.

I-for-you	The co-experienced 'I' that alters 'other' through engagement
I-for-me	The aestheticized 'self' that calls for recognition through other
I-for-us	A chorus where, for a moment in time, there is synchrony
I-for-thou	An 'I' that is understood, valued and accepted. There may be an authorial 'thou' implicated here who always understands

In this theorisation it is impossible to fully separate the 'I' from the 'other'. This complex view of the self proposes that meaning and identity are formed within relationships between self and 'other'(s). This is what Bakhtin means when he uses the term "form-shaping consciousness" – we are shaped and shaping others constantly – moment by moment. And this is where loving encounters play a vital role because they influence how we see ourselves reflected through others and are, in Bakhtin's view, a moral and ethical obligation for all.

Vasudevi Reddy (2008) examines shifts in the way the 'self' is now considered in the early years based on a series of experimental studies that have shown infants far more aware of themselves in relation to others than was previously understood. Drawing on studies that demonstrate aspects of self-other awareness, Reddy suggests that infants are not only aware of others but that they can strategically apply that awareness in their responses. Infants do this in several ways – following another's gaze and adapting their own behaviour according to the preference of another; eliciting laughter based on an awareness of the response of others' to redirect attention elsewhere (long before pointing); or by drawing on past experiences or objects of shared significance. These new insights coincide with Bakhtin's orientation towards the self as part of a complex dialogic whole that is only accessible through deep understanding and aesthetic appreciation of young children, their use of language (in all its forms) and the relationships that are shared.

A dialogic approach to love in the early years

Taking these ideas into the early years setting it is possible to see the tremendous importance of relationships to learning. For Bakhtin, these relationships are characterised by respect and appreciation through answerable acts of love. Love is not viewed here as a feeling that one can necessarily rely on but as a deed or an act that involves aesthetic appreciation of another. This means taking the time to carefully try to understand other in relation to the self. Aesthetic love is thus a complex process of both intimacy and evaluation – stepping into the relationship that is by necessity 'up-close and personal' while maintaining the capacity to step outside of the relationship to offer an evaluative eye (visual surplus). The pedagogical priority here is to do so without either subsuming the child into one's own way of being while maintaining one's own outsidedness in order to appreciate what is offered by the child. I believe this is one of the biggest challenges facing the early years teacher. In my view this approach is virtually impossible when teachers are oriented towards outcomes or objectives that require them to set an agenda for the child that is either too narrow or aligned to adult orientations for 'learning'. Taking this to the extreme, Alexander Lobok (2014) describes the teacher who fails to appreciate the differences between themselves and learners, as well as between learners themselves, as a mini-Hitler – responding to totalitarian orientations by invoking 'sameness' at the expense of creativity.

Towards the end of the previous chapter I invited you to watch footage of Zoe, her teacher and a doll that Zoe was caring for. I asked you to consider the significance of this event from a dialogic standpoint: its meaning to you based on *your* analysis, and what that meant for the way you now think about dialogic pedagogy in the early years. In this chapter I want to revisit that footage, taking into account key Bakhtinian principles of axiology, aesthetics and answerability – all features of a dialogic approach to love.

To do so I need to give you a few more important details about the event that are not immediately apparent. Visual surplus is Bakhtin's way of illuminating the additional insights we can give to one another, wittingly or not, through our own unique relationships with others. I deliberately resisted giving you additional details from my visual surplus earlier because I wanted you to develop your own point of view on what was happening here. But now I invite you to consider the same event, and its aftermath, through additional surplus – in this case mine, which you will now add to your own insights. In doing so I hope to introduce you to the significant role of dialogue (dialog) through an examination of axiology, its relationship to chronotope and answerability, and how this plays out in the early years. I hope that this, in turn, will illuminate the idea of *axiology* that both Zoe and her teacher bring to this event.

Zoe has been filmed for over four months by the time this footage takes place. Her mother and I have been meeting regularly, with Zoe present, to discuss our interpretations of the events that are revealed through the polyphonic screen. On one of these occasions Zoe's father and teacher are also present. We are all devoted to discussions about Zoe and, boy, does Zoe know it! On this particular occasion Zoe retrieves one doll for each of us – with the exception of her father – passing it to us as we talk. At this point I started to recognise that this act of passing over dolls was becoming a ritual every time we met. As soon as I arrived in the centre Zoe would present me with a doll – always the same one and always followed by her own engagement with the other dolls. I began to consider the possibility that Zoe might actually be authoring *us* through her acts, matching the dolls to each of us. Her teacher, who had dark skin and black hair, always received the doll that looked like her while her mother always received the golden-haired doll. I, on the other hand, was gifted the 'old' doll with hair that was falling out. I asked Alicia, Zoe's teacher, if she had noticed what Zoe appeared to be doing with the dolls. Alicia said that she had wondered but then thought, "Naaahh," dismissing this idea as far too sophisticated for an 18 month old.

On the morning of the filmed episode Zoe's mother and I had been discussing her interest in dolls. There had been a prior piece of footage, a week earlier, where Zoe carefully placed a doll in a basket and laid a blanket over top. Zoe's mother explained that this was something Zoe had seen at home with a family friend and her baby in the car seat. There was a discussion over rocking the baby and we laughed as Zoe interjected by bringing a doll over to us and singing "rock, rock." Two hours later filming commences.

If you wish to be reminded of this event watch the video again: it's called 'Baby rock'.

As you can see by the footage Zoe is sitting somewhat possessively beside the basket in which the dark-skinned doll rests. Another child attempts to place her doll in the basket but Zoe protests, throwing it onto the concrete. The other girl then picks up Zoe's doll but Zoe grabs it back and replaces it in the basket, which she then attempts to rock, just as we discussed earlier. Her teacher responds by moving to sit next to Zoe. Alicia picks up the baby earlier cast aside and holds it close, saying, "It's a bit dirty." Zoe places her hand over her mouth and says, "Dirty." Zoe, unperturbed, adopts another strategy. This time she points to a bug on the concrete. The teacher assumes that Zoe is referring to sand and they repeat the word "sandy," rubbing it with their feet. Zoe does not pursue this line of inquiry. They return to their babies – Alicia holding one and Zoe rocking the other in the basket. They sing a rocking song together. A peer arrives and attempts to take the doll and basket but Alicia intervenes. Zoe resumes rocking and is now offered a blanket by another teacher. She places the blanket over the basket and continues to sing "baby rock." "What a good mum you are," exclaims Alicia.

Now watch the next piece of footage, taken later in the same morning (see 'Eyes, nose' in the video companion).

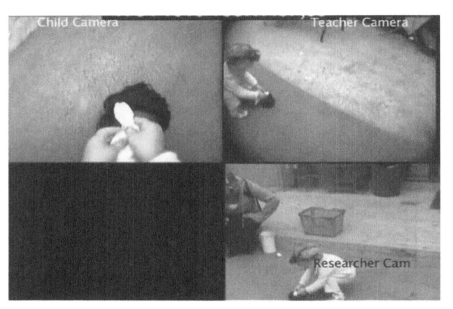

FIGURE 4.4 Eyes, nose . . .

By now Zoe has Alicia's undivided attention. She is feeding her doll using sand, a metal spoon and a jug while Alicia provides a commentary. "Oh, eye," says Zoe, rubbing sand off the doll's eye. "Is it sandy?" says Alicia. Zoe wipes it away vigorously, saying, "Dirty." "Is she all right? Is Baby all right?" asks Alicia. "There . . . there," says Zoe as she takes the doll out of the basket and tips out the sand. "There – all clean," says Alicia. Zoe rubs the basket, repeating "clean." Zoe picks up the doll, saying, "Eyes." "Did she get sand in her eyes?" asks Alicia. A peer rushes out to Alicia, who says, "Do you need a tissue?" She goes to get a tissue off the shelf. When she returns the peer has gone. Alicia says to Zoe, "Do you need a tissue for her eyes?" Zoe proceeds to clean the baby with the tissue, saying, "Eyes" then "Toes" while Alicia watches. "Bobo," says Zoe and turns around to see Alicia. She wipes the dolls bottom and says, "Poos." She drops the baby, saying, "Bubby, bubby," and places the tissue in the rubbish. Alicia claps. "More, more," exclaims Zoe, reaching up for the tissues, which are out of reach. "OK, one more, one more tissue," replies Alicia, raising her finger to signal one. "One more tissue, one more," she repeats as she passes the tissue box to Zoe. Zoe returns to the doll, saying, "Nose, nose," as she wipes the doll's nose. She looks at Alicia: "Snotty." "Are you wiping her nose?" inquires Alicia. Zoe then wipes the doll's hair – "Hair" – and then returns to the doll's bottom – "bottom" – as she wipes vigorously. "Poooo," exclaims Zoe. "Oh, ew," replies Alicia. "Dirty," says Zoe. Alicia laughs. "Dirty."

How do you 'see' this event with this additional visual surplus?

Let's consider the dialogic significance of this event when seen over a longer period of time and with the benefit of more than one perspective on what took place. In the footage we can see the teacher leaning forward intently to try to understand what is taking place. She is clarifying Zoe's sounds and considering them in relation to her body movements, the employment of artefacts and a shared history. From the previous video we (the teacher and I) have learnt that Zoe has received much positive reinforcement for using the rubbish bin, being clean, and that she has carefully observed her teacher caring for the babies in the early years setting. From everything we have learnt in our aesthetic encounters, there is a strong hint that Zoe is keen to please her teacher and gain approval in multiple ways through this event. It seems as if Zoe is drawing on every possible genre at her disposal to draw her teacher towards her. We can hear echoes of adults who have repeated the words (and intonation) "dirty" in episodes beyond our camera lens; and we have a reasonable idea that her teacher is responding through clarification and expansion of this play. Most importantly we can observe the intensity of this relationship, its rich legacy based on many hours of this teacher trying to understand what Zoe is presenting. However it is also evident that Zoe is working very hard to understand what matters to her teacher. It is, in my view, a loving encounter in a Bakhtinian sense where "aesthetic form is pronounced and justified by an aesthetically productive sympathy or love that comes to meet the co-experienced life from outside" (Bakhtin, 1990, p. 83). The effort of both Zoe and her teacher (as well as ourselves in trying to understand) is evident here. I want to suggest that Bakhtin's entreaty towards a loving encounter is evident in both the intention towards a shared meaning that values the multiple ways of conveying ideas and the attentiveness towards seeing more and being surprised, challenged or, in this case, amazed as Alicia identified in her subsequent dialogues about this event. I must confess that I too was blown away by what I saw through dialogic eyes. Were you?

Through such visual surplus we have the opportunity to not only 'see' the other in a more complex manner but also to learn more about ourselves and the relational perspective to us taken by another. Such insights contribute to a lifelong process of becoming that is characterised by constant flux. In this way it is impossible to consider any human being as an isolated subject (or lone 'I') in a vacuum of social isolation or as merely acting upon their environment. Along with this consideration we are also confronted with the significance of our own acts and their potential to expand or limit other (and vice versa). Bakhtin offers us a way of seeing ourselves through others but also reminds us that our acts – for better or for worse – have an impact on others (and vice versa). This is an important point also made by Julia Manning-Morton (2006), who suggests that a possible reason why it is difficult for early years teachers to talk about love is because they are uncomfortable with the intimacy a loving pedagogy, of necessity, invokes. This was certainly true for Zoe's teacher. During an event where Zoe attempted to cuddle her teacher in the presence of Zoe's parents, Alicia explained her conflicting feelings of discomfort and pleasure:

> I felt as if I was on show . . . Well, not on show but . . . it was a lovely feeling . . .
> but then, at the back of my mind . . . I kept thinking . . . "What are Mum and
> Dad thinking?" . . . I wouldn't want them to go away and think . . . I mean if I
> was a parent and I saw . . . my child reacting to someone like that . . . in a way
> I would be happy but . . . in a way I would be a bit jealous.
>
> *(Teacher interview, in White, 2009, pp. 176–177)*

The irony was that Zoe's parents were delighted to see that their daughter had a warm relationship with her teacher. Jools Page experienced a similar phenomenon in her PhD study of love when she interviewed six mothers about their experience of leaving their babies with an early years teacher. She found that each of the mothers, in different and quite complex ways, wanted the teacher to care for their child deeply. As one mother explains:

> Love is about not just being on the surface it's about knowing a child. So for
> me it's about . . . meeting Daisy's needs, it's all of them really not just the love
> thing. It's about the care side as well . . . love is there, I know that sounds daft
> to say that wouldn't be my sole priority because to me it's about the care and
> I know love comes with care but it's fitting the two . . . it's just that the caring
> and understanding and the needs of Daisy are far more important.
>
> *(Page, 2011, p. 318)*

So if parents and teachers value loving relationships, why are conversations about love so rare in early years pedagogy?

Talk of a loving pedagogy?

Of course there are many reasons why consideration of a loving pedagogy is so difficult for early years teachers to embrace. While theorists such as Dr Maria Montessori described the early years teacher as someone who ought to be concerned with "the work of love" (1924, p. 12) almost one hundred years ago, the term is now seen as 'inappropriate' in many parts of the world. In countries where there is a strong push for professionalism, talk of love poses a particular challenge because of its traditional allegiance to mothering, as opposed to teaching. Sandy Farquhar (2012) reminds us that the overarching nature of professional discourse objectifies education and trivialises emotional work. The consequence of such positioning is that any talk of love is silenced in the pedagogical realm. Recent literature in the early years provides consistent messages associated with the all-important relationships that exist between infants and their teachers in educational settings (see for example, McDowall Clark & Baylis, 2012; Recchia & Shin, 2012; Ulloa, Evans, & Parkes, 2010; White & Page, 2014). Responsiveness, attunement, sensitivity, care and love are all implicated in these.

It may also be challenging for parents to conceive of their child loving someone outside the home – a point raised by both Jools Page (2011) in her work with parents in the United Kingdom, and in my work with Zoe and her teacher. Jools argues for the notion of "professional love" (p. 317) – a positioning of love as an intellectual endeavour. While I don't think Bakhtin would share this intellectualised view of love, it is important to understand its genesis. Early years teachers have had to fight hard for recognition in education, sometimes at the jeopardy of important values such as love and care, which are seen as too emotional, overly feminized or 'soft' (to name but a few of the accusations portrayed in the literature). What is interesting about Bakhtin's notion of aesthetic love is that he views it as part of human experience – not something that only women and babies should be doing – "a meeting of two consciousnesses which are in principle distinct from one another" (Bakhtin, 1990, p. 89), comprised of admiration and faithfulness. Surely these are qualities that are central to any learning dialogue?

But many early years teachers do not struggle with the concept of love. When I asked infant teacher Rachel to explain the significance of her dialogue with the infants she worked with, she unashamedly conceptualised her pedagogy as a kind of love:

> It's a different love than from your own children . . . but it's still there, a, like a nurturing love. The thing is that, you know, they're in care . . . like five days a week. Nine-hour days or something, and so you think "if you were at home what would you be getting? Well, you'd be getting love from your mum, your dad, your grandparents" and so why not make our environment a loving place to be where there is physical touch, kisses?
>
> *(Rachel, in White & Mika, 2013, p. 101)*

Her pedagogy was characterised by open-ended responsive acts, generating valued genre (such as cuddles at bottle feeding time) that the infant could rely on as part of her authorship experience. Such dialogues are comprised of a sound, a touch, a look or even close physical proximity which invokes senses such as smell and taste. Together they present a very different type of dialogue than what might be seen in a classroom with older children or adults. They represent a stark shift in thinking to early years settings where there are 'no kissing policies' or in settings where

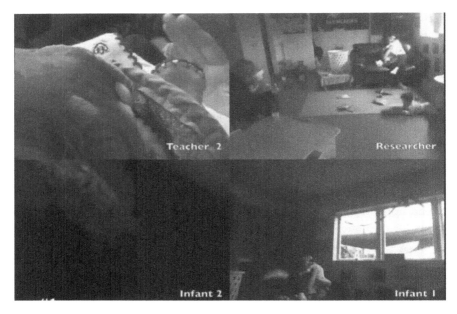

FIGURE 4.5 Bottle feed

additional money is asked from parents who wish their child to receive these types of affectionate overtures in their absence.

The following event reinforces Rachel's pedagogical conviction towards intimacy during Lola's bottle feed just before bedtime (see 'Bottle feed' in the video companion).

> Lola and Rachel, her teacher, sit together on the sofa, gazing into each other's eyes as Lola drinks enthusiastically. She pauses. "Had enough . . . enough," says Rachel, who leans forward and smiles, clicks her tongue, "EEEEEEnough," and laughs. Rachel holds Lola close to her cheek and kisses her, saying, "Mmmmmmm," while patting her rhythmically on the back. Rachel laughs and smiles as Lola makes the sound "ahhhhhhh." Rachel mimics the sound and together they sing in chorus, "Ahhhhhhhh." Lola leans into Rachel as she continues to pat her back. "Oh, cuddles," says Rachel, "cuddles, with Lola." Lola repeats the "ahhhhhhh" sound in synchrony with Rachel until the sound subsides and Lola sits up. Lola then leans towards Rachel for another cuddle, "Ah, more," as Rachel kisses Lola on the cheek several times, "More." Lola sits back up. "Are you tired? Do you need to go to bed again?" asks Rachel. "Or are you just, that's what we do, snuggles?" Lola sniffs loudly and presses her nose. Rachel wipes her nose and frowns saying, "Ah ho ah ho ho ho," and wiggles her head. They continue to look at each other closely.

When talking about this event afterwards Rachel was very clear about what she considered to be the value of this intimate dialogue, explaining its pedagogical significance:

> Not only emotionally am I filling her . . . I'm actually filling my emotional tank too because . . . we obviously work with children because we love them and we have a passion for working alongside infants and so that is, she is, we're filling each other's emotional tanks.

While Bakhtin would not have chosen to use the term 'filling a tank' to describe this emotional experience because of its implication of transmission, he might agree with Rachel that such acts are always emotionally imbued. This understanding lies at the heart of dialogic pedagogy and, by definition, is not limited to formal types of learning. The importance of this dialogue exists not so much in its ability to transmit information (or even feelings) from the teacher to the infant but to engage in exchanges that prompt curiosity and wonderment. Interactions like these position dialogic pedagogy at the heart of learning. They can (and do) take place across all domains of the early years curriculum, not least in routines which also play an important role in the setting.

Routine as prime time

From a dialogic standpoint routines that may on the surface seem 'uneducational' take on increased significance when a Bakhtinian approach to love as a deed is summoned. They become opportunities for teachers to engage in meaningful dialogue with infants, toddlers and young children in different ways than they might in other contexts. In our study with Lola and Harrison what we discovered was the nuanced nature of dialogue that included language such as sounds, touch, looks (especially watching others) and what the teachers described as 'being in the moment'. These were especially pronounced for the teachers during care routines but we also noticed that they were a feature of dialogues in playful encounters between infants, their peers and their teachers (White, Redder, & Peter, 2013). As one teacher – Lynnette – explained, dialogue is very subtle and her responses were based on careful attention to the cues offered by the infants themselves:

> So this starts off with the two infants being engaged . . . that must be when I put him down. See, Lola's sort of laughing at him, sort of trying to get his attention . . . or something. And that's him [Harrison] responding to her. She's making "tickedy" sounds there? Sort of "tick tick tick" . . . I was just stroking her hand. I obviously didn't say anything but . . . um, to try and get her to be gentle because she's grabbing him a little bit . . . I think he's looking towards us . . . Yep . . . Look at Harrison . . . he's really engaging as well, like he's making those vocal sounds – she's interested. So she backs off and immediately I take over with the vocal sounds, I thought that was interesting,

because I noticed that he wanted to talk and such, and Lola's lost interest in talking to him so I take over . . . You know, when you see it, it happens sort of instantly so I'm obviously watching this very closely, and responding to, to carry on that dialogue with him.

Here is the event that Lynnette is referring to. Note the complex language taking place here and its volitional tones (these cannot be conveyed without watching the footage itself: 'Tickedy sounds' in the video companion).

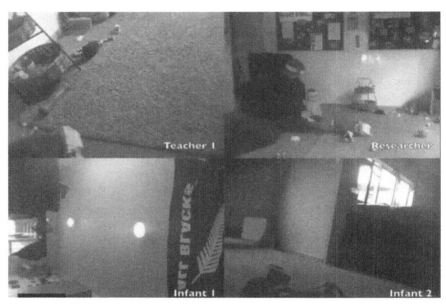

FIGURE 4.6 Tickedy sounds

Lynnette has placed Harrison on his back on the floor, passing him a rattle which he holds above his head. Lola is close by. Harrison looks at Lynnette and makes sounds. Lynnette jiggles his feet and mimics his sounds. Lola begins to laugh too, and leans forward to touch Harrison. Lola says, "Tickedy tickedy tickedy." Lynette puts her hand on top of Lola's and says, "Gentle hands." Lola leans forward over Harrison and Lynnette strokes her hand then picks her up and puts her on her knee. Harrison says, "Ooh ahhh," which Lynnette repeats, saying, "Ooh ahhh, ohh ahhh, says Harrison, ooh ahhh." Lola leans forward and Lynnette holds her hands and rocks her, singing, "Row row row your boat, gently down the stream . . . if you see a crocodile don't forget to scream." On the last word Lynnette lifts up Lola's hands and pretends to scream, then laughs. The song is repeated. Harrison then makes a grunting sound, "AHH AHH," and returns to the "ooh ahhh" sounds. Lola is still being rocked by Lynnette but eventually slides to the floor. She leans forward to touch Harrison, repeating, "Tickedy tickedy," and he responds with more sounds, "Hooow hoooow." He screams and calls out as Lola lies beside him and touches him. Lola starts to back away and Harrison calls out. Lynette leans forward and says, "Hey, heeeyyy," looking right into Harrison's face: "I need to go and look what the time is." Harrison responds with sounds and waving arms. "I do, I do," says Lynnette, to which Harrison replies: "Ohh ahhh." Lynnette replies, "Ohh ahhh," and Harrison responds with the same noise. The sound escalates into "OHHH OHHH," to which Lynnette replies with the same noise. Lola, having moved some distance away, turns to Lynnette and makes noises, "Gurgle gurgle," but there is no response. Lynnette passes Harrison his rattle and they look at one another. Harrison calls out loudly, "Ahhhhh, ahhhh," and Lynnette responds using the same sounds. Harrison screams and Lynnette rubs his stomach before standing up. Harrison calls out, "Ewww ewww ewww," watching her closely as she moves away. His sounds change as he calls out and then begins to make protesting sounds, waving his arms in the air, "Oooh hoooo," then screaming, until he sees Lynnette and returns to the softer "ewww ewww" sounds of earlier. "OK, Harrison," says Lynnette, walking back over to him. "Are you going to have a nice big sleep this afternoon?" Harrison answers with more sounds. Lynnette squats down beside him and jiggles his body with her hands – "Big sleeps, big sleeps" – at which Harrison squeals. "Take this off, fiddle fiddle," Lynnette says, trying to unclasp Harrison's bib. "Oh, it's not coming off. . . there it is." She leans forward and says, "Boo." Harrison squeals and smiles. "Ahh ha ha," repeats Lynnette. "Take your pants off?" and pulls his trousers off. "And your socks." Harrison's breathing is rasping. "You got your wheeze back," says Lynnette. "Need a new nappy? I think we'll go and have a look." Harrison replies: "Ahhh ahhh." Lynnette waves his legs in the air: "Go and have a look." Harrison laughs and so does Lynnette. "You're not supposed to be laughing at me, you're supposed to be tired." Harrison replies with a growly sound: "Ahhh ahhh." Lynnette leans forward and looks into his face and repeats the sound, which is then repeated back. Lynnette rubs Harrison's stomach and says, "Come on then." She picks him up: "Come on then, let's go." They go to the nappy room. Lola continues sitting on the floor close by – she has been watching this interaction and others taking place in another part of the room with older peers.

This event highlights the complex, emotionally laden dialogues that are possible between infants and their teacher when strong relationships exist in the early years setting. Dialogue alters according to the nature of the encounter and is often initiated by the infants then responded to by the teacher according to her pedagogical judgments in this particular moment in time. But, as we saw in the previous chapter, teacher responses are not neutral, nor are they beyond speculation. Love can also be manipulative, exploitative or alienating if imposed upon others according to what is 'best' according to the standards of the person who decides what is 'needed'. For this reason a highly ethical consideration must coincide with any engagement of this nature, as an awareness of one's answerability to the child, the family, society and perhaps even some higher authority (an 'authorial thou', as Bakhtin might suggest).

While exchanges like this can take place almost anywhere, the early years setting creates opportunities for different types of dialogue to thrive because it is characterised by a very different social context than might typically occur in a family setting. These dynamics create special challenges for teachers who seek to build loving relationships with children. Did you notice how Lynnette playfully (or was it forcefully?) distracted Lola from tickling Harrison by playing a game? How did she interpret that Harrison needed a sleep? What was joyful (or difficult) about this event for Lynnette? For Harrison? For Lola? And what genres were shared (or not shared) that made the dialogue possible? These questions are all part of the event that Lynette has played an important role in. Her 'careful watching' provides a clue that the positive nature of this event has not happened by chance but is born of her interpreted understanding of these infants, in this moment, through lingering lovingly in their lives. It is both intentional and intuitive practice. Both require a strong ethical awareness of the implications of the teacher's engagement (or, for that matter, nonengagement).

Role of the teacher

As we have seen, there are serious implications for pedagogy when the dialogic principles of love are brought to bear on learning. If we accept that relationships and associated axiologies play a vital role in development (for example the wiring of the brain, the acquisition of language) and learning (about one's worth, about the self in relation to other and the way one acts upon the world), then the teacher is seriously implicated. What we say, how we say it and how we feel about the children we work with is all deeply connected to their experience – indeed it *is* their experience for the time they spend in the early years setting, with long-term impact. I think this is what Paul Sullivan means when he describes "the duty of love" (2007, p. 11). Sullivan articulates this relationship as an intersection between spirit (sense of action) and soul (action in relation to other), drawing on Bakhtin to suggest that the soul gives form to the spirit through dialogic activity. Herein lies the nature of dialogic pedagogy.

In this conceptualisation of love the teacher is called upon to 'see' the child in ways that do not diminish or trivialise their personality. In the early years context this is a boundary encounter because the teacher relies on second-hand experience of the child's life beyond the centre. Bakhtin (1990) explains that a loving encounter takes special consideration of these boundaries; indeed they acquire new significance in such meetings. As a result there are many surprises in such relationships – sometimes difficult or painful while on other occasions joyful and exciting. As Alicia explains:

> It's something beautiful and something sad. You treasure that person more, it brings you all together and sometimes it's hard and sometimes there's a bit of sorrow there, sometimes a bit of anger . . . it's a lot of things all mixed into one. It's special and it's beautiful and . . . it's lots of things.
>
> *(Teacher interview, in White, 2011, p. 62)*

Loving pedagogical relationships call for teachers to speak *with* the child as much as possible, not *of* them. The latter can easily occur when teachers impose limits on a child because of preheld assumptions based on theories or 'knowledge' that prescribe what constitutes learning. In a dialogic approach the teacher is able to offer their insights while remaining open to those offered to them by *this child* in *this event-of-being* (rather than the 'universal child'). I think this is what early years teachers are trying to explain when they talk about pedagogical practices such as "watching over time" (Dalli & Doyle, 2011, p. 18) or "sensory pedagogy" (Johansson & Lokken, 2014, p. 886) – embodied practices that are often hard for teachers to explain. For Bakhtin, indifference or lovelessness does not have the capacity to cherish the child in ways that are necessary for aesthetic engagement: "Only in correlation with the loved is fullness of the manifold possible" (Bakhtin, 1993, p. 64). To linger lovingly is therefore more of a moral deed than an emotional response.

Now the role of the teacher shifts from the detached, rational, impartial, 'low affect' professional promoted by Lilian Katz (1984) over 30 years ago as distinct from the parent role. Yet this is not to suggest that the teacher should attempt to replace the parent in any way. The parenting and teaching columns in the model in Table 4.1 are derived from Lilian's distinction between both roles. In contemporary society characterised by diversity, I do not believe it is ethically appropriate for me to comment on how a parent 'should be' with their child. The dialogic pedagogy column highlights the shift that is necessary for the teacher to make in order to prioritise deeds of love as a pedagogical imperative for very young children.

In collapsing parent-teacher distinctions in terms of these role dimensions, I am making the point that being 'professional' and simultaneously loving are not disparate ideas. Of course significant differences remain. Unlike many parents of young children, teachers are not (and, in my view, should not try to be) the centre of the child's world and need to work closely with families to ensure that their relationships with the child are prioritised. Children do not need teachers' magnanimous intervention to be who they are, but they do need the dialogic space to explore the impact of their agency upon the world. On the other hand it would be equally 'unprofessional' (and potentially damaging) to be aloof or distant with young children because we know that relationships are very important to learning across many theoretical domains.

TABLE 4.1 Adapted from "Distinctions between parenting and teaching in their central tendencies on seven role dimensions" (in *More Talks with Teachers*, Katz, 1984)

Role dimension	Parenting	Teaching	Dialogic pedagogy
1. Scope of function	Diffuse and limitless	Specific and limited	*Specific and limitless*
2. Intensity of affect	High	Low	*High and low*
3. Attachment	Optimum attachment	Optimum detachment	*Optimum balance between engagement and evaluation*
4. Rationality	Optimum irrationality	Optimum rationality	*Poised resourcefulness*
5. Spontaneity	Optimum spontaneity	Optimum intentionality	*Both*
6. Partiality	Partial	Impartial	*Both*
7. Scope of responsibility	Individual	Whole group	*There is no alibi*

The benefits of love in pedagogy

The benefits of paying attention to the fullest expression of understanding children and ourselves in early years pedagogy, as a deed of love, are manifold. The effects of loving relationships can be felt both immediately and in the long term. The latter is harder to demonstrate and is another reason why it is so difficult to justify the importance of these intimate relationships to policy makers who seek scientific 'evidence' rather than interpretation. Relationships that are characterised by this aesthetic take time, energy and commitment. They are not easily achieved with outrageous ratios or group sizes, nor can they be realised in efficient encounters of indifference. What sets this kind of love apart is that it celebrates the different spaces, or necessary gaps, that exist between people. It does not seek to create synergy and, for this reason, is incongruent, confusing and uncertain. I think this is what Bakhtin means when he uses the term *nezavershennost* – unfinalisation.

Paying attention to relationships in this broader sense, from a Bakhtinian stance, is possibly the highest priority in early years pedagogy. Paying careful attention to the orientations of young children – where they are looking, how they are communicating with you and others, what they bring from other worlds – is therefore a further opportunity for dialogic encounter. It is an act of love requiring you to linger long enough to encounter the child as a personality in their own right, with the very real potential to challenge your previously held assumptions and beliefs. From a dialogic standpoint love therefore lies at the centre of pedagogy in the early years.

Looking back, moving forward

In this chapter the notion of love has been presented as a central tenet for early years pedagogy. Based on the idea that love is a deed rather than an emotion, it is possible to view the teacher in two interrelated ways: the first as intimate partner in the life of the child. What is said or not said and, most importantly, the *way* it is said has huge implications for the developing consciousness. This expands beyond words to the look or gaze that features so heavily in early years pedagogy and which implicates the teacher as fully responsible for their own actions. Trying to know the child – often through the painful realisation that one can never fully know – is a central quest for the dialogic teacher. Yet at the same time it is important to recognise that such knowing is based on a set of ideological assumptions and interpretations that shape both what can be seen, how it is seen and what this means in the moment of evaluation (which takes place whether or not it is conscious activity).

The second aspect of this love deed for the teacher is to create an evaluative distance from the child in order to separate one's own consciousness from theirs. We have explored some of the dangers when this is not possible and children are judged according to the teacher's priorities rather than their own. This risk is echoed in Bakhtin's notion of consummation – to be totally consumed is to lose oneself. The consequences, suggests Bakhtin, are that ideas are merely transmitted and the opportunity to learn from others, in this case the child, are seriously limited at best. At worst a society of clones are produced who have no voice beyond the voice of authority, and creativity is unable to thrive.

Taking this dual stance requires teachers to be self-aware as well as aware of others. As such this chapter concludes by inviting you to examine your relationships with others before moving towards any kind of assessment that you might make of another. Bakhtin allows us to hold both in animation – destabilising though this might be – and to embrace uncertainty as a legitimate and necessary approach to teaching and learning.

References

Bakhtin, M. M. (1984). *Problems of Dostoevsky's poetics* (C. Emerson, Trans.). Minneapolis: University of Minnesota Press.

Bakhtin, M. M. (1986). *Speech genres and other late essays* (C. Emerson & M. Holquist, Eds.; V. W. McGee, Trans.). Austin: University of Texas Press.

Bakhtin, M. M. (1990). *Art and answerability* (K. Brostrom, Trans.). Austin: University of Texas Press.

Bakhtin, M. M. (1993). *Toward a philosophy of the act* (M. Holquist & V. Liapunov, Eds.; V. Liapunov, Trans.). Austin: University of Texas Press.

Cresswell, J., & Teucher, U. (2011). The body and language: M. M. Bakhtin on ontogenetic development. *New Ideas in Psychology, 29*(2), 106–118.

Dalli, C. (2002). Constructing identities: Being a 'mother' and being a 'teacher' during the experience of starting childcare. *European Early Childhood Education Research Journal, 10*(2), 85–101.

Dalli, C. (2006). Re-visioning love and care in early childhood: Constructing the future of our profession. *The First Years: Ng Tau Tuatahi New Zealand Journal of Infant and Toddler Education, 8*(1), 5–11.

Dalli, C., & Doyle, K. (2011). Eyes wide open: How teachers of infants and toddlers recognize learning. *The First Years: Ng Tau Tuatahi New Zealand Journal of Infant and Toddler Education, 13*(2), 15–18.

Demuth, C., Keller, H., & Yovsi, R. D. (2012). Cultural models in communication with infants: Lessons from Kikaikelaki, Cameroon and Muenster, Germany. *Journal of Early Childhood Research, 10*(1), 70–87.

Dostoevsky, F. (1991). *The brothers Karamazov* (R. Pevear & L. Volokhonsky, Trans.). New York, NY: Vintage. (Original work published 1879–1880)

Emerson, C. (1995). Bakhtin at 100: Looking back at the very early years [Review of the book *Toward a philosophy of the act*, by M. M. Bakhtin, V. Liapunov & M. Holquist]. *Russian Review, 54*, 107–114.

Farquhar, S. (2012). Narrative identity and early childhood education. *Educational Philosophy and Theory, 44*(3), 289–301.

Freire, P. (1997). *Pedagogy of the heart.* New York, NY: Continuum.

Gergen, K. J. (1999). *An invitation to social construction.* London: Sage.

Haynes, D. (1995). *Bakhtin and the visual arts.* Cambridge: Cambridge University Press.

Hermans, H. J.M. (2012). Dialogical self-theory and the increasing multiplicity of I-positions in a globalizing society: An introduction. In H. J.M. Hermans (Ed.), *Applications of dialogical self theory* (pp. 1–21). San Francisco, CA: Jossey-Bass.

Hicks, D. (2000). Self and other in Bakhtin's early philosophical essays. *Mind, Culture and Activity, 7*(3), 227–242.

Johansson, E., & Lokken, G. (2014). Understanding and encountering children through the senses. *Educational Philosophy and Theory, 46*(8), 886–897.

Junefelt, K. (2011). Early dialogues as a teaching device from a Bakhtinian perspective. In E. J. White & M. A. Peters (Eds.), *Bakhtinian pedagogy: Opportunities and challenges for research, policy and practice in education across the globe* (pp. 159–178). New York, NY: Peter Lang.

Katz, L. G. (1984). *More talks with teachers.* Champaign, IL: ERIC Clearinghouse on Elementary and Early Childhood Education.

Lobok, A. (2014). Education/obrazovanie as an experience of encounter. *Dialogic Pedagogy and International Online Journal, 2.* Retrieved from http://dpj.pitt.edu

Loreman, T. (2011). *Love as pedagogy.* Rotterdam: Sense.

Manning-Morton, J. (2006). The personal is professional: Professionalism and the birth to threes practitioner. *Contemporary Issues in Early Childhood, 7*(1), 42–52.

McDowall Clark, R., & Baylis, S. (2012). 'Wasted down there': Policy and practice with under-threes. *Early Years, 32*(2), 229–242.

Montessori, M. (1924). The call (S. Radice, Trans.). *The call of education, 1*(1), 8–12.

Noddings, N. (2010). Moral education in an age of globalization. *Educational Philosophy and Theory, 42*(4), 390–396.

Page, J. (2011). Do mothers want professional carers to love their babies? *Journal of Early Childhood Research, 9*(3), 310–323.

Petrelli, S. (2013). *The self as a sign, the world, and the other: Living semiotics.* New Brunswick, NJ: Transaction.

Raikes, H. (1993). Relationship duration in infant care: Time with a high-ability teacher and infant-teacher attachment. *Early Childhood Research Quarterly, 8*, 309–325.

Recchia, S. L., & Shin, M. (2012). In and out of synch: Infant childcare teachers' adaptations to infants' developmental changes. *Early Child Development and Care, 182*(12), 1545–1562.

Reddy, V. (2008). *How infants know minds.* Cambridge, MA: Harvard University Press.

Rockel, J. (2009). A pedagogy of care: Moving beyond the margins of managing work and minding babies. *Australasian Journal of Early Childhood, 34*(3), 1–8.

Roth, M. (2013). An integrated theory of thinking and speaking that draws on Vygotksy and Bakhtin/Volosinov. *International Journal of Dialogic Pedagogy, 1.* Retrieved from http://dpj.pitt.edu/ojs/index.php/dpj1/issue/view/3

Ryoo, J. J., Crawford, J., Moreno, D., & McLaren, P. (2009). Critical spiritual pedagogy: Reclaiming humanity through a pedagogy of integrity, community and love. *Power and Education, 1*(1), 132–146.

Semetsky, I. (2012). Living, learning and loving: Constructing a new ethics of integration in education. *Discourse: Studies in the Cultural Politics of Education, 33*(1), 47–59.

Sullivan, P. (2007). Examining the self-other dialogue through 'spirit' and 'soul'. *Culture and Psychology, 13*, 105–128.

Trevarthen, C. (2009). The intersubjective psychobiology of human meaning: Learning of culture depends on interest for co-operative practical work – and affection for the joyful art of good company. *Psychoanalytic Dialogues, 19*(5), 507–518.

Ulloa, M., Evans, I., & Parkes, F. (2010). Teaching to care: Emotional interactions between preschool children and their teachers. *New Zealand Research in Early Childhood Education, 13*, 145–156.

Vygotksy, L. (1994). The problem of environment. In R. Van der Veer & J. Valsiner (Eds.), *The Vygotsky reader* (pp. 338–354). Oxford: Blackwell.

Wegerif, R. (2013). *Dialogic: Education for the internet age.* Abingdon: Routledge.

White, E. J. (2009). *Assessment in New Zealand early childhood education: A Bakhtinian analysis of toddler metaphoricity* (Unpublished doctoral thesis, Monash University, Melbourne, Australia).

White, E. J. (2011). Aesthetics of the beautiful: Ideologic tensions in contemporary assessment. In E. J. White & M. A. Peters (Eds.), *Bakhtinian pedagogy: Opportunities and challenges for research, policy and practice in education across the globe* (pp. 47–67). New York, NY: Peter Lang.

White, E. J. (2012). Cry, baby, cry: A dialogic response to emotion. *Mind, Culture and Activity, 20*(1), 62–78.

White, E. J. (2014). Interpreting metaphoric acts: A dialogic encounter with the very young. In I. Semetsky & A. Stables (Eds.), *Pedagogy and edusemiotics: Theoretical challenges/practical opportunities* (pp. 51–68). Rotterdam: SensePublishers.

White, E. J., & Mika, C. (2013). Coming of age?: Infants and toddlers in curriculum. In J. Nuttall (Ed.), *Weaving Te Whāriki: Aotearoa New Zealand's early childhood curriculum document in theory and practice* (2nd ed., pp. 93–113). Wellington, New Zealand: NZCER Press.

White, E. J., & Page, J. (2014). *Navigating the Scylla and Charybdis of infant educational research: Reconciling the 'group care' agenda.* Manuscript submitted for publication.

White, E. J., Redder, B., & Peter, M. (2013). To be or not to be: Is that the question in infant play? *The First Years: Ngā Tau Tuatahi New Zealand Journal of Infant and Toddler Education, 15*(2), 16–20.

White, E. J., Redder, B., & Peter, M. (in press). The work of the eye in infant pedagogy: A dialogic encounter of 'seeing' in an education and care setting. *International Journal of Early Childhood, 47*(2).

Wyman, A. (2008). Bakhtin and Scheler: Toward a theory of active understanding. *Slavonic and East European Review, 86*(1), 58–89.

Zack, E., Barr, R., Gerhardstein, P., Dickerson, K., & Meltzoff, A. (2009). Infant imitation from television using novel touch screen technology. *British Journal of Developmental Psychology, 27*(1), 13–26.

Zinchenko, V. (2009, June). *Consciousness as the subject matter and task of psychology.* Keynote address to the Second International Interdisciplinary Conference of Perspectives and Limits of Dialogism in Mikhail Bakhtin, Stockholm, Sweden.

5

TEACHING AND PLAY

In a book about the early years there is perhaps no more important topic than play. In many parts of the Western world there appears to be a general consensus that play is the modus operandi for infants, toddlers and young children. However, there is much less agreement about the complex *nature* of play and its *purpose*. In Western early years education today, play is often described as the primary means through which teachers can help the child learn. That children have been playing perfectly well without such intervention for centuries seems to have been forgotten in this discourse. This point is at the centre of a dialogic orientation – that play is such a natural event – makes it a rich palette for understanding others and ourselves in the social world. The pedagogical provocation for teachers is to consider how to 'be' in these events, and the extent to which types of engagement, or nonengagement, contribute to the experience. In the chapter that follows you are invited to consider the potential for play to be a great deal more than a source of cognition or received learning and the opportunities that are available to adults prepared to stand in awe of children's tremendous strategic capacity to alter their own and others' worlds.

What is play from a dialogic standpoint?

Bakhtin's specific attention to play is less prominent throughout his texts than many of his other ideas. He loosely describes play as something that happens when the theatrical 'footlights' are turned off and, in doing so, conjures up an image of events that take place outside of a performance or public display with no relationship 'between playing and the artistic event' (Bakhtin, 1990, p. 74). In this depiction of play the players do not have a set script that has been rehearsed to perfection and they are not performing for the benefit of others. Things could be said in ways that might not be entertained in the official show and the players might be free to take on a range of different, perhaps multiple, roles than those assigned in the earlier designated script. Play is characterised by impromptu creativity and skill, relying on the wit of the players rather than a pre-established convention, although convention may be summoned at certain points of the event.

Thinking about play in light of Bakhtin's wider corpus from a twenty-first century Western standpoint opens up possibilities to explore its rich potential in the social world of infants, toddlers and young children. At once it becomes evident that while each different play event has its own set of rules (as Vygotsky also suggested) it is, like all language, negotiable and always in a state of flux. What is of most interest to dialogic pedagogy is not so much the rules themselves but the way that they are established (disestablished, negotiated or violated) in dialogue through *genre* and maintained or transgressed through *chronotope*. Both of these ideas are examined later in this chapter in relation to play.

When we talk about play using a Bakhtinian lens we do not compartmentalise it as symbolic versus literal (or *dialectic*) in the way that Vygotksy might have us do. Play takes multiple forms and has multiple genres – none are any less significant or valuable than another because they all have a role in the social experience. They often appear simultaneously. It stands to reason, then, that we would avoid any suggestion that any play is 'anti' or 'un' social. Even what Piaget might call solitary or parallel play is, from a Bakhtinian point of view, still social. Whether or not there are others in the room does not dismiss this idea because the player may be calling upon unseen others, historical, authorial others or perhaps even nonliving others to join the event. Karin Junefelt (2008) discovered this phenomenon in her video work with a sight-impaired 8-year-old boy who summoned the voices of his parents in play with his doll. Taken from this view it becomes very difficult to assert that the boy is playing alone even though this is what it may seem like to the distant observer. James Wertsch (1991) calls this *hidden dialogicity* – a concept that significantly expands on Vygotsky's notion of private speech to suggest that internal speech is not merely a developmental process. Bakhtin argues that everyone uses language in this way – it is not just the domain of the child:

> The second speaker is present and invisibly, his words are not there, but deep traces left by these words have a determining influence on all present and visible words of the first speaker.
>
> *(Bakhtin, 1984, p. 197)*

Suspending developmental limitations in this manner makes it possible to consider even the youngest infant as capable of communication through play in a way that Vygotsky and Piaget could not. A Bakhtinian approach to play is not limited to certain developmental periods that mark its meaning. Instead it is viewed as a social act that, like other forms of communication, orients itself towards or away from shared meaning. In contrast to Vygotsky, play is not viewed as a means of promoting higher psychological thought nor is it seen as a less sophisticated 'activity' than real learning. While Bakhtin shares Malaguzzi's idea that there are multiple languages that are employed, for him these are not merely used as a random form of individual expression. Language is viewed as a way of positioning oneself in the social world. It stands to reason, therefore, that the role of the teacher in play will be markedly different from this perspective. Indeed Alexander Lobok is highly critical of teachers who attempt to plan for play outside of this dialogic entreaty. For him, interference of this nature is more likely to stifle creativity than enhance it:

> To confess honestly, among the various kinds of methodological handbooks for kindergarten teachers, what concerns me most is the unflinching conviction, on the part of their authors, that any game in which adults play with children must have clearly defined didactic goals and objectives. But day-to-day play and day-to-day stories are like life: always richer than any of our conscious goals and objectives.
>
> *(Lobok, 2012, p. 105)*

In an examination of play Bakhtin (1990) invites us to "step across the footlights and take up a position" (p. 79) thus ceasing to be a mere spectator of play, or seeking to manipulate play to some external learning agenda or script, while recognising that any other position in play cannot be taken for granted. A Bakhtinian approach to play grants primacy to the players themselves – both on and off the stage. It is a special kind of *postupok*.

Play as *postupok*

You may have realised already that a dialogic approach to play does not suggest that play is only the domain of the child. Play is a lifelong pursuit and is not separate from its dispositional relationship to playfulness. How often have you toyed with the idea of changing your image or the way you want people to see you (or think they see you in any case) through dressing up or a new haircut or job? Have you ever enjoyed a moment of realisation that you had altered the way people saw you through some social exchange that positioned you differently – either temporarily or perhaps forever? I will never forget the day I dressed up as 'Granny' for the children at kindergarten – for a moment in time I was that person and all that this entailed – much to the delight of the children. For many months afterwards, the children would ask, "Where is Granny today?" knowing full well that Granny was me! The delight we shared in that secret concealment was not only valued but also altered the basis of our future relationship and became a valued part of the kindergarten chronotope.

> A few days after Granny's visit, 3-year-old Taylor spied a piece of cake in the staff room. She asked me if she could eat it for morning tea. I replied, "I'm sorry but that's Granny's cake. She needs it for sustenance because she is so old." She smiled at me and seemed to accept this rationale. However five minutes later Taylor returned, having gone to the dress-up clothing box and retrieved a shawl and wig (the same one 'Granny' had worn). She was bent

over and, in a quavering voice said: "Can I have a piece of cake?" How could I resist giving it to her!

(Teaching notes, 1989)

In my Western reading of Bakhtin's concept of *postupok* this lifelong process of 'becoming' can be closely aligned to play. Unlike the literal Russian meaning of this word, the interpretation of play may or may not be employed as a full-blown deed of self-sacrifice, but there is always some kind of deed involved.

The notion of a deed positions play as an ethical act of 'doing' because it has an effect on others. For Bakhtin, such an effect is the essential element of being seen and heard: in other words, answered. To have an effect is, in essence, to exercise agency over the world. We will explore agency in more depth in the next chapter but, for now, it is important for you to know that Bakhtin's interest in agency is closely concerned with his idea of answerability explored in chapter 3.

Remember that for Bakhtin there is always an 'other' − even if they are not present. Play is therefore a central way of being with others or of bringing others into being. Imaginary friends or *ventriloquised voices* from home (notice how often young children play out parent conversations on the telephone or mobile phone, for example) are rife in early years settings. Each are examples of addressing others and being addressed through different roles − playing out histories, events and experiences in ways that can alter their meaning or perhaps provide a way of dealing with their consequences. Perhaps, for this reason, Brian Edmiston has described play as a "workshop for life" (2008, p. 10) where meaning-making possibilities are rampant and unrestrained.

In a New York study by Lynn Cohen (2009) four children play out the idea of going on an aeroplane with a baby. They encounter an imaginary problem when Elena suddenly announces that they are going on a "grown-up plane" which does not allow babies. Elena's act of making this suggestion, which is made possible through the play event, responds to the ethical dilemma the game has posed. It is also a dilemma many children experience in real life but here, in play, there are possibilities for these children to resolve the situation in ways that may not be available to them in the 'real' world of adults. After much discussion the group decide that the baby can go on the grown-up plane but that they must sit at the back. Jessenia proudly announces the resolution: "Baby, you can come with us" (p. 337). Her deed, as a conscious decision to alter the situation, is to facilitate ways to include the baby and, in doing so, to reach an equitable outcome. The problem has now been solved and, as Lynn explains, the children have created a means of encountering convergent viewpoints through play, devising strategic outcomes that satisfy the rules of the game or, as has happened here, inventing new ones to solve the irreconcilable problem of taking the baby on an 'adults-only' aeroplane.

But such impact is not always so amiable. It can sometimes be very painful for those involved, or even for those watching. In the following situation, Zoe is trying very hard to join in to pretend play with the 4-year-old girls she so admires (see the video 'Bark chip eggs').

Zoe carefully watches two 4-year-old girls dressed in pink hula skirts place bark chips into egg cartons. They have set up a pretend shop in their early learning centre and are studiously 'selling' eggs. "Two dollars, please," says one of the girls to the other, holding out more bark chips in her hand. They exchange 'money' across a table, and sort out their 'produce'. After several minutes Zoe picks up a piece of bark chip and steps forward with her hand out, offering 'money' too. "No, Zoe, you can't play," says one of the girls. "Go away." The teacher, having heard this rejection, suggests to the girls that perhaps Zoe could join in. The girls are adamant that their play is for them alone, stating clearly: "No, we don't want Zoe here." The teacher helps Zoe find more egg cartons and supports her in setting up shop nearby. The older girls visit the shop and 'taste' some of Zoe's eggs. Zoe beams as her wares are sampled. Her teacher stays close to support her in this play.

(Marjanovic-Shane & White, 2014, p. 130)

Postupok in this example is exercised by the teacher, who makes a conscious decision to assist Zoe into the play while simultaneously upholding the wishes of the 4 year olds not to have their game interrupted. The nature of the teacher's engagement in play is framed within the relationships that exist between the teacher and these children, not in some external rituals of 'best practice'. It is an ethical stance

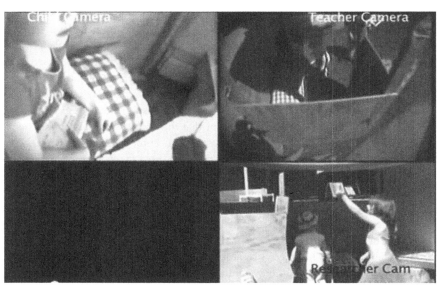

FIGURE 5.1 Bark chip eggs

that draws on the teacher's knowledge of these children in tandem with her percep-
tions of their orientation towards play. For this teacher, play is a mutually voluntary
pursuit – that is, you cannot *make* people involve others in their play. In this sense it is
a private affair and the teacher has responded to the older girls' desire to be left alone
accordingly, yet she is equally attuned to young Zoe and her priorities to enter into
the play. Teachers in the early years often struggle with the potentially exclusion-
ary aspects of play – particularly in settings where democratic processes are highly
valued. Yet, from a dialogic standpoint, the experience of being excluded presents
an opportunity, and challenge, for children to encounter boundaries through play,
provided there is dialogue to support their experience. In this case Zoe's teacher
provides her with a means of understanding the genre of pretend play and satisfying
her desire to participate by entering into the play herself. While she can, and does,
play a part in suggesting a potential role for Zoe in the group, and in providing some
cues as to the genre Zoe needs to adopt to be successful in this type of play, the
teacher cannot presume that her suggestions will be accepted by the others. Both
the girls and Zoe need to make up their own minds about who the play will involve
and how it will take place – it is this freedom that marks its magic.

Eugene Matusov (2009) has criticised Vivian Gussin Paley (1992) for her famous
intervention of placing a sign in her kindergarten classroom saying "You can't say
you can't play." In her book Vivian presents the dilemma in her class of some children
being excluded from play. Based on her ideologic orientation towards a 'democratic
classroom', Vivian weighs up the cost for each child in taking this stance, arguing
(undemocratically in the end) that it is fairer not to exclude. Eugene's disagreement
starts and ends, in my view, with the notion of play as an ethical deed that cannot be
manipulated by outsiders because it represents an opportunity to explore and experience life's challenges through dialogue. In play such intervention is particularly
unwelcome due to the fact that the very essence of play is that it represents a source
of freedom for the players. Yet, in the case of young children, it does not mean that
teachers do not have an important role to fulfil.

Returning to the event of Zoe and the shop, it is clear that the girls are free to
choose whether Zoe joins in or not. Even though, with the support of her teacher,
Zoe is able to engage in the object of the pretend play (that is, the bark chip, egg
cartons and even the space that has been set aside for a pretend shop), she is ultimately denied the opportunity to play with the 4 year olds. They vacate the area
and pick up their intimate game elsewhere. What is your response to this outcome?
Should the teacher attempt to make the girls aware of the impact of their exclusive
play on others? Perhaps they are already aware of this and unconcerned? Either way,
vital clues as to the positioning of 'other' in the early years setting are revealed and/
or concealed through this play event. If Zoe wants to play with the big girls she has
some serious strategising to do and, with the help of her teacher, she can take this
'step up' (postupok) in her play. Seen in this way play is far from a mere pastime or
trivial pursuit but a serious effort by those involved. It is also a cultural event that
requires sensitivity and awareness of the wider social and historical spaces in tandem
with the unique children who are involved in each play. *Postupok*, as a deed of great

significance for children in their play, should not be trivialised as 'mere play' but viewed as very serious pedagogical work for all involved.

'Making a step' through play

Translated literally, *postupok* means to 'make a step' or proceed. Pi-Chun Grace Ho and Anna Stetsenko (in press) explain:

> Every deed that together forms a seamless stream of life as an active project of "coming forward through doing," as "postuplenie" . . . it captures diverse connotations and conveys the sense of a process-like, continuous (uninterrupted) and dynamic (ever-changing and cumulative) unfolding and active pressing forward in carrying out one's life, as a stepping forward through deeds, as a becoming-through-doing.

When children (just as adults) enter into a play experience, they have the opportunity to take important steps towards a different way of being that might not otherwise be available to them. A 4-year-old girl who is known by the adults in the centre as 'the sensible one' always taking a reliable, responsible position, suddenly emerges from the dress-up corner as a silly clown with a painted face, throwing balls in the air. A 3-year-old boy who tends to stay in the background quietly observing the adventurous play of others becomes a raging lion by waving a furry puppet and roaring loudly. Animals are often employed in play to support children in catapulting themselves into a different way of being seen by others (and perhaps even themselves). How often have you seen young children pretend to be a pet dog or cat, possibly as a means of positioning themselves in a care-receiving role, or become an all-powerful superhero at times when autonomy may otherwise be quite limited? Some theorists call this identity formation but for Bakhtin it is much more sophisticated than this – for him identities are suspended and negotiated rather than arrived at for all time. You may recall from earlier chapters that Susan Petrelli (2013) describes this dialogic principle as a logic of otherness, based on the notion of subjectivities in play whereby identities shift in relation to the people we are with. In this sense play is yet another process of authoring and being authored, as discussed in chapter 3, that takes place in the social world. Rupert Wegerif (2007) outlines this important theoretical shift from identity to difference in dialogic theory, suggesting that meaning has no limits and is never fixed when taken from this view. If we accept this standpoint then we must also accept that play like any other act is never isolated from others – even when it appears to be solitary. There may be invisible others involved who are summoned from other spaces – perhaps even those who we have yet to imagine (did you have an imaginary friend as a child?). All is not what it seems.

Play is a very special dialogic space for authoring because it offers a means of trying out different identities, testing limits and exploring possibilities. Because its purpose is so often elusive to adults (despite the fact that many adults claim

FIGURE 5.2 Shoe fetish

to 'know' its meaning with a great deal of certainty), play presents children with unique opportunities to claim and even exploit alternative ways of being. Moreover, children author themselves and others through play in subtle, creative ways. It is this mutual co-authoring that I draw your attention to in the section that follows. You are first invited to watch the video 'Shoe fetish', which shows the following event.

We had filmed an extended episode during the late summer afternoon in the centre. Eighteen-month-old Zoe spent a considerable amount of time retrieving three sets of her 4-year-old female peers' pink shoes that she found strewn about the place. She carefully picked them up and tried them on, then placed them carefully on the lower level of the shoe rack. One of the 4-year-old girls, who owned a pair of these shoes, took all the shoes off the lower level and placed them on a higher rack where Zoe could not reach. Zoe tried, in vain, to reach them over a long period of time. Eventually she went over to her teacher and pointed to the shoes. Realising her desire, the teacher retrieved the shoes and Zoe proceeded to try them on – one after the other – taking them on and off, on and off and negotiating the Velcro attachments. This was a scene that she repeated on many occasions over subsequent days – always with those same pink shoes.

A week later I sat with Zoe's mother to discuss the footage, with Zoe present. Luckily I videoed this event also and could see Zoe in the background as we were talking. I said: "I've noticed that Zoe seems to have a shoe fetish." Her mother laughed and agreed. "But," I said, "it only seems to be the pink shoes of certain girls." Zoe's mother explained that these girls were friends of the family who spent a lot of time with Zoe outside of centre. "Oh, that probably explains it," I replied. "But I find it interesting that she never tries on the dress-up shoes." Later, analysing the video footage I watch Zoe as she listens to our conversation (Bakhtin would suggest that she is eavesdropping – a point I return to in the next chapter). While her mother and I are talking about Zoe's shoe preferences Zoe walks to the dress-up corner and retrieves a set of gold grown-up shoes, sits down on the floor and puts them on. She looks intently at me as she does so.

It is possible to contend that Zoe might be 'stepping out' in several different ways through this play event and its aftermath. Whatever stance she hopes to present it is clear that she is co-authoring the event in a variety of ways. Firstly she seems to be exploring her gendered position within the setting – pink shoes are for girls after all, aren't they? Her determined play with the shoes, despite the barriers presented by others and in the face of multiple other objects at her disposal, suggests that *these* shoes are representative of something more for Zoe. Perhaps she was exploring ideas of literally putting herself in someone else's shoes, particularly someone whom she saw as sharing aspects of her future self. But there is more to this story from a Bakhtinian point of view – she also presents another aspect of her personality in determining that she is not interested *only* in those shoes, after all. Here, I suggest, she is 'stepping out' to claim her stance as more than what I declared (or authored) her to be – liberating herself as golden and grown up as well as pink and girlish. Of course I can never know that this was her intention, but it is through the act of trying to understand that we gain so many insights about ourselves and others. In Zoe's case I was reminded of the importance of not finalising her intentions and recognising her orientation and agentism as separate from my own. Stepping out through play, in this instance as for many others, offers vital cues for adults who are interested to learn about the way children wish to be seen and heard.

Play is a conscious, value-laden, answerable act

But what marks one play event as significant, and who decides its value? As Bakhtin (1993) explains, while life is full of continuous acts, *postupok* represents a "constituent moment of my life" (p. 3). From this statement we can imagine points in our own lives where it seems as if everything up until that point has led to some movement, or step, in a different direction. So it is with play. Moments where you might feel as if a light goes on in some way – perhaps a shared realisation or epiphany, or maybe an encounter where you feel strangely out of place. For Bakhtin, there is great significance in both ends of this pole. In play we get the opportunity to experience both in multiple forms of social exchange. We can be that raging lion or shopkeeper for a temporary moment in time as a means of testing ourselves against others. Conversely, we can deliberately set out to alter a situation with a strategic word, action or nonaction.

Bakhtin (1981) gives us a means of making sense of this complex and often confusing process through the notion of *double-voiced discourse*. Here language is summoned from outside the direct play experience to bring other perspectives and dimensions into the act. Through such means players have the opportunity to test different points of view and to play them out. A classic example of such discourse is those moments where young children take on the role of authority figure in a parodying fashion – it can be very revealing to observe a young child playing 'teacher' by waving a finger at the children only to realise that this is what *you* have just done during group time. In a 2012 New Zealand study by Lia de Vochdt two children did just that in play when they took on roles of teacher and student during a re-enacted group session:

M: Put your hand up and cross your legs. [in a firm voice] (Maddy is sitting on the teacher's chair next to a children's paint easel with a chart depicting images of the weather, days of the week, dates etc. She crosses her own legs under her chair, watching J.)

J: (Shuffles back on his bottom, all the way to the back wall.)

M: Put your hand up. (M speaks in a firm voice and puts her own arm up.)

M: Jonathan, would you like to come over here? [in a sweet voice] (Again, as she did earlier, as if selecting him, making beckoning motion with her hand.)

J: (Walks slowly up to M with big steps with his cap in his hand and pulling knees high up. He stops right in front of the chart.)

M: (Follows him with her eyes and chuckles a few times.)

M: Jonathan, what number are we up to? (M is asking in her sweet voice again.)

J: (Points to a number in the section of the chart that has the dates of the month.)

M: I know, 32! [in a pleased, affirmative voice] (She motions him with her arm to go back again and sit down.)

J: (Walks back and sits on his bottom)

M: Which day is it?

J: (Comes running forward to the chart and points)

M: It starts with an M, pah . . . pah? (Pointing to a word and mouthing the first letter, P.)

J: Sunday! [calling out] (Hops from one foot to another a few times.)

M: Sunday! [affirmative, in a pleased voice] (She claps her hands a few times.)

M: How about, do you want to read a book with me? (M is standing facing the chart and tries to take it out from under the board clips, but then puts it back up again. She briefly glances at the teacher and the child who are discussing where the centre rabbit has gone. M sits down on the stool next to the easel again.)

M: No, you go over there. (She points J where he has to sit down and she waits until J has gone there.)

M: Put your hand up . . . Jonno, would you like to come over here? [again in the sweet voice she used earlier] (She cocks her head and watches J. J runs towards the chart.)

M: It is . . . (Pointing to pictures with different types of weather and pausing.)

J: It is snowing! I love snow. [in a high pitched funny voice] (Spreads out his arms wide, turns around.)

M: Nooo. [M stretches the word out, smiles] (She cocks her head.) (de Vochdt, 2014)

The teacher is therefore very important in play when considered dialogically. Lia suggests that the children in the event just described are not merely playing amongst themselves but are actually addressing the teacher even though she is not physically present. A teacher who is open to the dialogic meanings offered in play therefore has an opportunity to see themselves and others authored through the visual surplus of children as much as they might offer their own point of view. They may not like what they see but play provides a means of re-examining ourselves and our relationships with others. As Rachel Rosen (in press) explains, this dialogic approach to play opens up the possibilities "to explore new social imaginaries about who children and adults are and might be; as well as to critically engage with questions about the worlds that we do not want to live in as well as those we do."

However you look at it, though, the teacher is not invisible. Indeed, Po Chi Tam (2012) suggests that even the mere gaze of the teacher when children are in play nearby has a profound influence on the type of play that transpires. Highlighting examples from her dialogic observations of teacher Mabel and her group of 20 4–5 year olds, Po Chi analyses the different types of play that transpire depending on the role of the teacher. These range from reproduction of the teacher's agenda (where the teacher has prescribed the play plot in advance and children step outside of the play frame to reinforce the teacher's rules) to disarray (where children confuse the teacher by pretending to play according to the rules while actually circumventing them). The latter is also an example of carnivalesque, as I explain in the next chapter. By bringing these different types of play together, Tam suggests that children are deploying a process of *bricolage* – a creative deployment of the teacher's wishes alongside those of the individual or peer group in order to develop new, more sophisticated play frames (we will explore this idea further in the next two chapters). As teachers, even our most subtle response plays a vital role in the types of play that take place in early years settings. We are, indeed, answerable. Let's look at an example of such deployment by 2-year-old Harry as she strategically finds her way into play through a doll (see the video 'The dolls').

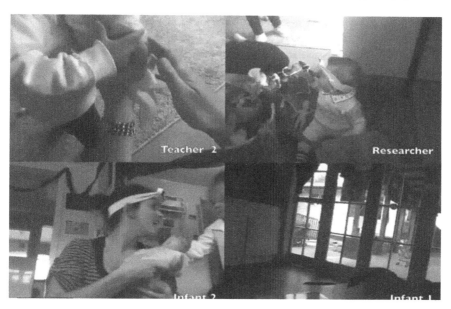

FIGURE 5.3 The dolls

Two-year-old Harry provides us with an early example of answerability in play. She has witnessed the teacher playing peek-a-boo with 8-month-old Lola and seeks to join in. She moves around the periphery of the game for some time, watching carefully how it is played out. A combination of strategies are employed in this game, including the layering of a scarf over the dolls head and an exclamation of "boo!" At the centre of the play is the doll that Lola has in her possession. Recognising the centrality of the doll to the play itself, Harry takes the doll from Lola and attempts to enter into the play. This she does successfully and very strategically while at the same time ensuring that Lola has a turn – perhaps recognising that this is her teacher's agenda.

(Marjanovic-Shane & White, 2014, p. 129)

It is interesting to note the key teacher's intense involvement within this play event. Further analysis of these interactions over a period of three hours showed that more instances of teacher-infant and infant-teacher responses took place in play than in routine events. This is especially interesting when you consider the fact that teachers in this centre claimed that their pedagogy was influenced by a Pikler philosophy, advocating for *less* involvement in play. Their rationale for this was based on Anna Tardos's (2012) idea that infants should develop the habit of occupying themselves with objects as a source of freedom. Although Anna does not deny the natural affinity babies have to others and the joy of playing together, I think this is a dangerous proposition for early years teachers to adopt as a monologic pedagogical tenet. A dialogic approach to play could never isolate objects from their orientation in the social setting – remember that the object is merely a means of imbuing the social situation which forms the basis of all play, in Bakhtinian terms at least. A sensitive infant teacher is not going to deliberately ignore potential opportunities to engage in dialogue, regardless of the social context. It is, therefore, unsurprising that our study revealed a very different type of pedagogy than what was espoused by the teachers who subscribed to this approach (White, Redder, & Peter, 2013). Instead, we discovered that teachers took every opportunity to become involved in play, even in spite of themselves and their philosophical heritage.

I cannot blame these teachers for getting involved in play (in fact, from a dialogic point of view, I applaud them). I am constantly amazed at the efforts even the very youngest child will go to in order to be involved, and involve others, in play. Using every strategy at their disposal, the smallest infant will take every opportunity to engage others in their iterative and extremely creative acts of play. Such resourcefulness suggests that very young children are far more socially capable, perhaps even manipulative, than might previously have been postulated. Most certainly, it is difficult to deny their absolute orientation towards other through play and the variety of ways in which they make their claim. This strategic orientation forms the basis of Bakhtin's theory of genre.

Genre and play

Bakhtin describes genre as "the drivebelts to meaning" (Bakhtin, 1986, p. 65). By this he sees genre as the compilation of a series of language forms which are carefully employed to generate meaning (or in some cases to deliberately thwart meaning). For example, when I talk on the telephone to my son I use a very different tone of voice, style of delivery, body language and vocabulary than I would if I were addressing a lecture theatre full of students. If I want to say something privately to someone in a social setting, or confess a secret I really don't want to share, I might employ a whisper, cover my mouth with my hand or use close body contact with my confidante. In using each particular form I am hopeful that those I converse with will share those conventions. These give us a shared sense of meaning that expands well beyond the exact words that are spoken. The use of genre is no different in play.

Think of all the different types of play that exist in an early years setting. Each has its own set of rules of encounter, although these may differ from place to place. One very important genre that can be employed in certain types of play – carnivalesque – will be explored in the next chapter. The different language forms that carnivalesque employs are centred around the body – belching, farting, shouting, raucous laughter or some form of ridicule are often observed in this genre. The genre employed for a more serious activity such as block play would certainly not welcome such language combinations, as Lynn Cohen (in press) has shown in her studies of block play. Similarly depending on the type of dramatic play, a set of social conventions will be imposed that establish the rules. For instance Po Chi Tam (2012) describes the genre of "boutique shopping" she observed in her study. This genre, she explains, was comprised of a series of "greeting-looking and trying on clothes-request and offer of service-transaction-salutation" (p. 248). The current trend in United States for play-world encounters, where children engage in storytelling as a means of engaging with others, is another increasingly popular play genre in early years pedagogy. Ageliki Nicolopoulou, Aline Barbosa de Sá, Hande Ilgaz and Carolyn Brockmeyer (2009) describe its forms as voluntary storytelling that is dictated and then formally acted out in groups. In the latter case the genre is much more teacher-initiated at the outset, while at the other extreme (in carnivalesque genre, for instance) play is child-initiated. In a similar vein Elin Odegaard (2011) suggests that co-narration, where stories are constructed between adults and children, is a special kind of genre. I'm sure you can think of many other genres that are specific to each type of play and which have their own set of meanings and ways of participating. Perhaps they are valued differently across cultures? Most of the studies that exist today suggest that children who can grasp each genre that is valued in the early years setting (by adults, children or both) are likely to be more successful in entering, and sustaining, play. If we accept the early years setting as a microcosm of life, there is perhaps no more important feat than this.

In my studies I wanted to understand the different play genre that took place for 18-month-old Zoe in an early years setting. I discovered those that were brought to the centre from home but were not well understood in the centre (which I called outside-in genre) and those that were viewed as acceptable within the centre (which I called inside-out genre). The latter were closely aligned to the genre described by Po Chi Tam and Lynn Cohen, and included 'mat-time' – a daily ritual that required all of the children to sit on the mat, legs crossed, and sing songs. Play was, on the surface of things, limited to the teacher's agenda in this genre, although sometimes children were able to suggest songs or games that could be played (if it was their turn to choose). Like her peers, Zoe worked hard to be involved in this genre but would often deviate from expectation if the requirements of sitting too long took precedence.

A great deal of *underground* dialogue took place during these events – some of which we will discuss in the chapters that follow. However, these were rarely valued by the teacher. Instead, genre based on adult orientations at mat time or in response to the centre plan featured heavily in centre documentation and, when children conformed, their participation was highly valued by the teachers. The extremely creative events taking place in the underground simply did not feature.

Outside-in genres – drawn from the home but not standard in the early years context – were more difficult for teachers to see. On one occasion Zoe was sitting beside her teacher reading a book outside. A trike rushes past and Zoe turns to jiggle her body and call out (it is indistinguishable to either myself or her teacher). Her mother later explained that she was calling out, "Go, Taylor, go" (see the video of that name), and that this was a game she played with the family dog down the

FIGURE 5.4 Go, Taylor

driveway. Her family enjoyed this play experience on a regular basis. Neither Zoe's teacher nor I saw the significance of this subtle language act, but it was of immediate significance to her family on this basis.

If we are seriously committed to dialogic approaches to play it seems to me that it is important for us to try to engage with the genre children bring to their experience, and the significant meaning each holds. Entry into play, or recognition of play that matters, should not always be on adult or centre terms. Children bring with them, from diverse worlds, multiple often competing priorities from experiences teachers know little about. Surely an important role for the teacher is therefore to enter into dialogues – with children and families – about the language combinations they see children using in the early years setting, especially those they do not understand. Conversely it may also be important to support children, and their families, to understand each genre that is valued in the centre – its various forms and meanings – as a source of engagement and perhaps, negotiation. As Elin Odegaard explains:

> Such practice can create a culture of learning where the child participating in the co-narrations can learn that their stories are worth telling. However, it is a continuous challenge for teachers to include and empower every child

as learners and at the same time support a group identity . . . Extending children's knowledge and building up expectations must not be undervalued.

(Odegaard, 2007, p. 62)

Once children have a strong grasp of valued genre across sites they can use them strategically and creatively. Lynn Cohen (in press) suggests that this requires a great deal of appropriation (of the words and actions used by others in the particular event), unidirectional and varidirectional discourse (as the appropriate language games are employed) and revoicing (when children redefine the language using their own voice) if the play is to be accepted in a specific context. In Lynn's case the context was block play, where 5-year-old children had to learn the dialogic principles of engagement to effectively participate.

But children can also use their knowledge of genres in even more sophisticated ways. They can, in effect, 'play' with the genres themselves. This capacity to alter play according to children's priorities is evident in the way genres can be manipulated to carry out certain agendas by exploiting the way they are utilised. We can see examples of such genre use in children's capacity to engage in what Ivy Schousboe (2013) calls "evil play" to generate private humour at someone else's expense(as we shall see in chapter 6) or to transform the play event into a real-life outcome (remember Taylor at the beginning of this chapter). Having a repertoire of genres at one's disposal is therefore a very important source of agency through play.

Chronotopes at play

While genre can be thought of as a relationship between the language forms employed and their meaning, Bakhtin's chronotope provides a way for us to understand the importance of context on how any genre is interpreted. As explained in chapter 2, chronotope considers the time, space and 'value' dimensions of each genre. It is a coordinating device that allows us to understand why one genre might be successfully employed in one social setting, with one group of people, but not in another. Why, for instance, would some acts be more acceptable during a centre mealtime (as several studies suggest) but not during mat time, for example? Who decides and on what basis? What happens if I fart loudly at mat time? If I misread the chronotope and make fun of the teacher when she is being very serious, what will be the consequences? Many serious historical moments could be analysed from this perspective – often with dire consequences for those involved. Comedians such as Mr Bean, Ricky Gervais and the Monty Python crew, for instance, built their humour on this premise. But it is not so funny for those who experience its reality (such as Karl Pilkington, who so often becomes the butt of the joke – or is he playing along?).

As we have already established, from a Bakhtinian perspective, play is complex, multi-voiced and in a constant state of flux. Yet if we return to the idea of *postupok* that began this chapter, it is reasonable to assert that play is also a way of positioning oneself, or stepping out, in response to others. Chronotope acts as a means of framing the positioning of each player by creating boundaries through the strategic use of genre. Once a boundary is established in play, it becomes possible to create surprises, disagreements or even to shock others – in order to be noticed and, in doing so, to be answered.

Four chronotopes of play

Ana Marjanovic-Shane (2011) identifies four distinct chronotopes in play that, she believes, are strategically employed in play as boundaries that exploit the relationships between imagination and reality. These are:

1. The Reality Chronotope. This chronotope only emerges in play. In everyday life outside of play, reality is what everyone experiences but in play it is utilised at strategic moments – perhaps to step outside of a game, to summon an important idea that will add to the play or to bring order to the chaos of play in the imaginary chronotope. Genres that are characterised by authority are utilised here – perhaps facts from books are summoned or a parent voice is introduced.

2. The Imaginary Chronotope. The Imaginary Chronotope is the primary location of play where fantasy is necessary to expand possibilities well beyond what is real. While it might be employed in other chronotopes it is really at home in play, as a valued way of operating. In this chronotope there is no such thing as a lie because everything is made up anyway. The types of genres that flourish in this chronotope are those that suspend truth such as fantasy play or the introduction of an imaginary friend.

3. The Community of Players Chronotope. The community of players chronotope exists in the co-creation of the boundary between imaginary and reality chronotopes. At this boundary the players share a mutual understanding of imaginary and real worlds in play, and utilise them to their common purpose. Here carnivalesque has its home – all hierarchies and rules are suspended; and an understanding of the creative interplay that is taking place is shared. Those that do not share in this chronotope do not have access to the fullest appreciation of the play context. We will explore this idea further in the next chapter.

Brian Edmiston (2010) takes this idea of co-creation very seriously in his work, or should I say play, with young children. Based on his experiences with Michael, his son, Brian summons Bakhtin's notion of answerability to highlight the importance of their joint engagement in play and the ethical challenges that arise through such encounters:

> On occasions, playing with Michael led to me being addressed in encounters that could become both more emotionally and ethically challenging for me . . . I tried to answer with honesty and integrity, relying on what I ethically believed rather than on moral abstractions. Bakhtin (1990, p. 1) reminds me that by turning to my life for answers my worldview will change.

(p. 208)

FIGURE 5.5 Brian Edmiston at the centre of play

Brian argues that his involvement within the play experience provides opportunities for learning that would not be available to children without him. Here he is with a group of preschool children more recently, exploring volcanic activity based on a child's provocation. You can see how central he is to the experience – perhaps a tad too central from a dialogic point of view?

4. The Audience Chronotope. Although we have already established that play, for Bakhtin, takes place when the footlights are off and the audience has gone home, there is still a silent audience in play. They are not part of the experience – perhaps they misinterpret the genres at play and their use – but who receive meaning by watching others. Children who reside at this chronotope benefit from watching others, being on the periphery of the experience and, of course, taking steps to become involved when they are ready. This chronotope is especially important for those who do not share the same culture as the community of players, and who may benefit from taking the time to understand the genres and their negotiating properties in play before stepping into the game. Without such understanding it is likely that they may be unwelcome or even excluded from the game.

Teachers may also reside in this space on occasions when they seek to understand what is happening rather than intervening. Faith Guss (2011) reminds us that this is an aesthetic position that involves "listening and learning . . . to sense the complexity of possibilities" (p. 123). This locale is often a good place for intensive

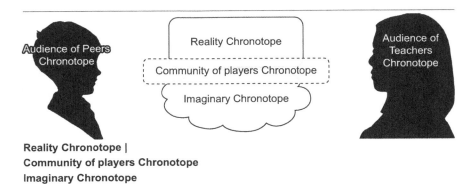

Reality Chronotope |
Community of players Chronotope
Imaginary Chronotope

FIGURE 5.6 Chronotopes at play

observation in order to gain insight about a child, a group of children, interests, social structures, language and so on. It is also the groundwork for lingering lovingly, as we discussed in the previous chapter. It represents "an ethical decolonisation of the pedagogy of play" (Guss, 2011, p. 124). This position is very different to the one Brian Edmiston writes about as a parent, highlighting the very different pedagogical role of the teacher in the early years.

As we can see, each chronotope holds potential for meaning-making in and around the periphery of play. There are opportunities for discovery at each boundary, and one may not stay in the same space across all types of play experiences. For instance, an interesting genre that is increasingly evident in early years setting is the language form of code-switching where children who speak two or more languages are able to move strategically across words and ideas in ways that are inaccessible to monolinguistic speakers. The additional advantage of multiple verbal languages provides a greater repertoire of possibilities to strategically engage (or not engage) with others, and is a point that is beginning to attract the research interest of scholars in the early years. (For example, you might be interested to read the work of Anne Kultti and Ingrid Pramling Samuelsson, 2014, in which children with more than one language were able to communicate in more complex ways with multilingual peers.) This should not be surprising to us when we consider the sophisticated examples of multiple, synchronous language use we have seen in infants and toddlers as they negotiate their bodies in creative ways to 'step out' into the social world.

Looking back, moving forward

This chapter has revealed a very different view of play than the traditional theories you will find in most textbooks on the subject. Taking a dialogic stance, play becomes a further opportunity to reveal oneself in the social world, to be authored by others and to explore different ways of being seen. It is made up of a series of genres that, taken together, form chronotopes that are able to interact with one another without long-term consequence. Seen in this way play is a strategy for testing limits and boundaries, perhaps even crossing boundaries just for a moment.

As we have seen through the various examples in this chapter, play is often subtle and mysterious but it can also be performative, manipulative, exclusive or, as seen by others such as Schousboe, it might be thought of as downright evil. While the invitation is there for all who choose to participate there is no guarantee that they will be successful in their attempts. In this regard play can be painful and deeply confusing, but it can also be outrageously fun. In a Bakhtinian approach to play there is complexity and depth that sometimes deliberately evades the eyes and ears of adults. In my view this provides a rich context for learning that sometimes exceeds the boundaries of adult 'seeing'.

So where does this leave teachers? If we conceive of play as *postupok*, a deed that offers a way of stepping out and engaging in an answerable act, there are serious implications for adults in the early years. Firstly I suggest that there is an invitation to celebrate the remarkable capacity of even the youngest infant to engage in sophisticated levels of play. With this realisation comes the responsibility for adults to become keenly attuned to the subtle messages that are being conveyed, explored, challenged, negotiated and interpreted through play in all its many forms. Secondly, there may be opportunities to support children in developing the necessary genres for participation or to attempt to understand the diverse meanings that might be given to any one form of language. Some of these genres rupture the rigid logic of adult interpretation and actively exploit the boundaries that undoubtedly exist between children and adults in early years settings.

Finally, and perhaps most importantly, Bakhtin reminds us that play, in the final analysis, belongs to the players – it is their story not ours. Therefore we need to be cautious about the assumptions we make regarding what we think children are 'learning' from play, their 'interests' or 'theories'; they are likely to be far more complex than we could ever imagine. This does not mean that teachers should step out of play altogether but that they should recognise its dialogic properties, the chronotopes that support or thwart its meaning and the tremendous influence adults can have in this regard. I think this is one of the greatest challenges early years teachers face. Granting children's multiple voices legitimacy in such spaces is a central part of a dialogic approach to play. It is also part of the loving deed discussed in chapter 4. As a dialogic entreaty there is no separation between the two. I hope that you will consider taking up Bakhtin's challenge and step across the footlights from time to time so that you, too, might learn to play. Whether you do or do not get involved, you are nonetheless implicated.

References

Bakhtin, M. M. (1981). *The dialogic imagination* (M. Holquist, Ed.; C. Emerson & M. Holquist, Trans.). Austin: University of Texas Press.

Bakhtin, M. M. (1984). *Problems of Dostoevsky's poetics* (C. Emerson, Trans.). Minneapolis: University of Minnesota Press.

Bakhtin, M. M. (1986). *Speech genres and other late essays* (C. Emerson & M. Holquist, Eds.; V. W. McGee, Trans.). Austin: University of Texas Press.

Bakhtin, M. M. (1990). *Art and answerability* (K. Brostrom, Trans.). Austin: University of Texas Press.

Bakhtin, M. M. (1993). *Toward a philosophy of the act* (M. Holquist & V. Liapunov, Eds.; V. Liapunov, Trans.). Austin: University of Texas Press.

Cohen, L. E. (2009). The heteroglossic world of preschoolers' pretend play. *Contemporary Issues in Early Childhood, 10*(4), 331–342.

Cohen, L. (in press). Layers of discourse in children's play: An examination of double-voicing in children's social interactions. *International Journal of Early Childhood, 47*(2).

de Vochdt, L. (2014). *Exploring dialogic research as a tool for early childhood teachers to respond morally to children's utterances.* Manuscript submitted for publication.

Edmiston, B. (2008). *Forming ethical identities in early childhood play.* London: Routledge.

Edmiston, B. (2010). Playing with children, answering with our lives: A Bakhtinian approach to co-authoring ethical identities in early childhood. *British Journal of Educational Studies, 58*(2), 197–211.

Guss, F. G. (2011). Meeting at the crossroads: Postmodern pedagogy greets children's aesthetic play-culture. In S. Rogers (Ed.), *Rethinking play and pedagogy in early childhood education: Concepts, contexts and cultures* (pp. 112–126). Abingdon: Routledge.

Gussin Paley, V. (1992). *You can't say you can't play.* Cambridge, MA: Harvard University Press.

Ho, P. G., & Stetsenko, A. (in press). Play as authoring: A dynamic pathway to becoming agentive actors in co-creating one's identities and the world. *International Journal of Early Childhood, 47*(2).

Junefelt, K. (2008). Mikhail Bakhtin: A missing link in hypotheses about children's linguistic and cognitive development. In M. A. Pourkos (Ed.), *Perspectives and limits of dialogism in Mikhail Bakhtin: Applications in psychology, education, art and culture* (pp. 197–221). Rethymnon, Greece: University of Crete.

Kultti, A., & Pramling Samuelsson, I. (2014). Guided participation and communication practices in multilingual toddler groups. In L. J. Harrison & J. Sumsion (Eds.), *Lived spaces of infant-toddler education and care: Exploring diverse perspectives on theory, research, practice and policy* (pp. 133–145). Dordrecht: Springer.

Lobok, A. (2012). Preschool education bullied: An experiment in establishing a dialogue with a kindergarten educator. *Journal of Russian and East European Psychology, 50*(6), 92–114.

Marjanovic-Shane, A. (2011). You are 'nobody'! The three chronotopes of play. In E. J. White & M. Peters (Eds.), *Bakhtinian pedagogy: Opportunities and challenges for research, policy and practice in education across the globe* (pp. 201–226). New York, NY: Peter Lang.

Marjanovic-Shane, A., & White, E. J. (2014). When the footlights are off: A Bakhtinian interrogation of play-as-postupok. *International Journal of Play, 3*(2), 119–135.

Matusov, E. (2009). *Journey into dialogic pedagogy.* Hauppauge, NY: Nova Science.

Nicolopoulou, A., Barbosa de Sá, A., & Ilgaz, H., & Brockmeyer, C. (2009). Using the transformative power of play to educate hearts and minds: From Vygotksy to Vivian Paley and beyond. *Mind, Culture and Activity, 17*(1), 42–58.

Odegaard, E. (2007). What's up on the teachers' agenda? A study of didactic projects and cultural values in mealtime conversations with very young children. *International Journal of Early Childhood, 39*(2), 45–64.

Odegaard, E. (2011). On the track of cultural formative practice: A chronotopic reading of young children's co-narrative meaning-making. In E. J. White & M. Peters (Eds.), *Bakhtinian pedagogy: Opportunities and challenges for research, policy and practice in education across the globe* (pp. 179–200). New York, NY: Peter Lang.

Petrelli, S. (2013). *The self as a sign, the world, and the other.* New Brunswick, NJ: Transaction.

Rosen, R. (in press). Imaginaries of childhood and neo-liberal 'value': Double-voiced responses to violently themed imaginary play. *International Journal of Early Childhood, 47*(2).

Schousboe, I. (2013). The structure of fantasy play and its implications for good and evil games. In I. Schousboe & D. Winter-Lindquist (Eds.), *Children's play and development* (pp. 13–27). New York, NY: Springer.

Tam, P. C. (2012). Children's bricolage under the gaze of teachers in sociodramatic play. *Childhood, 20*(2), 244–259.

Tardos, A. (2012). 'Let the infant play by himself as well' (A. Kajtar, Trans.). *The First Years: Ngā Tau Tuatahi New Zealand Journal of Infant and Toddler Education, 14*(1), 4–9.

Wegerif, R. (2007). *Dialogic education and technology: Expanding the space of learning.* New York, NY: Springer.

Wertsch, J. (1991). *Voices of the mind: A sociocultural approach to mediated action.* Cambridge, MA: Harvard University Press.

White, E. J., Redder, B., & Peter, M. (2013). To be or not to be: Is that the question in infant play? *The First Years: Ngā Tau Tuatahi New Zealand Journal of Infant and Toddler Education, 15*(2), 16–20.

6

TEACHING AND LAUGHTER

A very special kind of playfulness is illuminated in this chapter. Bakhtin's work on laughter is perhaps his most popular in the Western world today. However it is not merely a light-hearted analysis of comedy or humour. Central to Bakhtin's concept of carnivalesque is its relationship to the 'underground culture' where officialdom and hierarchy is temporarily suspended and convention is, for a short time, open to ridicule and debasement. Carnivalesque provides a means of revealing, suspending and unsettling the limitations of monologic truth. Laughter and ridicule becomes a mechanism for temporarily entering into the contradictory, ironic and counterpoint nature of reality. In this chapter you are invited to consider some of the many ways in which young children engage with carnivalesque in early childhood contexts – as rituals, feasts and festivals of laughter. The role of the peer group will be considered as a unique and sometimes exclusive culture that exists in group settings of this nature. The chapter invites teachers to consider the role(s) they might play in such contexts by exploring 'horizontal' and 'vertical' approaches to pedagogy.

Through carnivalesque Bakhtin gives cause to celebrate the essential ungraspability of human beings while simultaneously offering pathways of potential 'knowing' by paying attention to the subtle genres in and around social acts. In the context of very young children, this chapter invites adults to consider the possibility that the young child can not only present and re-present herself as a complex agent in her own right – well beyond the interpretive gaze of adults around her – but she can also exercise her authorial right to invoke dialogic loopholes as "the retention for oneself of the possibility for altering the ultimate, final meaning of one's own words" (Bakhtin, 1984, p. 233). A key mechanism for this invocation is through the strategy of eavesdropping, described by Bakhtin (1984) as an attempt to "outguess and outwit all possible definitions of his personality others may offer" (p. 59). In this chapter eavesdropping is presented as one of several intentional alteric (that is, form shifting and shaping) acts employed by young children in early years settings.

Bakhtin (1984) described this capacity as the ultimate right to claim one's authorial loophole by employing chameleon-like strategies in order to alter understanding and thus challenge the ultimate authorship of a developing person by another.

Despite all its seriousness I hope you will finish this chapter with a smile on your face and in awe of the amazing capacity for children to outwit adults – who so often think we know best.

Why laughter?

I was first inspired to think about the importance of humour in a serious way (excuse the pun) when I was working with a group of early years students a few years ago in Hamilton, New Zealand. We were watching a piece of video footage featuring a toddler who was repeatedly throwing crayons onto the floor, much to the delight of his 3-year-old peer. As each crayon was tossed into the air, the toddler shouted, "Uh oh!" in a raucous and repetitive fashion as he boldly watched the reaction of those around him. His peer eventually joined in the game, thus increasing its intensity, despite adult attempts to distract the play to another domain. I was interested to see how the students would theorise this event and asked them to analyse it using whatever theoretical lens they liked. I was utterly amazed at their response: most summoning behaviourist theories to suggest that the toddler needed to learn the correct way to use crayons and that the teacher ought to intervene to re-establish order. They were critical of the teacher's lack of response and thought that she had missed an opportunity for positive behavioural guidance.

What these students did not see, and perhaps *could* not see because of the theoretical lens at their disposal, was the strategic humour of this experience. In my view their desire for order and acceptable behaviour masked their capacity to celebrate all the wonderful things that were happening in this joyful event. I resolved to write a piece that would provide them with another way of looking at this act – you are now reading it. I hope by the end of this chapter you will see what I mean and how central these ideas are to dialogic pedagogy and the role of the teacher.

Humour and young children

Humour plays a very important role in the early years of life. Several early years theorists have categorised laughter as a form of social development, often sparked by conceptual incongruities (see for example, Loizou, Kyriakides, & Hadjicharalambous, 2011; Piaget, 1953; and Winner, 1988). The sorts of ambiguity that invoke acceptable forms of laughter can be found in early games of peek-a-boo, chasing, making funny faces or sounds (Sroufe & Wunsch, 1972), clowning, teasing or role-reversal (Tallant, 2013). They can also be employed by children to experiment with words (e.g. rhyming and nonsense), concepts and genres. The following example highlights the complex ways one 4-year-old experimented with both ideas and genre during a story-telling episode in a Cyprus classroom:

> Once upon a time, there was a rooster who wore glasses and sometimes wore clothes and sometimes doctor's clothes. He wore doctor's clothes because he was a veterinarian . . . One time when he was putting his clothes, instead of putting doctor's clothes he put a tie and went to his office.
>
> *(Loizou et al., 2011, p. 72)*

Clearly this kindergarten child has some understanding of the conventions surrounding different professions. As the authors explain, he or she is now manipulating these to create incongruency and subversion of rules that he or she considers to be aligned to specific societal roles. Here we begin to see the remarkable capacity of very young children to work creatively with ideas and to examine ideas through juxtaposition of seemingly disparate or ambiguous ideas. In my view this is creativity at its best.

Reddy (2008) suggests that these sorts of events are funny for young children not merely for their own sake but because they can be shared with others as a means of intersubjectivity: "Funniness exists only in relation" (p. 214). For humour to be appreciated by someone else, its ironic potential must be known. By this I mean that social partners must share in the fact that something is funny because it lies beyond the dominant discourse and can be toyed with accordingly. The point of the exercise is not merely an individual cognitive encounter but a deliberate act of invoking a response. Consider the following example Reddy shares from a mother of an 11-month-old infant:

> She stomps along (away from her father) waving her arms, shrieking with laughter doing da da da and he then chases after her, stomping his feet and making lots of noise and she shrieks with laughter and he scoops her up and swings her round and pushes her down again . . . And even when she's coming towards him she does exactly the same and then he just steps over her and she continues and she thinks this is incredibly funny, laughing hysterically as she sort of staggers off down the hall, laughing and sort of, she is laughing so much that she can't always keep her balance.
>
> *(Mother of Fiona, in Reddy, 2008, p. 201)*

What becomes immediately evident in this excerpt is the opportunities this game offered for Fiona to initiate and sustain a shared moment of joy. Her beginning invitation, through laughing and shouting, invites her father into the fun, which he responds to by pretending not to notice. We are not told but it might be possible to consider the idea that this game is a ritual Fiona and her father share regularly – one that she can predict and anticipate from this particular relationship.

In a similar vein Reddy (2008) describes teasing as an important aspect of humour for very young children. In these sorts of encounters there is an element of testing that takes place. Infants, toddlers and young children alike can explore the limits of their relationships through such means – taking a few risks and playing on the boundaries of their known (often adult-centric) world. Here is an example of a 14-month-old infant doing just that, as told by his mother:

> . . . On a previous occasion he had accidentally touched a hot pan . . . He knew it was painful . . . Today I was paying little attention to him and he slowly reached out a hand towards the pan (looking at me with a slight smile on his face . . .): I said "no, hot!" immediately, but he didn't withdraw. I looked up and found him looking at me with a slight, playful smile . . .
>
> *(Reddy, 2008, p. 210)*

The kinds of humour that have been presented so far take place in intimate moments between adults and children or peers who know each other well (a point also raised by Ana Marjanovic-Shane as central to understanding play). But there may also be humorous exchanges that take place because not everyone knows the 'rules of encounter', or appreciates their significance. They may also occur when meaning is "related by some common conditions of life . . . By the bonds of brotherhood on a high level" (Bakhtin, 1986, p. 166). Such forms of laughter form the basis of carnivalesque.

Carnivalesque laughter

> You who laugh it up and down
> Laugh along so laughily
> Laugh it off belaughingly
> Laughter of the laughing laughniks,
> overlaugh the laughathons
> Laughiness of the laughish
> laughers counterlaugh the laughdom's laughs!
>
> *(Khlebnikov in Markov, 1968, p. 7)*

In this poem by the famous Russian poet Velimir Khlebnikov a complex view of laughter is portrayed. This poet was much admired by Bakhtin (2002) and it is possible to see the irony portrayed in these words that position laughter as much more than a guttural sound. This was certainly true in Bakhtin's conceptualisation. For him, laughter represented a form of social commentary, a means of pushing beyond boundaries or even operating outside them completely. Laughter existed for its own sake, but it also provided a welcome relief from the monologic certainties that pervade human lives.

I can imagine that humour would have been very much needed in 1940s Stalinist Russia – not so much as a source of light relief but as a means of social commentary and a means of retaining a sense of one's agency in authoritarian regimes. Bakhtin's route to understanding was via French satirist François Rabelais, who wrote about the medieval society that he was a part of, and the use of carnival as a context for laughter, which offered temporary suspension from the very serious monologic world of that era. As Bakhtin explains:

> Carnival is a pageant without footlights and without a division into performers and spectators. In carnival everyone is an active participant, everyone communes in the carnival act. Carnival is not contemplated, and, strictly speaking, not even performed; its participants *live* in it, they live by its laws as long as those laws are in effect, that is, they live a *carnivalistic life*. Because carnivalistic life is life drawn out of its usual rut, it is to some extent "life turned inside out" . . . "the reverse side of the world."
>
> *(Bakhtin, 1984, p. 122)*

Tracing the Renaissance period through to Enlightenment, Bakhtin describes the ways laughter and all its iterations came to be considered inappropriate in a society that privileged certain forms of production over others. Bakhtin contended that embracing the grotesque (the body and all its extremes) as well as the beautiful (what was accepted by society as important) opened up a dialogic means of encountering the world. The former did not disappear simply because it was not valued; instead Bakhtin contended that it went underground, only to emerge in times of carnival festivities where the official culture was temporarily suspended – such forms of humour retained an important place in society. In his 1964 doctorate, *François Rabelais in the History of Realism*, Bakhtin tried to examine this phenomenon, suggesting that carnivalesque offered a temporary means of speaking into the dominant culture by temporarily suspending, revealing and de-crowning its authority. The body provides a central tool in his armoury.

Emphasising the body

> While roaring with laughter, we give in to the rhythmical contractions of the diaphragm, generate spasms and bizarre sounds that may contaminate and distort the integrity of social order.
>
> *(Vlieghe, 2014, p. 149)*

Laughter is, without doubt, a bodily experience. One cannot avoid paying attention to the body when laughing – even if just to catch breath. Carnivalesque is the bodily manifestation of humour. Here there is no rational meaning to be interpreted in order for laughter to be appreciated; rather a collective experience is shared between bodies. Joris Vlieghe (2014) explains that this kind of humour is different from the individual act of laughing at sophisticated jokes or incongruous situations and is instead a collective experience that might even be offensive, savage or cruel. For this reason Merete Moe and Alexander Sidorkin (2014) suggest that a fuller appreciation of dialogue can be difficult in the absence of a consideration of carnivalesque because the body is *always* involved.

Bakhtin summons the grotesque body to this dialogue by invoking Rabelais's characters, such as Gargantua and Pantagruel – horrific figures who behave in an uncouth manner that is provocative and impermissible in the official domain. These characters belch and fart as they please and much comedic attention is spent on the lower body and all its faculties. Young children share this fixation: discussions about defecation, genitals and other body parts feature heavily in the conversation of children in early years settings. They serve as a source of humour not in spite of but *because* they negate or de-crown cultural norms and hierarchies. Brian Sutton-Smith recalls his childhood memory of throwing cow pots (large clumps of faeces found on New Zealand farms) at his peers:

> You put your hand on top, scoop it out on the dry part and then throw it in each others' faces. It was difficult as it would break and get on your clothes and your mother would go nuts. That was combined with horse dung grenades. Use your imagination.
>
> *(2012, p. 6)*

This game is not only fondly recalled because of the sensory properties of the faeces shared among peers but perhaps, too, because of the horror it evokes in the adults. This kind of humour would make no sense to Brian's mother, and neither should it. If it did, the joy of the experience might be diminished since it is fuelled by its counterpoint. The very point of carnivalesque is its deliberate location outside of the official discourse. For this reason carnivalesque cannot be appropriated by those who represent this discourse. The humour exists *because* of the social struggle of opposition. The laugher of carnivalesque is in no way a means of "social glue" (Vlieghe, 2014, p. 157) but rather a way of "sensuously interact[ing] with truth from many angles" (Sullivan, Smith, & Matusov, 2009, p. 329). This kind of interaction is an essential ingredient of humour for young children in early years settings – as we will soon see!

Carnivalesque in the early years

If you walk into almost any early years setting you can hear the sound of children's laughter. Yet the significance of humour is seldom featured in discussions about children's learning and, perhaps for this reason, is barely present in many early years curriculum documents (see for example, Tallant's (2013) critique of EYLC, the United Kingdom curriculum).

Carnivalesque has especially fertile soil in the early years setting because there are numerous people to laugh at, with or about in relation to others. There is also, whether we admit it or not, an authoritative discourse in place (one that will be discussed more in the following chapter) which, coupled with a peer group culture, creates unique opportunities for carnivalesque to thrive. Remembering that a key distinction between carnivalesque, as a genre, and other forms of humour is that it

FIGURE 6.1 Down low – too slow

takes place outside the official discourse, often in groups who share commonality, it is not difficult to see why. Watch the video 'Down low – too slow' for an example of early years carnivalesque in action.

Gemma offers her hand to Clayton, saying, "Down low," then quickly pulls it away, laughing – "too slow." She repeats the action and is joined by Jacob who repeats, "Down low." Clayton turns to Jacob and attempts to hit his hand. Both Gemma and Jacob repeatedly offer their hand and pull it away, repeating, "Down low, too slow." Clayton nudges Jacob's body as Jacob moves back. Clayton now offers his hand, but as he is taller the other two, cannot reach. "No, I'll go down" – he puts his hand down low at which point both Gemma and Jacob attempt to hit it. "Ohhhh, too slow," says Clayton, as everyone laughs. "Up slow, too slow," repeats Clayton, raising his hand. Jacob repeats this action and attempts to hit Clayton's hands several times. By this time Gemma has returned to her artwork. "Why don't you try to get two of them?" suggests Clayton and holds both hands out on either side of his body. Jacob dives at his arms but misses. "Oh, you missed them," says Clayton, moving out of the way. He offers his arms again. Jacob lunges forward and nudges Clayton in his stomach "Yes!" "No," responds Clayton, holding out both hands in front. Gemma now moves forward to touch both hands – "Gotcha" – and puts her hands on her hips, smiling. "Nah," says Clayton and runs across the room, chased by Jacob.

Notwithstanding the obvious skills that the children are conveying through this act, it is also clear that there is an element of risk for some of them. The humour of the event is richer because it offers the opportunity to hit one another in ways that are 'almost' acceptable (since 'down-low-too-slow' is a well-known joke children share with teachers). You can see the delight in their body language as the game progresses, but its sheer joy appears to be centred around the limits that are tested and the use of a language act that has been sanctioned by the adults, for alternative purposes. I even wondered if these children were actually 'taking the piss' out of their teachers, but only they will know. That this event takes place at the art table – a place typically set aside for quiet pursuits – seems to make it all the more desirable and it is clear that the experience soon outgrows this context as Jacob and Clayton move outside of that space onto other pursuits.

Despite the obvious presence of carnivalesque in early years settings, there are almost no documented studies that help us to interpret its significance in the lives of children and teachers. Perhaps this is because carnivalesque is often considered inappropriate, out of place or is dismissed in educational settings because it is interpreted as "a corporeal event" – something that takes place in the body – and is seen in isolation of learning (yes, surprisingly the old Cartesian mind–body split still exists today). It can be seen as a distraction or perhaps even as offensive by adults who do not appreciate its role. Alternatively its absence may be the result of the gross underestimations that are so often made concerning young children and their capabilities. How could we possibly conceive of such sophisticated acts in children so young?

Yet carnivalesque plays an important role in the life of a young child. This is especially true when they enter into early years settings where a polyphonic symphony of subjectivities resides. People come and go from this setting, bringing with them a variety of discourses that may or may not have a voice in this setting. There are a lot more children in one (often quite contained) space than is typically the case in society, and the play-based chronotope of the early years sets the scene for "free and familiar contact among people" (Bakhtin, 1984, p. 123). At the same time, children are part of a very serious official educational context in which rules are established and maintained. This creates an interesting tension for children to explore. As Tim Lensmire (2011) explains:

> As we become more serious, we risk undermining the sort of joyful, playful relation to the world and each other that would actually allow us to look fearlessly at the world and tell the truth about it.
>
> *(p. 125)*

The early years setting, to some extent, mirrors the tensions Bakhtin describes between the freedom of the Middle Ages and the emergence of purposefulness in the Renaissance period. In this historical epoch, he argued, laughter went underground because it, like all aspects of the body, was seen as inferior to the mind. The joy of carnivalesque therefore lies in the capacity of such laughter and debasement to de-crown officialdom, leading to "transformations and renewals" (Bakhtin, 1968,

p. 394). For this reason it is the strategic, underground element of laughter that defines it as carnivalesque.

Consider the following event that took place after an interview with Zoe's mother:

> During an interview, Lynette explains Zoe's increasing interest in humour. She describes a game Zoe plays with her dad at home after he released wind (a term colloquially described as "farting"). In this game, Zoe would try to squeeze out some wind too, after saying "Daddy part, Zoe part." This exchange would end in raucous laughter. A week after this interview, Zoe is in the sandpit at the centre and releases wind loudly. She laughs and turns to look at the researcher [me], saying "Zoe part." We laugh together. This joke was to become part of our subsequent relationship.
>
> *(White, 2011, p. 382)*

Zoe's interest in farting was not shared by the teachers at the centre. Like many aspects of carnivalesque that are associated with the body and the grotesque, acts of this nature did not appear to have a place in the curriculum and, indeed, were often looked upon disapprovingly. It seemed as if what mattered in the centre context was the provision of 'activities' and the way children responded to 'the plan'. In the absence of dialogue between Zoe's mother and the teachers it was not possible for Zoe's interests, such as this, to be known by the teachers. I speculate that Zoe shared this experience with me because she had been part of the interviews that took place between her mother and myself. This meant that she had a clear understanding that I was not one of the teachers and not, therefore, part of officialdom.

The kinds of humour that take place outside of the dominant (authoritative) discourse in the early years setting can be likened to those that Dostoevsky described in his famous book *Notes from the Underground*, which "gives subtle life to this voice from under the floorboards with all its withholdings, second thoughts, loopholes, special pleadings; and admirable too" (Pevear, in Dostoevsky, 1993, p. xi). This kind of 'under the floor' dialogue counter has been variously described by early years writers as counter discourse or subculture (see for example, Robinson & Diaz, 2006). By invoking this underground metaphor there is an additional opportunity to recognise that the balance of power is never equal in the early years setting. Children are not as powerful as adults in determining what takes place. No matter how many choices teachers might offer children in early years settings, children cannot choose whether or not to attend (that is their families' choice) and they seldom determine the curriculum in its entirety, no matter what the rhetoric might tell us. As we shall see in the next chapter, this choice is not always up to teachers either.

Yet in other respects children can be very powerful in early years settings by invoking carnivalesque genres that enable them to progress their agenda alongside the official discourses that exist through playful exchange. Lynn Cohen (2011) suggests that these kinds of dialogues children engage in represent Bakhtin's (1984) notion of double-voiced discourse: "In carnival style, children use a double-voiced discourse in playful dialogic interactions to free themselves from the authority of adults and to develop a better understanding of their social significance" (Cohen, 2011, p. 186). Lynn maintains that double-voiced discourse occurs when children encounter situations where they are faced with conflicting discourses which they may not subscribe to. They can then summon voices that they perceive represent the alternative ideas they are exploring alongside those they perceive to be valued by adults in the setting. Children call upon this strategy as a means of negotiating their way through the ambiguity, allowing them to suspend its ambivalence while simultaneously avoiding any direct challenge to adults or the official discourse they serve. It is really very clever.

So clever, in fact, that at times children's power (like anyone else's) can be potentially dangerous or scary – even to the children themselves. When any discourse takes away the ability of another to speak, it can become monologic and shut others down. It is not difficult to imagine situations in early years settings where individuals or groups exclude or ridicule others in the guise of 'fun' – this is especially true in settings where there are vast age, experience and/or cultural differences. Herein lies the conundrum for the dialogic teacher who, in celebrating the individual, must also take into account the wider group. The following example by Ivy Schousboe provides an important catalyst for thinking about this tension: two 4 year olds try to persuade 2-year-old Maria to drink 'medicine' that is actually pee in a soda water bottle (which Maria knows):

> Now the little one is to take its medicine and she must be coaxed into taking it: "Here you are, Maria, here is your soda pop!" they say in very sweet voices. To their blank surprise, the little one refuses to even touch the bottle. However, that does not stop the game. The big ones recover from their surprise. It fits well into the game that the little one refuses to take her medicine – that also happens in the real world. It is not *supposed* to be easy. And the big ones appeal and threaten long within the framework of the game: "Yum! It's soda water. – I wish it was mine! You are only to take a sip, otherwise you'll get ill." The little one grows more and more resistive and frightened but remains adamant. At last the big ones realize that the little one has dropped out of the game. They are scandalized: Maria is mean, for they had *agreed* to play doctor. Now they threaten and deride Maria in earnest. They will never let her play again, she destroys everything. Looking very pedagogical they explain to an adult: "We are not playing with her any more. She is too young."
>
> *(Schousboe, 2013, p. 16)*

While Schousboe describes this event as "evil play," I do not think that the girls are deliberately being mean or nasty; rather, they are testing the limits of their agency in play and experimenting with their authority. In such cases teachers have an important role in supporting those who, for whatever the reason, may have less access to their personal agency in any particular moment while maintaining the carnival atmosphere. As Paul Sullivan and others (2009) explain: "The regime of carnival, described by Bakhtin, should not be equated with simple relaxation or full elimination of the teacher's authority" (p. 333). I could imagine an important dialogue taking place between Maria, her teacher and the 4-year-old girls to support the ontologic goals of the children, within or perhaps outside of the group. Perhaps in this dialogue democratic alternatives can be explored within the carnivalesque atmosphere that has been established. This calls for a creative approach indeed since any imposition of authority could either be rejected or discursively adopted only to be later refuted in the underground.

At other times children who share mutual understanding can enjoy "the source of carnival as the source itself" (Bakhtin, 1984, p. 131). This statement suggests that there is joyfulness in the moment – in and of itself – which resists being analysed or otherwise tampered with by outsiders. In an early years setting there are many opportunities for this kind of humour to be shared with peers. In the following excerpt you can see Zoe chasing a balloon in the wind, accompanied by onomatopoeic sounds (see 'Balloon running' in the video companion):

> She chases the balloon and runs to her two-year old peer, continuing with the noise. She touches her peer and together they run, making the same noise, as they chase the balloon. When they catch it they laugh, release the balloon, and repeat the experience.
>
> *(White, 2012, p. 6)*

What stands out in this event is the unspoken, joyful and embodied nature of the dialogue. It is as if these two toddlers share in an unwritten code that surpasses

FIGURE 6.2 Balloon running

adult understanding. When asked, neither Zoe's teacher nor parent could see any-thing significant at all about the event yet, from a carnivalesque standpoint, we can celebrate the encounter as another lived experience of dialogue in the life of the children involved. As such, it represents a process of formation – *obrazovanie* – as discussed in chapter 4 (Lobok, 2014). This event can therefore be reinterpreted as one that may be highly significant in the life of the child – even if we cannot name and frame its significance ourselves.

Once we have the means through which to appreciate the sophistication of car-nivalesque while suspending certainty, it becomes possible to celebrate children's acts more fully. Children will draw upon the genres at their disposal in order to navigate their way through the expectations of adults alongside their own understandings. By turning these on their head, children have an opportunity to experiment with ideas and their authority. For adults who understand what is happening there are many riches to be found.

Po Chi Tam's (2010) dialogic observations of teachers in a drama classroom led her to some important discoveries about the kinds of conditions through which carnivalesque might be supported by teachers. Teachers, she suggests, need to be committed to a spirit of "creative imagination, free expression and a creative pro-duction of the genre through learning in a playful way" (p. 184). While there are many ways this might be experienced, Po Chi advocates for consideration of less structured physical spaces and programme flexibility as an echo of the open, unfi-nalised nature of experience that characterises carnivalesque. She does not, however,

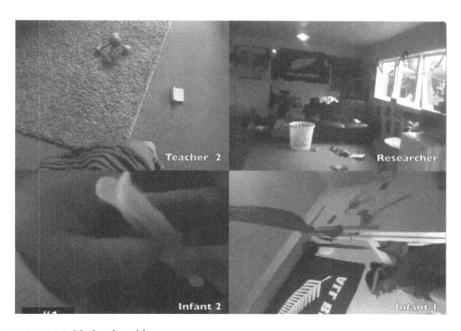

FIGURE 6.3 Under the table

suggest that the teacher can or should suspend all authority but that they should be prepared to be mocked or de-crowned as "a necessary condition for the birth of new forms of power and meaning, as well as the death of the old forms" (p. 187). The following encounter between Rachel, 10-month-old Lola and her nearly 2-year-old peer highlights such a meeting place in an early years setting.

Lola steers herself under a low table. "Under you go, under the table," says her teacher, Rachel. Lola exerts a great deal of effort to manoeuvre herself until she goes out of sight. Rachel laughs. "She's gone right under, like *right* under." Two-year-old Zoe leans in to watch. "Where's she gone Zoe?" Rachel lifts the table-cloth and says, "Booooo," laughing. She calls, "Lola, Lola," and reaches out her hand. "Do you need to come out, do you need to come out? Come on." She touches Lola's hand and rubs it. "Come on. Do you need to come out? Are you feeling stuck yet?" Lola does not answer – she discovers a peg under the table, which she looks at closely. The teachers talk on the outside: "Where's Lola gone? She's happy under there . . . Oh, how funny." Under the table Lola laughs and says, "Tickley tickley tickley," as she turns the peg over. The teachers laugh while Zoe leans close to look under the table. "It's a bit low for me to bend down, I can't crawl on my belly at the moment," explains Rachel (who is pregnant). "Can you make sure Lola's OK under there, Zoe? Have a look under the table and make sure Lola's OK – cos I can't get that far down." Lola can be heard breathing heavily. "Are you right under there, Lola?" asks Rachel and leans forward, singing, "Lola, Lola." Rachel sits up – "she is not worried" – while at the same time Lola says, "Boo . . . boo . . . boo."

Perhaps it is in the midst of all this seriousness and effort that carnivalesque thrives. Lola is literally immersing herself in the underground now, entering into a private space from which she can speak "from under the floorboards." Her preference is upheld by the teachers and becomes a legitimate part of the curriculum – as important as any other form of learning – but on Lola's terms. As a result teachers can share in the humour while appreciating that they do not necessarily understand its depth for Lola (for instance, the significance of the peg and the amusing "tickley" sound). This suspension of certainty in relationships with others is characteristic of all forms of dialogic understanding, but is brought to a new level in carnivalesque genres.

But, of course, there are some spaces in the early years setting where the kind of responsive openness to children's priorities we have just seen is not so easy. It is, perhaps, no coincidence that almost all the early years studies where I could find examples of ridicule, deviance or slapstick humour were oriented around meal-times (see for example, Albon, 2010; Brennan, 2007; Johansson & Berthelsen, 2014;

FIGURE 6.4 Fist banging

Junefelt, 2010; Loizou et al., 2011; Odegaard, 2007). Mealtimes are often the most structured, rule-based events that take place in play-based early years settings. When teachers are preoccupied with such authorial orientations there is an even stronger need for children to reclaim their agency through invoking the festival spirit of carnival. Bakhtin appropriated the medieval "feast of the fools," where food created another opportunity for emphasising the body and all its carnivalesque qualities, for this type of festivity. I think it is a very apt title for the next event, which takes place at lunchtime in an early years setting (see the footage 'Fist banging').

> A 4-year-old boy begins to rhythmically bang his fist on the table, and laughs. His actions are followed by his peers. Zoe watches their actions closely. The banging becomes louder and louder as the children laugh heartily . . . The teacher returns and tells them to "Stop." The banging ceases with the exception of Zoe, who looks intently at the teacher and offers one last loud BANG with her fist.
>
> *(White, 2014, pp. 907–908)*

Again you can note the lack of verbal language required for this event to make its statement as an underground act that arises out of the 'bonds of brotherhood' shared between Zoe and her peers in this moment. I have often speculated as to what might have happened if the teacher had joined in the fist banging. Perhaps it would have lost its effectiveness altogether since, it seems to me, that events such as this are significant *because* they resist authority. The teacher, when interviewed about the event, described Zoe as "being quite testy" (White, 2009, p. 140) – challenging the authority of the teacher while simultaneously seeking participation within the peer group. In both respects, Zoe was highly successful through this genre. Not only did she gain entry into an older peer group but she also established herself as someone who was willing to resist the status quo. This same tension was identified by Eva Johansson and Donna Berthelsen (2014) in their mealtime study:

> A tension existed for the teachers as to how to have control over the event and to follow the traditional rules for mealtimes, on the one hand and, on the other hand, to allow the children some agency so that a shared and joyful atmosphere could be created.
>
> *(p. 86)*

Recalling the dialogic tenet that tensions are an important component of dialogic pedagogy, such moments warrant our urgent attention – both in practice and in scholarship. The carnivalesque adventures that take place in such contexts are not only opportunities to celebrate children's agency but also clearly essential for the complex experience of life in the 'centre village' that makes up an early years setting. Perhaps they are also an opportunity for teachers to reflect on the extent to which 'control' is necessary in a dialogic setting.

Deborah Albon suggests that mealtimes are also places where the most contentiously ethical dialogues can take place. Explaining a lunchtime scene where two boys are using a piece of garlic bread to pretend to get married while kissing each other at the table, Deborah describes her surprise at the teacher's response:

> She told them that boys cannot get married and that they should be eating their lunch. I gently asked, "Can't they?" and there seemed a momentary pause . . . Interestingly, this also seemed to halt the children's playfulness.
>
> *(Albon & Rosen, 2014, p. 109)*

Such challenges do not only take place at meal times in early childhood settings, but the practice of sitting together in a confined space to share food is one of only a few places where pedagogy is made quite so public. In this case what started out as a humorous exchange became a deeply serious examination of gendered assumptions. For teachers this can be deeply confronting but is nonetheless central to pedagogy if we are serious about our work and its educational significance in the lives of children. Yet again the teachers are implicated.

As we have seen in this chapter, carnivalesque (and of course play as we saw in chapter 5) is an essential way of recognising children's remarkable, often mindblowing, capacity to play with ideas imaginatively and strategically by orienting language (in all its forms) towards and away from others. For Bakhtin, both orienting aspects of the personality are important and unreducible in the final analysis. However, just when we think we have it all sewn up in relationship with others, a person can present and re-present themselves as an ungraspable personality. They can influence the extent to which others can share in their world and, equally, confound any final analysis (as we saw in the examples earlier in the chapter). They can construct, deconstruct and reconstruct the way others will see them, "authoring dynamically changing relational selves (Edmiston, 2010, p. 209). This is an important feature of dialogic pedagogy. Seen in this light, children have the opportunity not only to reveal themselves through language but equally to conceal. The ultimate means of doing so can be seen, and celebrated, in Bakhtin's employment of the dialogic loophole.

The dialogic loophole

> A loophole is the retention for oneself of the possibility for altering the ultimate, final meaning of one's own words . . . This potential other meaning, that is, the loophole left open, accompanies the word like a shadow.
>
> *(Bakhtin, 1984, p. 233)*

Once again inspired by Dostoevsky's characters, Bakhtin here presents the loophole as cause for celebrating the mystery and unknowability of a personality. It is also a deliberate, agentic act that allows individuals to alter the way they are seen by others, thwart any finalisation of their personality and "outguess and outwit all possible definitions of his personality others may offer" (p. 59). The loophole can be employed in a number of ways. Bakhtin describes manoeuvres such as a sideways glance or a shift in focus that may be employed by an individual to present themselves as "ambiguous and elusive even for himself" (p. 234). Clark and Holquist (1984) expand on this concept:

> Dialogism is a metaphysics of the loophole. And although the loophole is the source of the frustration, pain and danger we must confront in a world so dominated by the unknowable, it is also the necessary precondition for any freedom we may know.
>
> *(p. 347)*

Perhaps you can think of occasions where you have exercised this loophole when others have finalised your personality in some way based on a fixed evaluation? As we have already established, finalisation is a dangerous approach to take in early years pedagogy – there are surprises at every corner when we work dialogically with young children.

Another way that the loophole might be summoned is in the employment of eavesdropping. Bakhtin describes this strategic approach as a way for someone to find out what others are thinking about them. I found many examples of young children doing this in my research when I paid attention to their subtle cues and discovered their manifestations. But of course I was a researcher in an early years setting with no other commitments besides trying to understand a small number of children. I wonder how often busy teachers with large groups of learners miss these remarkable agentic feats, focusing instead on certain professional or theoretical claims about what is happening in a generic sense rather than on *this* child (as personality not product) in *this* moment of meeting. In a dialogic approach teachers trust that even the youngest children are the ultimate experts on their own learning. They can merely glimpse the fullness of each learner with a sense of awe, respect and awareness of their important (and answerable) role in the life of this child. Retaining a sense of mystery and wonder is key to dialogic pedagogy but so, too, is accountability, as we shall see in the next chapter.

A serious pedagogical topic for the early years

> When laughing together in the classroom, it does not really matter that we are together with others we did not choose to be with, with persons that have completely different ambitions, opinions or social and cultural backgrounds, or with teachers that are always at a distance because of their professional status. We find ourselves as equals, and this may profoundly alter the quality of the relations students have not only with each other but also with teachers. In that sense the possibility of a truly *new* future is created.
>
> *(Vlieghe, 2014, p. 159)*

Laughter is a very serious pedagogical topic in the dialogic early years setting indeed. In consideration of dialogic pedagogy it is not something that teachers can manipulate to their own educational ends, as some writers have suggested (see for example, Gartrell, 2006). As part of a dialogic relationship, engaging with children's humour is less a case of imparting knowledge than trying to understand and appreciate 'other'. Such understanding can only be revealed if the learner wishes it to be; and we have seen many examples of children's efforts to deliberately conceal themselves or their valued ideas from adult eyes. Yet, as Paul Sullivan and others (2009) suggest, teachers are not dismissed from the call for answerability. They still need to be vigilant about the potential of carnivalesque events to privilege some individuals or groups at the expense of others by striving for a balance between carnivalesque and democracy, especially in early years settings where individual differences may be developmentally, as well as socially, constrained. Bakhtin's (1968) call for both horizontal and vertical roles is very helpful in this regard.

This model reinforces the idea that teachers can and do play an important role in carnivalesque even though they may not always share in the laughter. It is not merely a case of ignoring what is happening or overlooking the role that adults (and the authoritative discourses that they represent) play. The *concrete, visible model of the earth* represents the significance of the body, the underground and all that sits outside the 'official' curriculum; while the *pathos of advance* signals a special role for the teacher

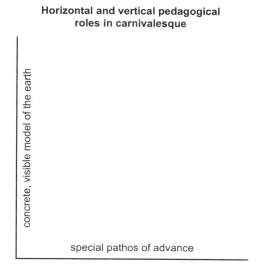

Horizontal and vertical pedagogical roles in carnivalesque

y-axis: concrete, visible model of the earth

x-axis: special pathos of advance

FIGURE 6.5 Horizontal and vertical pedagogical roles in carnivalesque

that is intentionally and ethically attuned to the best interests of learners. Mary Johnsson (2013) suggests that this dual emphasis means teacher choices (for intervention, nonintervention and so on) need to be justified in terms of their significance and consequences for learners. This role might call upon a myriad of responses: laughing with children in shared exchanges, provoking further hilarity, playfully pretending to disapprove, looking the other way, intervening to support those who are at risk or maybe sometimes accepting that you are the butt of their joke as a means of light relief or adjusting power imbalances. Such an approach "challenges the contestability of taking the next step together among those who choose to step together" in order to "celebrate and value the multiple and shifting ways in which we learn" (p. 1260). In this way intersubjectivity is not the only means to engagement – alterity is also upheld as legitimate in the learning relationship. This is complex work that requires moment-by-moment responsiveness or, as Rachel Rosen reminds us, answerability. This poignant example of her experience in an early years setting highlights this complexity and returns us to an emphasis on our own subjectivities as teachers:

> My bum is an area of sustained interest, especially for a small group of boys. It manifests as friendly slaps on my bum, 'bumping into' my bum, pushing me on my bum when manoeuvring in play, and peals of giggles when Jesse said "I saw your bum!" (despite it being completely covered). When it first happened I felt desperately uncomfortable, uncertain how to respond to these 'intimate' interactions with young children.
>
> *(Albon & Rosen, 2014, pp. 45–46)*

Rachel explains how she later considered the uncomfortable boundaries that children were presenting her with in terms of sexuality, innocence, intimacy and safety. She concludes: "Perhaps discomfort is a good thing for provoking an embodied reflexivity – but I have tried to worry away at my initial reactions, questioning in part the 'adult' spin I was putting on children's actions and fascinations" (p. 46). This is revealing work indeed.

In the context of early years settings all of this leaves the teacher as someone who must strive to 'meet' children in unsettling, sometimes difficult spaces in order to authentically work with their agency, on their terms:

> A teacher who is prepared to meet the inquisitive activity of children, to face children's questions, to deal with children's initiative, with children's creativity, and with children's individuality . . . Is the teacher prepared to work with the personality, independence, cognitive interest, and self-actualization of the child? Is the teacher prepared to develop the cognitive interests of the child? If the answer is yes, the child will be educated. Otherwise, the child's educational impulses will fade very soon and education will become, for such a child, nothing but a drag and a headache.
>
> *(Lobok, 2012, p. 107)*

Alexander Lobok suggests that contemporary education in the early years is too preoccupied with logic and that the wonder and magic of creativity can be lost to this process if teachers are not prepared to meet children on their own terms in this manner. Such magic is only accessible to adults who are willing to look and listen to complex voices and their many forms. As a Bakhtin scholar Alexander is not dismissing the significance of logic as a means of understanding but rather suggesting that it is not the most important priority for very young children. Perhaps instead of asking questions like "how does this fit into my understanding of science?" or "how can I manipulate this play experience into some kind of learning that makes sense to me?" a more appropriate provocation might be found in quiet speculation, response to the child's urgent curiosities and perhaps even, dare I say it, appreciating the moment as a dialogic event in and of itself.

Looking back, moving forward

This chapter has identified a special kind of humour that orients laughter as a dialogic event of exchange. With Bakhtin's help, we now have access to a richer and perhaps more celebratory appreciation of children's capacity to engage in alternative discourses that adults may not always have access to. As such there are opportunities to re-explore the significant role of adults – as catalysts, provocateurs and, in some cases, idiots in the lives of young children. How patient they are with adults who seek to know them more! Once again we return to ourselves, our awareness of the subtleties offered in dialogues with children and their potential for richer meaning (or nonmeaning) in the dialogic space of learning encounters.

- How open are you to children's humour, especially when you are potentially the butt of the joke or the humour does not appeal to you personally?
- In what ways does your pedagogical orientation take into account the loophole?
- Returning to the example of the toddler at the beginning of this chapter – what features of carnivalesque might you now be in a position to appreciate in the act of throwing crayons?

References

Albon, D. (2010). *An ethnographic study examining food and drink practices in four early childhood settings* (Unpublished PhD thesis, London Metropolitan University, England).

Albon, D., & Rosen, R. (2014). *Negotiating adult-child relationships in early childhood research.* Abingdon: Routledge.

Bakhtin, M. M. (1968). *Rabelais and his world* (H. Iswolsky, Trans). Cambridge, MA: MIT Press.

Bakhtin, M. M. (1984). *Problems of Dostoevsky's poetics* (C. Emerson, Trans.). Minneapolis: University of Minnesota Press.

Bakhtin, M. M. (1986). *Speech genres and other late essays* (C. Emerson & M. Holquist, Eds.; V. W. McGee, Trans.). Austin: University of Texas Press.

Bakhtin, M. M. (2002). *Besedy s V.D. Duvakinym* [M. M. Bakhtin: Conversations with V. D. Duvakin] (2nd ed.). Moscow: Soglasie.

Brennan, M. (2007). Young children breaking the rules: A sociocultural interpretation. *Early Childhood Folio, 11*, 2–4.

Clark, K., & Holquist, M. (1984). *Mikhail Bakhtin.* Cambridge, MA: Harvard University Press.

Cohen, L. E. (2011). Bakhtin's carnival and pretend role play: A comparison of social contexts. *American Journal of Play, 4*(2), 176–203.

Dostoevsky, F. (1993). *Notes from the underground* (R. Pevear & L. Volokhonsky, Trans.). New York, NY: Alfred A. Knopf.

Edmiston, B. (2010). Playing with children, answering with our lives: A Bakhtinian approach to coauthoring ethical identities in early childhood. *British Journal of Educational Studies, 28*(2), 197–211.

Gartrell, D. (2006). A spoonful of laughter. *Young Children, 61*, 108–109.

Johansson, E., & Berthelsen, D. (2014). The birthday cake: Social relations and professional practices around mealtimes with toddlers in child care. In L. J. Harrison & J. Sumsion (Eds.), *Lived spaces of infant-toddler education and care: Exploring diverse perspectives on theory, research, practice and policy* (pp. 133–145). Dordrecht: Springer.

Johnsson, M. (2013). Practitioner meets philosopher: Bakhtinian musings on learning with Paul. *Educational Philosophy and Theory, 45*(12), 1352–1263.

Junefelt, K. (2010). The dialogic impact of early language development and thought. In K. Junefelt & P. Nordin (Eds.), *Proceedings from the Second International Interdisciplinary Conference on Perspectives and Limits of Dialogism in Mikhail Bakhtin* (pp. 60–74). Retrieved from http://www.nordiska.su.se/polopoly_fs/1.30109.1344252792!/menu/standard/file/publication_2010_bakhtin_conf_sthlm_2009_correct_ISBN.pdf

Lensmire, T. (2011). Too serious: Learning, schools and Bakhtin's carnival. In E .J. White & M. Peters (Eds.), *Bakhtinian pedagogy: Opportunities and challenges for research, policy and practice in education across the globe* (pp. 117–128). New York, NY: Peter Lang.

Lobok, A. (2012). Preschool education bullied: An experiment in establishing a dialogue with a kindergarten educator. *Journal of Russian and East European Psychology, 50*(6), 92–114.

Lobok, A. (2014). Education/*obrazovanie* as an experience of encounter. *Dialogic Pedagogy and International Online Journal, 2.* Retrieved from http://dpj.pitt.edu

Loizou, E., Kyriakides, E., & Hadjicharalambous, M. (2011). Constructing stories in kindergarten: Children's knowledge of genre. *European Early Childhood Education Research Journal, 19*(1), 63–77. Retrieved from http://dx.doi.org/10.10080/1350293X.2011.548939.

Markov, M. (1968). *Russian futurism: A history.* Berkeley: University of California Press.

Moe, M., & Sidorkin, A. M. (2014, March). *The polyphonic embodied self.* Paper presented at Nordic Educational Research Association (NERA) Conference 2014, Lillehammer, Norway.

Odegaard, E. (2007). What's up on the teachers' agenda?: A study of didactic projects and cultural values in mealtime conversations with very young children. *International Journal of Early Childhood, 39*(2), 45–64.

Piaget, J. (1953). *The origins of intelligence in the child.* London: Routledge & Kegan Paul.

Reddy, V. (2008). *How infants know minds.* Cambridge, MA: Harvard University Press.

Robinson, K., & Diaz, C. (2006). *Diversity and difference in early childhood education: Issues for theory and practice.* Maidenhead: Open University Press.

Schousboe, I. (2013). The structure of fantasy play and its implications for good and evil games. In I. Schousboe & D. Winter-Lindquist (Eds.), *Children's play and development* (pp. 13–25). New York, NY: Springer.

Sroufe, L. A., & Wunsch, J. P. (1972). The development of laughter in the first year of life. *Child Development, 42*, 1326–1344.

Sullivan, P., Smith, M., & Matusov, E. (2009). Bakhtin, Socrates and the carnivalesque in education. *New Ideas in Psychology, 27*, 326–342.

Sutton-Smith, B. (2012). From the streets of Wellington to the Ivy league: Reflecting on a lifetime of play. *International Journal of Play, 1*(1), 6–15.

Tallant, L. (2013). *No laughing matter: An exploration of the significance of young children's humour* (Unpublished master's thesis, Roehampton University, London, England).

Tam, P. C. (2010). The implications of carnival theory for interpreting drama pedagogy. *Research in Drama Education, 15*(2), 175–192.

Vlieghe, J. (2014). Laughter as immanent life-affirmation: Reconsidering the educational value of laughter through a Bakhtinian lens. *Educational Philosophy and Theory, 46*(92), 148–161.

White, E. J. (2009). Assessment in New Zealand early childhood education: A Bakhtinian analysis of toddler metaphoricity (Unpublished doctoral thesis, Monash University, Melbourne, Australia).

White, E. J. (2011). 'Now you see me, now you do not': Dialogic loopholes in authorship activity with the very young. *Psychology Research, 1*(6), 377–384.

White, E. J. (2012). Cry, baby, cry: A dialogic response to emotion. *Mind, Culture and Activity, 20*(1), 62–78.

White, E. J. (2014). 'Are you 'avin a laff?': A pedagogical response to Bakhtinian carnivalesque in early childhood education. *Educational Philosophy and Theory, 46*(8), 898–913.

Winner, E. (1988). *The point of words: Children's understanding of metaphor and irony.* Cambridge, MA: Harvard University Press.

7

TEACHING AND ACCOUNTABILITY

After the jocularity of the previous chapter, this chapter takes a more serious turn. Summoning a heteroglossic view of pedagogy we explore the complex accountabilities that take place in an early years setting and their impact on relationships. This is an important agenda because teachers cannot ignore their many accountabilities: (1) to higher authorities such as the state who represent societal priorities; (2) to the profession that establishes parameters for themselves and colleagues; (3) to families who hold expectations about the care and education of their children; and most importantly (4) to the children themselves, who may not share the same priorities. Engaging with this heteroglossia exposes the constant and essential ideological battle that takes place in any social setting between order and disruption – an ebb and flow of encounters that make up the early years setting. The interplay between 'official' early years practices, what Bakhtin describes as authoritative discourse (AD), and those that are personally relevant to individuals, known as internally persuasive discourses (IPD), is examined through this view. Battle lines are drawn between discourses and their associated ideologies – thus setting the scene for an examination of the oppositional and sometimes ironic discourses in early years pedagogy. AD demands adherence, has a strong legacy and, unless challenged by IPD, dominates the heteroglot without question. In this chapter you are invited to examine the place of AD and IPD in contemporary accountability practices that permeate the early years heteroglot. In doing so you will confront the associated ideologies that can be challenging for children and, at times, adults too. The role of the adult in upholding what is valued – by whom, for whom – and associated ideologies that underpin pedagogy is offered for reflection.

A dialogic approach to discourse

A chapter on this topic may at first seem out of place in a book based on Bakhtin philosophy and theory. After all, Bakhtin did not concern himself with aspects of institutional power in the way philosophers such as Michel Foucault (1961, 1984) did. In fact, as Craig Brandist (2014) explains, Bakhtin rejected any allegiance to systems that, from a cultural-historical point of view, shed light on the material dimensions of human experience in institutions. Bakhtin's emphasis was always on human relationships and the tensions between linguistic forces at play, but he did not specifically address institutions, let alone early years settings. For those who seek a systemic means of understanding power, this absence will be disappointing. At the very least it is limiting for those who seek to analyse institutions as systems or power constructions. For that you are reading the wrong book!

Yet it may come as a surprise to you, as it did to me, that Bakhtin explored several important concepts that assist us in thinking about our work within and beyond organisations, with particular emphasis on the discourses individuals bring to their dialogue. Perhaps unsurprisingly to you by now, Bakhtin's route to a dialogic analysis of these powerful discourses is offered through the careful study of language where values and beliefs are betrayed by speakers:

> Each word . . . is a little arena for the clash and criss-crossing of differently oriented social accents. A word in the mouth of a particular individual person is a product of the living interaction of social forces.
>
> *(Voloshinov, 1929/1973, p. 41)*

What we can clearly see in this statement by Voloshinov – a member of the Bakhtin Circle – is an orientation towards the study of language as a means of exposing the constant interplay of *social forces*. This is exactly what Bakhtin means when he introduces concepts of multidiscursivity (linguistic variation/diversity – *raznojazyycie*), multivoicedness (*raznorecie*) and diversity of individual voice (*raznogolosie*). Brigitta Busch (2014) explains that these terms have been translated into the notion of 'heteroglossia' in the West.

Heteroglossia

Heteroglossia can be loosely interpreted as a process through which discourses, as social forces, compete to be heard. Bakhtin (1981) describes this concept as "another's speech in another's language, serving to express authorial intentions but in a refracted way" (p. 324). The use of refraction is noteworthy – suggesting a change in direction due to different conditions or medium. When we think of refraction of a prism, for instance, scientists tell us that the light actually bends when it passes through this new medium. If we apply this imagery to our relationships we see that the way we encounter the world is profoundly affected by the different discourses we are exposed to, as conditions that shape our direction.

In an early years context heteroglossia takes on special significance in this accord because it suggests we can never encounter other discourses (or people for that matter) without being affected in one way or another. This idea lies at the heart of Bakhtin's chronotopic threshold where meeting places become opportunities for transgradience – we will revisit this idea shortly. Carolyn Shields (2011) explains heteroglossia in an educational context along these lines:

> Heteroglossia is not a poster on a wall with people of different colours hold-ing hands but a way of acknowledging the fundamental diversity of the uni-verse. It reminds us that we live in community, and that education must take account of, and serve, the *whole* community.
>
> *(p. 242, my emphasis)*

By "whole" I don't think Carolyn is merely talking about teachers or manage-ment in educational settings. In an early years context there are many different people, each with diverse – sometimes personally or professionally conflicted – ideological orientations, who make up "an assembly of heterogenous chronotopes which interact or outweigh each other" (Moe & Sidorkin, 2014, p. 2). There are also, as we have learnt from Bakhtin, many different 'voices' within each individual and in relation to others.

Consider, for example, an early years setting without any forms of accountabil-ity. It can be very helpful for parents to know that teachers are required to meet certain generic standards of quality (as far as we can assert what that is) in the education and care of their child. Yet because authoritative discourses are uncon-testable by their very nature, they can shut down alternative, internally persuasive discourses if we are not attuned to their limiting potential. Not least, they can rob teachers of their ability to make judgements – even when they might be in the best interests of children – because their associated actions exceed the parameters of officialdom.

> For this reason Bakhtin introduces heteroglossia as a means of opening up the potential of dialogue to provide scope for alternative, personally relevant, discourses. In Bakhtin's conception of heteroglossia we are given the oppor-tunity to consider the competing discourses at work within (and around) an early years setting as an opportunity to grow. Bakhtin is not suggesting some sort of revolutionary overthrow of authorial discourses because they exist for a reason. For dialogue to occur, an organization must think of itself as a set of several incommensurable chronotopes. Organizational cultures are cyclical, with mutually exclusive but also complementary chronotopes alternating.
>
> *(Moe, 2014)*

Bakhtin describes this heteroglossic process through the employment of another metaphor borrowed from physics – this time using the notion of centripetal and centrifugal forces that pull towards and away from a central core. Both are impor-tant aspects of dialogism.

Bakhtin's metaphorical use of this scientific metaphor is interesting on more than one level. On the surface it presents the obvious tensions that exist in the social setting – between intersubjectivity (shared, centralised meanings) and alterity (oppositional meanings) that exist within the heteroglot. On another level, as Deborah Talbot (in press) explains, the centripetal force acts as a 'throwing out' mechanism when it gains momentum in relationship with oppositional forces. Through such tension it is possible to launch oneself outside of the immediate space in order to think and act differently. Such launching offers an opportunity to transgress privileged meanings to encounter other discourses that give rise to revisioned ways of seeing the world – it is, therefore, a dialogic process. The potential for this to occur is dependent on the extent to which alternative discourses have the opportunity to influence one another as authentic forces in the social setting, thus building a momentum that allows threshold encounters to occur. As we might imagine, this is not possible when there is one dominating force that eliminates all other voices, as in the case of authorial discourse.

1) Authorial discourse

> The authoritative word is therefore . . . organically connected with a past that is felt to be hierarchically higher. It is, so to speak, the word of the fathers. Its authority was already acknowledged in the past . . . therefore authoritative discourse permits no play with the context framing it, no play with creative stylizing variants on it. It enters our verbal consciousness as a compact and indivisible mass, one must either totally affirm it, or totally reject it.
>
> *(Bakhtin, 1981, pp. 342–343)*

Where authorial discourse – what Bakhtin describes as the "word of the fathers" – has supreme status there is little opportunity for dialogue. Instead we live in a monologic world of obedience and allegiance to one discourse. For Bakhtin this is problematic because there is no interplay of voice and, by association, no room for creativity. Merete Moe and Alexander Sidorkin (2014) liken AD to the organisational culture in an early years setting – one which marks out the vision, goals and valued practices of the institution. But this is only one of many discourses at play in that heteroglossic space.

While I agree that total allegiance to authority is problematic – particularly when taken to the absolute extreme in the kind of totalitarian society Bakhtin knew for much of his lifetime – I also think there is hope. Children have a remarkable capacity to respond to authorial discourse in an early years setting even when they may not appear to have any voice. Carnivalesque, as discussed in the previous chapter, is one strategy of many that children have access to in the play-based learning environments that characterise early years settings. Here the peer group can act as a powerful underground culture in ways that adults do not always realise – its secrecy is what makes it powerful. Children very quickly figure out that if adults know what they are doing (or think they know) then power belongs to the adult. In the following example the children artfully respond to the authority of the adult by pretending to play a game that the teacher approves of, under her watchful eye, while in reality upholding their own agenda:

Researcher:	What're you playing?
Sean:	We're playing the 'zyun zyun hyun' game.
Howard:	We're making a big circle!
Researcher:	How do you play the game?
Sean:	Make a small circle first, then make a big one. Lastly, do an exchange. (Pointing at Howard's fishing rod, and turning his rod to demonstrate.)
Researcher:	What comes next?
Sean:	Just wave it, and wave it! If . . . if you stop in the middle, the strings will get into a knot. (Howard noticed that the teacher was staring at them as they were not actually playing the fishing role-play. He immediately knelt down near the pond and pretended that he was fishing. He shouted out loudly, 'Wow! I got a fish!')

(Tam, 2013, p. 255)

As Po Chi Tam explains: "The children had to counter-scrutinize the moves of the teacher and devise their own solutions . . ." This is very creative practice that suggests children are artfully claiming chronotopes for themselves that sit outside of the official discourse or AD – whether adults recognise this or not.

2) Internally persuasive discourse

Bakhtin does not suggest that we should try to get rid of authorial discourse but instead alerts us to its monologic potential. However he also draws our attention to internally persuasive discourses (IPD) that exist in the heteroglot. These are the discourses that draw from different chronotopes, and by definition contest authorial ones in encounters that are "constantly present in organisations of social and governmental life" (Bakhtin, 1981, p. 99). The ideal interplay is not one winning over another, as is often considered desirable in education, but maintaining an openness to their contestability. In spaces where only one voice is heard, this is not possible and opportunities are lost. This is not to say that IPD do not exist, but rather they disappear from the dialogue and do not reach their fullest capacity to contribute to the dialogic space. In my study (White, 2011a) the teacher described these hidden forms of IPD as metaphorical dust that gets swept under the carpet. She explained those aspects of practice that comprised the 'dust' as ones that did not align with the curriculum espoused by management in their portrayals of the setting. These contrasting social forces and their manifestation made up the reality of this unique centre heteroglot in this New Zealand early years setting, yet those that were hidden were never discussed in a public way and were often covered up as 'poor practice', trivialised or dismissed as irrelevant. I wonder if you have experienced this too.

When teachers or managers in early years centres ignore this 'dust' in favour of the pristine 'mat' that they wish to portray, there is much less potential for the dust to make them metaphorically sneeze. Everyone is compliant and there is no room for alterity. In situations where early childhood managers and other authorities operate on a principle of low trust or exert a great deal of pressure on teachers based on external accountabilities, teachers can become discursively 'obedient'. They are seen to fulfil the requirements publicly but underneath there are murmurings, secrets and practices that betray their real point of view. I have witnessed these secret dialogues in staff rooms when those who represent AD are out of earshot or appearing in practice when those who represent authority leave the building.

Moe and Sidorkin (2014) convincingly argue that the quality of preschools relies on the dialogic understanding that these struggles are often incommensurable and in a constant state of change or flux. This is very different from the typical approaches to the study of organisations as a cohesive whole that give priority to consensus. For Bakhtin, it is how meanings are negotiated at sites of struggle that is of central importance because the struggle often generates something new. Instead of always orienting towards consensus, it is dissensus that gives rise to a fuller appreciation of individuals within, between and beyond groups or chronotopes. In this space, obedience is not always welcomed, or warranted, and teachers act as dialogic partners with important views of their own while still listening to others.

Teachers and children in the heteroglot

As we have seen in previous chapters, early years settings are a boiling cauldron of living relationships for children and adults alike. They represent significant meeting places for diverse people, cultures and ideologies. As societies become more and more diverse and complex, any notion of the universal child is seriously disruptued. As such, relationships are influenced by the people who attend the setting as well as those – seen or unseen – who animate their lives (past, present and future). Alongside these direct relationships early years settings are increasingly monitored by official bodies that play a significant role in determining what takes place and how the centre is perceived by others. Teachers are highly accountable to these authorities. They must also bear allegiance to the early years profession itself – characterised by codes of practice, curriculum and regulations. In early years practice such professionalism has been hard won and is therefore very important to many teachers. Each alliance brings with it a set of practices, beliefs and attitudes that are ideologically oriented to particular societal demands. It is for this reason that dialogue is seen as so important in terms of teacher accountability in the early years since it is not a question of allegiance from a dialogic standpoint but rather one of generating meanings out of the complex diversity that makes up any early years institution.

Somewhere in the midst of all these alliances resides the child. But neither the individual child nor his or her peer group exist in a utopian garden of innocence despite what many child-centred theories might suggest. Nor do children merely respond to adult intervention – from a dialogic standpoint there is more than one side to the story. Children are directly and indirectly influenced by the ideologies that exist in the setting, even though adults are not always aware of this. There are a number of reasons for our ignorance – partly due to psychological, developmentalist views that limit the capacity of young children to be aware of 'other' (as discussed in chapter 4), partly due to the methods that seek to understand their experience by emphasising the individual in isolation of others, and partly as a romanticised reluctance to view young children beyond notions of innocence and naivety. But regardless of how adults might see things, young children in early years settings are part of the heteroglot and experience its complexity as much as we do.

This complexity is highlighted by Fikriye Kurban and Joseph Tobin, who analyse the following dialogue between two 5-year-old German-Turkish girls in a German kindergarten and Fikriye, who is Turkish. Although the girls, according to their parents, did not speak Turkish or pray consistently at home and had lived in Germany all their lives, they describe their sense of 'otherness' in the early childhood setting:

Ayla:	We speak Turkish. We speak Turkish so they won't understand and they will go away.
Fikriye:	Do the teachers let you speak Turkish?
Selda:	Yes, but not at lunchtime.
Fikriye:	Why?
Selda:	Because they are big. They don't understand. They don't know Turkish.
Fikriye:	Do you go to Mosque?
Ayla:	Yes, I go to Mosque.
Selda:	I go to Mosque, too.
Fikriye:	What about the Germans?
Ayla:	No. They don't.
Fikriye:	Why?
Selda:	Because they are not Turkish . . . Germans go to, there is this thing [tracing a cross with her finger on the table]. They go there.
Fikriye:	Have you been to Turkey?
Ayla and Selda:	Yes.
Fikriye:	Do you like it there?
Ayla and Selda:	Yes.
Fikriye:	Do you like to live in Turkey or in Germany?
Selda:	In Turkey.
Fikriye:	Why?
Selda:	Because we have a lot of friends there.
Fikriye:	But you have friends here, too.
Ayla:	Here, it's only us.
Fikriye:	Do the German kids like you?
Selda:	They like us.
Ayla:	No they don't. They don't like our body (*Vücudumuzu sevmiyorlar*). You know I am fat.
Fikriye:	No, you're not fat.
Ayla:	Oh, yes, I am.

(Kurban & Tobin, 2009, p. 26)

Kurban & Tobin's interpretation of this dialogue highlights the point that there are tensions in the early years setting for these children who experience alienation keenly, even though they have never lived outside of the dominant culture. This is exemplified in Ayla's statement about her body and being fat – which Kurban and Tobin suggest could be an indication of her embodied identity within the wider cultural context, signifying her lack of acceptance by others who do not share the same history, ethnicity or experience. If this were true – and of course we can merely speculate here – we can begin to appreciate young children's experience of deep-seated societal prejudices and their powerful force in early years settings as an important part of learning. To ignore these powerful discourses is to ignore children's realities in the contemporary early years heteroglot. In a contemporary globalised society it is also important to celebrate what Ofelia Garcia and Camila Leiva (2014) describe as "translanguaging," which is possible for children who draw from more than one culture and for whom new realities are possible through the creative use of different languages all at the same time (a phenomenon linguists call code switching).

But such differences are not limited to official languages. In their edited volume Adrian Blackledge and Angela Creese (2014) present case after case of linguistic diversity in classrooms around the world that are characterised by languages that exceed ethnic domains. Contemporary examples of hip-hop, text-speak and computer-mediated languages express ideas interchanged with conventional forms of language in learning environments, as a powerful contemporary presence in learning contexts. These dialogues suggest that no learner is purely monolingual since each of us draws from the multiple language systems at our disposal – past, present and future. As Brigitta Busch (2014) explains:

> . . . the linguistic repertoire not only reflects the synchronic juxtaposition of language practices associated with different social spaces (home, school, place of origin, temple, etc.) but also reflects a diachronic dimension: it points backwards to past language experience and forwards to expectations and desires linked to the future. It encompasses not only what a speaker 'has' but also what can be felt as an absence, a blank (e.g. the grandparent's Czech, the grandfather's Chinese).
>
> *(p. 35)*

This complex view of language use sets the scene for a much more sophisticated consideration of the multiple forms of communication, and associated opportunities for dialogue, that young children bring to the early years setting.

The early years teacher and the heteroglot

As an early years teacher you are inescapably part of this complex heteroglot. At times it can seem confusing because there are so many different ways to look at ourselves and each other in accordance with the variety of discourses at our disposal.

Some we may even be unaware of. For Bakhtin this idea is portrayed in his conception of 'ideology' (*ideologiya*) – a specific way of thinking that betrays itself through
language. From a dialogic standpoint there are many ways such a betrayal manifests
itself. In my studies I noticed that teachers often drop their voice to a whisper, speak
from behind their hand as an aside or giggle nervously when they say something
that is not consistent with authorial discourse. Here is an example in my dialogues
with Alicia, who revealed her concerns about assessment practice. Note the use of
her hand as her IPD is revealed:

> I often don't record those (personal moments that I notice about children)
> because I don't feel that they are authentic because . . . what if I am seeing it
> wrong? (puts hand over mouth) . . . it's almost like making a story up for the
> sake of it because I *need* a learning story to go in my profile.
>
> *(Teacher interview in White, 2009, p. 169)*

Why do you think this teacher subscribed to this kind of assessment practice
even though she did not consider it really captured the child's experience? The reasons are many: the centre prescribed this particular approach because they wanted
to promote consistency of assessment documentation among staff, they wanted to
please the authorities that regularly came to evaluate the setting, and they were keen
to produce records that were based on (nationally prescribed) desirable outcomes.
The teacher was merely complying with the demands of the setting and its wider
context. Alicia's confession here also suggests that she is unsure how to write about
the things that really matter to her because she is unsure of the legitimacy of her
IPD. The prescriptive nature of assessment documentation in the setting meant that
she did not feel that her own insights had a place – at least not unless they could
be somehow linked to the official curriculum. Ironically the parents I interviewed
said that they preferred more informal dialogues about their child. So the question
remains as to why this practice maintained prominence in the setting. Surely the
authorial discourse is not that powerful? Or is it? (For a further discussion on this
issue see White, 2011a and 2011b.) Can you think of other instances in the early
years where practices are upheld even when those who are upholding them do not
see their value?

Parent voice can also be shut down in early years contexts where those who
represent AD convey the attitude that they know best. This may not be done deliberately but is part of what I consider to be one of the dangers of contemporary
'professionalisation' of the early years. Teachers who have qualifications and expert
knowledge can easily be fooled into thinking that they know children better than
their own families. Michel Vandenbroeck, Tom Boonaert, Sandra Van der Mespel and Katelijne De Brabandere (2009) describe this as a new phenomenon they
call "the pedagogicalization of parents" (p. 68). Based on unfortunate assertions
that early childhood education can provide an antidote to impoverished family life,
parents can be viewed as "an object of intervention as well as domination" (p. 68)
masked as a kind of autonomy. Such assertions are really an excuse for blaming

individuals rather than viewing issues as interdependent relations and an opportunity to explore IPD:

> In our view, relational citizenship inevitably includes a statement on respect for diversity, not as a tolerance towards those who deviate from prevailing norms, but as a reflection about the norms that create deviations and exclusions.
>
> *(Vandenbroeck et al., 2009, p. 74)*

Easier said than done. Remember the German and Cameroon mothers in chapter 4? How might a dialogic teacher create the kind of heteroglossic spaces that would assist them in understanding that the Cameroon baby who does not cry is not necessarily any 'happier' (or sadder) than the German baby who does? Such consideration requires us to suspend some of our so-called expertise on child development to consider the social experience of this child in this place. There is also cause for us to examine our own culturally based ideologies – what if the teacher is German herself? Being able to meet others who do not share the same ideologies as ourselves is an opportunity for greater understanding. On the basis of this understanding teachers can then try to ensure that priority is given to each child within the setting rather than trying to force the child (or family for that matter) to fit into what is deemed important to the setting, or teacher. In a Bakhtinian sense the 'setting' has no agency, but the people within it (and beyond it) most certainly do. As early years contexts become more and more diversified, this is a very important agenda indeed.

Bakhtin's principle of 'otherness' might also play an important role in providing alternative ways of understanding early years practice in light of this increasingly complex community of others that exist in and beyond the centre heteroglot. Summoning the notion of intergenerationality, she suggests that there are important opportunities for teachers to consider alternative pedagogical approaches through dialogue across generations of families that draw on local people and places. Traditional Western notions of child-centredness, for example, might be usefully reconceptualised through such encounters, opening up possibilities to develop new pedagogies that take into account the personal meanings children bring with them from other people and places.

As we have seen, however, it can be very difficult for teachers to act in ways that might be less 'obedient' to the privileged pedagogies or programmes that are held sacrosanct, and to management practices that dictate rosters or routines. Carolyn Shields (2011) explores reasons why it is so difficult for educational leaders to exercise greater agency within organisations with the help of Bakhtin's novelistic depiction of the chronotope he calls "adventure time." In adventure time the individual is at the mercy of external factors with no hope of changing their situation. As Carolyn explains: "They [educational leaders] have no time to reflect on the distinctive needs of their particular student body nor how to address them, opting instead, for the most part, for commercialized packaged programs and prescriptive responses" (p. 229). The opportunity to linger lovingly, as we discussed in chapter 4, seems a distant utopian dream in such spaces.

Conversely, biographical time represents a more open approach that relies on the integrity of those within it. Here past, present and future are taken into account and the status quo is questioned in light of these contexts. Carolyn asserts that such an approach calls for a different type of communication:

> Take[ing] care to reject purely individualised solutions to systemic issues, to examine how rules and policies reflect power relations that, when inequitable, may contribute to the continued marginalization or exclusion of minoritized students.
>
> *(Shields, 2011, p. 230)*

Bakhtin (1981) asserts that the route to such forms of communication lies in our increased awareness of the reified nature of certain forms of language and, in doing so, recognising its profound influence on "how the world is seen and felt, ways that are organically part and parcel with the language that expresses them" (p. 367). In an early years setting this revised way of communicating would direct more attention to the voices brought by 'others' into the heteroglot – children, families and even the personal discourses of teachers themselves. Lively debates could take place between policies *and* the people who make them, live them and are impacted by them, giving primacy to responses and their interpretations rather than demanding allegiance. This includes children, who have much to contribute if we are prepared to linger in their presence. Pedagogies of this nature form the basis of Bakhtin's approach to creativity:

> Creative understanding does not renounce itself, its own place in time, its own culture; and it forgets nothing. In order to understand, it is immensely important for the person who understands to be located outside the object of his or her creative understanding – in time, in space, in culture.
>
> *(Bakhtin, 1986, p. 7)*

Bakhtin goes further than merely pontificating on creativity here. He actually provides a concrete means of aesthetically engaging with others in the heteroglot. His route to such engagement is through the chronotope.

Chronotope in the early years heteroglot

As I have, I hope, clearly established by now, chronotopes can be thought of as a means of defining the significance, and associated potential, for divergent voices to compete in any given heteroglot. As such, chronotopes can act as a kind of optic for reading discourses that meet to shape experience in the heteroglossic space. Bakhtin (1981) suggests that they can be identified through four key features:

1   function and quality – the story they tell, or their 'plot';
2   representational significance – what they look like in the heteroglot;
3   distinguishing features – what sets them apart from other chronotopes;
4   semantic significance – their interpreted meaning. (Cited in Bemong & Borghart, 2010)

Chronotopes are inseparable from their experience in time and space. They are also given presence, and prominence, through the value that is given to them. Michael Holquist (2009) goes so far as to suggest that chronotope sits at the heart of not only culture but knowledge creation as a whole. Identified combinations of context + practice + assigned value orient the chronotope in pedagogy, providing a means of understanding "organizing centers for the narrative events" (p. 183).

Chronotopes are a particularly useful way of thinking about the early years heteroglot because they allow us to explore learners' dialogic participation and subsequent learning in and outside of the educational setting (White, 2013). Carolyn Shields (2011) further suggests that chronotopes provide a way of understanding historical and contemporary epochs – why, for example, one approach is favoured over another at a particular point in time. By granting a "route to the formation of knowledge as a process of 'ideological becoming' – an ontological position" (White, 2013, p. 268), it becomes possible to understand and encounter difference and diversity. This is best realised in Bakhtin's notion of the chronotopic threshold.

The chronotopic threshold represents the junction at which negotiations take place, and whereby "the sphere of meaning is accomplished" (Bahktin, 1981, p. 258). Gary Morson and Caryl Emerson (1990) argue that these negotiations are constant; chronotope shapes subjectivity in relation to cultural rules, dialogic principles and accepted (or contested) modes of being, all of which become visible only in the event of dialogue with 'other' (Holquist, 2009). Since children and teachers alike are exposed to the polyphonic complexity of multiple subjectivities in an early years heteroglot made up of rules and accepted modes of being, there is great value in opening up possibilities for meeting with alternative discourses on this threshold.

Encounters at the chronotopic threshold create opportunities for transgradience. Rather than seeing the child's learning as a product of one dominant culture that they will assimilate, there are fresh challenges at this intersection. Here teachers pause to understand and create ways of negotiating with children and families about the complex domains of meaning (*znachimost*) that exist within each chronotope – across and between dynamic settings. The quest is not to win over alternative views or to shape them into a dominant way of being but rather to meet them at the threshold. Here ideological clashes and contradictions can become a source of learning for all, and teachers are willing to make changes to practice on this basis. Mikhail Gradovski and Ingrid Lokken (in press) explain that reflection plays an important role in this process as what was initially considered to be a conflict becomes a source of "dialogical inquiry for rethinking current structures, standards and experiences needed for a particular practice." Seen in this light, pedagogy might be seen as "continuous joint work at the boundary" where differences act as a constant source of potential insight and provocation to practice. Thus, while early years teachers cannot dismiss the undeniable presence of authoritative discourse, they can bring it to the threshold in order to meet with alternative chronotopes.

In my work with several New Zealand teachers I found these same types of threshold encounters in early years settings where there was a strong commitment to negotiated responses to the official discourses through reflection, leading to thoughtful practices:

> Teachers drew upon their knowledge of what was *right* according to regulations, centre philosophies and, in the absence of specialist theoretical knowledge, their own prior experiences. They then weighed these up against official requirements, parental preferences, and relational knowledge of each individual child. Contemplating these against the social and political context in which their work was located, pedagogical choices made by teachers were characterised by a series of converging and diverging points of view. Each suggest that the lived experiences of infants in education and care settings are oriented by the negotiating role of the teacher who resides at the interface. It is here where choices must be made in the everyday reality of these contexts.
>
> *(White, 2014, p. 214)*

Yet as we saw earlier in this chapter, such threshold experiences are not possible when one discourse has dominance in the heteroglot. This is the case when rules and regulations take precedence over people, where certain pedagogical practices dominate over what really matters to the learner, where certain language forms and meanings are given priority over others, and where the personally vested truths of children and their families are ignored. You can see this happening when certain rituals are imposed upon others, where 'themes' or topics of inquiry promote the interests of individuals or groups over others, and where prescribed learning outcomes matter more than what is really happening for learners. It is also highly evident in the privileging of certain forms of verbal language over other, more subtle ways of communicating (such as the body and its gestures or alternative sounds). I think this is where infants fare worst in early years settings because adults do not (or cannot) always take the time to consider what they are trying to say. There are many reasons why this is the case.

A lack of heterglossic awareness is also evident when teachers allow themselves to be personally confronted by behaviours that they do not understand. To the teacher who fails to understand their significance from a dialogic standpoint, these behaviours can be seen as disruptive or unhelpful in the early years setting because they do not meet with either the AD or IPD of the adults. In fact one of the biggest challenges graduate teachers tell me they face in their first year of teaching is dealing with 'negative' or 'unacceptable' behaviour. Most of the literature on the topic asserts that behaviours can, and should, be shaped through interventions that will suppress, shape or change behaviour (remember my students in chapter 6 as they watched the toddler throwing crayons?). But the ontological question is seldom asked: "Why is this behaviour unacceptable? And to whom?"

Taking a dialogic approach to the issue it becomes necessary to consider the chronotopes at play in any event and, the extent to which teachers are able to meet these at the chronotopic threshold. This became very clear to Alicia when she realised, after several weeks of frustration, that Zoe was not randomly biting other children in the centre but was, in fact, doing it every time she (Alicia) went on a break. At that time the setting was dominated by rosters that meant teachers had to take breaks at very specific times in order to fit in to a schedule (this schedule and its timetable represent a certain kind of chronotope). Teachers had expressed frustration, even anger, at Zoe's biting – placing her in 'time-out' (physical isolation) every time incidents took place. What had not occurred to the teachers was that Zoe was drawing on a genre at her disposal to convey her IPD rather than being deviant.

The chronotope Zoe was drawing from was based on a relationship orientation: she wanted to spend time with her favourite teacher. Once the teachers took the time to work this out through observation, discussion with other staff and deep personal reflection, they were able to respond more thoughtfully and, in my view, appropriately by explaining to Zoe what was going to happen at various parts of the day. They were able to ensure that she had the opportunity to spend valued time with Alicia and other staff to build positive relationships. Although teachers were not prepared to suspend the schedule altogether (they could not conceive of such practice in this chronotope), they did decide that breaks could be better coordinated to support the routines of children. They found ways of interpreting Zoe's language to see clashes – like biting – as opportunities to understand one another anew. This revised understanding was reflected in a note the teacher wrote at the time, expressing her relationship with Zoe following this threshold encounter:

> Later that afternoon I enjoy cuddles with you. You are very cuddly. We look into each other's eyes. You feel like a baby at this moment. You fixate on my mole. You touch my mole with your fingertips. You say "mooollllee" accentuating the sound, which always cracks me up laughing. I reply "yes, that's my mole, it's still there." We have a little chuckle together . . .
>
> *(Teacher's letter to Zoe, in White, 2011a, pp. 60–61)*

What this example highlights, I think, is the answerable basis of dialogic pedagogy in the early years. The idea that there is no alibi is truly implicated here because there is no way the early years teacher can remove him or herself from accountability – to the child, to the family, to society and to themselves. However, such an entreaty calls upon teachers to examine their own ideologies, and those of the AD, alongside others. Knowing that there is always room for alteration gives us permission to consider ourselves and others as individuals who are full of potential, able to make mistakes or to change our minds (recall Dostoevsky's loophole in chapter 6). Most importantly, this note conveys a commitment to linger lovingly with Zoe using the genres that are important to her – casting back to the episode of the mole in chapter 4, you will appreciate the depth of this encounter. There is a strong sense of vulnerability on the part of the teacher here; we see two subjectivities trying to understand one another deeply, respectfully and with regard for the person rather than any prescribed outcome or agenda. This kind of 'professionalism' is all too rarely espoused in early years practice. Yet in a dialogic approach early years teachers are free to embrace the fact that they are part of an ongoing polyphonic dialogue that changes every day and alters our view of the world. Such alteration does not happen by chance though; teachers must be willing to listen and look, as well as speak into (and sometimes from the outside of) dialogic meeting spaces of difference and uncertainty. These are thresholds of opportunity indeed.

Looking back, going forward

This chapter offers, perhaps, the most profound challenge to early years teachers who espouse 'communities of practice' and naïve forms of 'democracy' based on one cultural standpoint as a sole means of creating harmony at the centre of their pedagogy. The reality that heteroglossia allows us to see is that harmony is only one of several possibilities for any individual or group in any moment in time and thus reassigns democracy to a new dimension characterised by a consideration of internally persuasive discourses in conversation with official ones. At times harmony can also be dangerous because it assumes a 'sameness' that frankly does not exist without some form of cost for someone eventually. In responding to the multiple accountabilities facing the teacher, it is neither possible nor desirable to please all of the people all of the time. There will be moments where teachers have to speak out as advocates for others or themselves – sometimes at great personal cost. At the end of the day teachers are humans too, with their own internally persuasive discourses that cannot, and should not, be ignored in the heteroglot. This doesn't mean that they always take precedence, of course, but that they are always part of the dialogue – spoken or unspoken. As we have seen, honest recognition of this reality is an important aspect of teacher reflexivity.

There will be other occasions where teachers will not 'see' what is going on – especially when it takes place in the underground – often because there is too much focus on serving the authorial empire. At other times the authorial discourse must be summoned because the early years setting is located within, and accountable to, society. Ongoing vigilance to retain a balance between both is a key component of answerability to the diverse community that makes up the early years heteroglot. Knowing that teachers can never, and should not strive to, create a monocultural climate means that it is possible to encounter the heteroglot as a living dialogue with difference. Bakhtin's chronotopic threshold provides a means of doing so through careful consideration of the time, space and axiologies that locate certain discourses in the setting and which may or may not create spaces for alternatives to speak. With this comes openness, honesty and, above all, dialogue.

But teachers are not alone in this complex space of competing discourses. Children, too, must negotiate their way through complex and oppositional forces that position them outside or inside familiar chronotopes. This journey can be painful at times and deeply satisfying at others. But it is always a source of learning in a dialogic sense. Children have strategies of their own that they put to service in this task as we have seen at various intervals throughout this book – through play, through laughter and by metaphorically speaking 'through the floorboards' into the adult world. Teachers who are vigilant about these different ways of revealing (and concealing) IDP have the opportunity to consider their tremendous potential to contribute to the life of the early years setting, and to our deeper appreciation of children through loving pedagogical deeds. The interplay between IDP and AD *is* the early years setting. The extent to which voices can be heard in this locale relies on teachers who are prepared to "utilise their personally and professionally vested truths and response to those of others, unleashing internally persuasive discourses within the official realm" (White, 2011a, p. 6). Dialogic pedagogy thrives in such spaces.

References

Bakhtin, M. M. (1981). *The dialogic imagination* (M. Holquist, Ed.; C. Emerson & M. Holquist, Trans.). Austin: University of Texas Press.

Bakhtin, M. M. (1986). *Speech genres and other late essays* (C. Emerson & M. Holquist, Eds.; V. W. McGee, Trans.). Austin: University of Texas Press.

Bemong, N., & Borghart, P. (2010). Bakhtin's theory of the literary chronotope: Reflections, applications, perspectives. In N. Bemong, P. Borghart, M. De Dobbeleer, K. Demoen, K. De Temmerman, & B. Keunen (Eds.), *Bakhtin's theory of the literary chronotope: Reflections, applications, perspectives* (pp. 3–17). Ghent: Academia Press.

Blackledge, A., & Creese, A. (Eds.). (2014). *Heteroglossia as practice and pedagogy*. Dordrecht: Springer.

Brandist, C. (2014, January). *Bakhtinian pedagogy: An historical perspective*. Keynote address to the Fourth International Interdisciplinary Conference on the Limits and Perspectives of Mikhail Bakhtin, Ngaurawahia, New Zealand. Retrieved from http://www.youtube.com/watch?v=cLMdgMOqHI4&list=PLGnuRFj6PKk6Tx3q1v7-muZWBV50_17DZ

Busch, B. (2014). Building on heteroglossia and heterogeneity: The experience of a multilingual classroom. In A. Blackledge & A. Creese (Eds.), *Heteroglossia as practice and pedagogy* (pp. 21–40). Dordrecht: Springer.

Foucault, M. (1961). *Madness and civilisation*. London: Routledge.

Foucault, M. (1984). *The Foucault reader* (P. Rabinow, Ed.). Harmondsworth: Penguin.

Garcia, O., & Leiva, C. (2014). Theorizing and enacting translanguaging. In A. Blackledge & A. Creese (Eds.), *Heteroglossia as practice and pedagogy* (pp. 199–216). Dordrecht: Springer.

Gradovski, M., & Lokken, I. M. (in press). Creation of an environment to experience chronotopic thresholds. *International Journal of Early Childhood*.

Holquist, M. (2009). The role of chronotope in dialog. In K. Junefelt & P. Nordin (Eds.), *Proceedings from the Second International Interdisciplinary Conference on Perspectives and Limits of Dialogism in Mikhail Bakhtin* (pp. 9–16). Stockholm: Stockholm University.

Kurban, F., & Tobin, J. (2009). 'They don't like us': Reflections of Turkish children in a German preschool. *Contemporary Issues in Early Childhood, 10*(1), 24–34.

Moe, M. (2014). *Dialogic relations in healthy organizations.* Manuscript submitted for publication.

Moe, M., & Sidorkin, A. M. (2014, March). *The polyphonic embodied self.* Paper presented at Nordic Educational Research Association (NERA) Conference 2014, Lillehammer, Norway.

Morson, G. S., & Emerson, C. (1990). *Mikhail Bakhtin: Creation of a prosaics.* Stanford, CA: Stanford University Press.

Shields, C. (2011). Bakhtin's 'novel' proposal: Lessons for educational leaders. In E. J. White & M. A. Peters (Eds.), *Bakhtinian pedagogy: Opportunities and challenges for research, policy and practice in education across the globe* (pp. 227–245). New York, NY: Peter Lang.

Talbot, D. (in press). Bakhtin remixed as teachers talk about their learning in the 21st century. *Knowledge Cultures.*

Tam, P. C. (2013). Children's bricolage under the gaze of teachers in sociodramatic play. *Childhood, 20*(2), 244–259.

Vandenbroeck, M., Boonaert, T., Van der Mespel, S., & De Brabandere, K. (2009). Dialogical spaces to reconceptualise parent support in the social investment state. *Contemporary Issues in Early Childhood, 10*(1), 66–77.

Voloshinov, V. (1973). *Marxism and the philosophy of language* (L. Matejka & I. R. Titunik, Trans.). Cambridge, MA: Harvard University Press.

White, E. J. (2009). *Assessment in New Zealand early childhood education: A Bakhtinian analysis of toddler metaphoricity* (Unpublished doctoral thesis, Monash University, Melbourne, Australia).

White, E. J. (2011a). Aesthetics of the beautiful: Ideologic tensions in contemporary assessment. In E. J. White & M. A. Peters (Eds.), *Bakhtinian pedagogy: Opportunities and challenges for research, policy and practice in education across the globe* (pp. 47–67). New York , NY: Peter Lang.

White, E. J. (2011b). Dust under the whāriki: Embracing the messiness of curriculum. *Early Childhood Folio, 15*(1), 2–6.

White, E. J. (2013). Circles, borders and chronotope: Education at the boundary? *Knowledge Cultures, 1*(2), 25–32.

White, E. J. (2014). A dialogic space in early childhood education: Chronotopic encounters with people, places and things. In J. Sumsion & L. Harrison (Eds.), *Lived spaces of infant-toddler education and care: Exploring diverse perspectives on theory, research, practice and policy* (pp. 191–202). Dordrecht: Springer.

8

DIALOGIC PROVOCATIONS

Throughout this book you have been confronted, over and over again, with Bakhtin's notion of dialogism, its many layers of meaning for early years pedagogy and some associated provocations. First and foremost Bakhtin's dialogic principles do not provide any excuse for teachers, or anyone else for that matter, to disassociate themselves from being heavily implicated in the learning experience of life. This is especially important for early years teachers, who work intimately alongside increasingly diverse children and families as partners in complex learning dialogues. There is nowhere to hide in this regard as Bakhtin's dialogism emphasises relationships with people over systems or processes. We are all implicated and involved, with moral responsibility for our acts as events of being in the lifelong process of ideological becoming that speaks into a contemporary world in time and space.

In dialogic pedagogy the teacher resides in several spaces within and outside of the pedagogical relationship. Not only do they occupy an intimate place in relationships with learners but teachers also play an evaluative role which positions them on the outskirts of intercourse – as observer or even stranger at times. From a Bakhtinian standpoint both positions are essential in the interpretative experience that constitutes dialogic pedagogy. The following model attempts to summarise this complex positioning:

Located in various spaces on this quadrant the dialogic teacher also navigates between horizontal and vertical positions where meanings are often unknown yet earnestly sought. In this location the teacher plays a precarious role in orienting themselves towards the priorities of each learner while maintaining democratic processes that are fair for all. Determining what is 'fair' or 'unfair' is clearly a moral concern that the teacher must contemplate beyond their own world view through dialogue with others in time and space. The extent to which teachers reside in any particular place at any particular time is thus informed by individuals in the social event rather than through the transmission of prescribed pedagogical objectives.

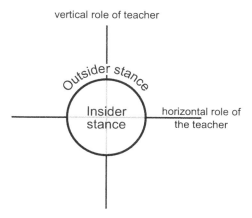

FIGURE 8.1 Positioning of teacher in dialogic pedagogy

Responsibility lies with the teacher to support learning in its broadest sense. Rather than using instrumental strategies to manipulate learning towards a preordained end point, the teacher is called upon to exercise courage, honesty and wisdom in each moment. In this, there is no alibi, as Bakhtin tells us, yet there is also no certainty that what we do is 'right' either. A combination of background knowledge, understanding of human development and theory is thus brought to bear on relationships which must simultaneously remain open to the possibilities and alternatives that children offer in learning events. Being prepared to be altered in dialogic pedagogy is not only the attitude for children but for teachers too – it is 'poised resourcefulness' at its best.

As a teacher you may feel somewhat burdened by this complex combination of answerability and uncertainty. There are no 'activities' or 'curricula' that can supersede this human encounter. Yet within this entreaty Bakhtin offers us a joyful optimism. It is not so much a question of 'being' dialogic as one of reclaiming what we, as humans, already possess – the capacity to engage with others. What so often stands in the way are the very scaffolds that education has erected in the form of rules, programmes, methods or structures that prioritise privileged theories and practices over responsive relationships in the local setting with real people. As recipients of this heritage teachers are called upon to shed the weightiness of some of these layers and free themselves to focus on the relationships they are in rather than the utility of those relationships in the future or the outcomes necessary to achieve set learning goals.

While we cannot claim an alibi for our acts in the early years setting and beyond, Bakhtin also offers a counterpoint to such seriousness through his related ideas concerning the joy of laughter, carnivalesque, play and playfulness. Being spontaneously responsive is unpredictable but it is also imaginative work that calls upon our whole being. It is simultaneously confronting because teachers may find themselves in the unsettling position of not knowing, feeling destabilised or perhaps even becoming the butt of a joke. Temporarily suspending hierarchies and certainties through playful encounter creates opportunities to see anew and, in so doing, to recognise the agency of young children: as group members, as persons of culture and as individuals with equal rights to our own. In a dialogic world there is room for diversity and difference (even resistance) to be celebrated rather than stifled or, worse from a Bakhtinian stance, ignored. Yet there is also a deep regard for 'other' and a careful attunement towards their priorities as well as our own. Speaking through the underground has as much legitimacy in a dialogic landscape as does official discourse. In dialogic pedagogy all voices have the potential to be seen and heard – including those that do not harmonise with our own. They become opportunities for learning and give hope for a future generation of thinkers who are able to voice opinions, take risks, resist dogma and live in a diverse world without seeking to enculturate others into their own point of view. This is an especially important agenda in a global society that, at the time of writing, appears unable to tolerate alternative ideologies to the point of waging war on them.

Bakhtin's lifelong philosophical works provide us with a means of reclaiming these dialogic principles through deeply interrogating the multiple ways we meet with others and how such meetings shape meaning. In the early years these give us permission to linger in the lives of children, to learn more about them and their families, and to take the time to understand ourselves as dialogic partners. We can do this by engaging in lively dialogues that really matter to those concerned and that open up thresholds for new ways of being – for teachers and learners alike. It is here, not in the exclusive domain of master theories that tell us how children think or how we should act, that the nexus of learning is forged. In this way dialogic pedagogy is very optimistic and forward-looking – always anticipating response, and forever open to alteration. (remember the loophole?). In essence, Bakhtin helps us to emphasise the creative potential of human relationships that resists finalisation and provides opportunities to 'see' anew. By recognising and perhaps even challenging the ideological limitations we bring to our seeing, it becomes possible to transgress many of the barriers that may hold teachers back from engaging in mutually animating relationships with learners. This is a possibility that has potential for all levels of society and through which children have the opportunity to play an authorship role in their own lives as a primary form of agency.

Despite such optimism there are many aspects of early years practice that dialogism cannot assist us with. These are left to other thinkers, theorists and philosophers – past, present and future. For instance, Bakhtin's stance asserts a position of dialogue that emphasises subjectivities in play and has little tolerance for the complex power issues that might stand in the way. Here he proposes a heteroglossic polyphony of voices over monologic dogma, and turns our attention towards educational experience as a conversation about diversity, difference and open encounter. While there is no doubt that Bakhtin may have been sympathetic to any resistance to contemporary ideological strongholds that seek to reduce early years pedagogy to little more than schoolification, he cannot aid us in escaping from prevalent rationalist discourses that ring in monologic tones outside of our own (moral) efforts. More-over, Bakhtin will not help us to explain cognitive function as an isolated concept or to respond to the call of authorial discourse to provide certain answers to questions that need not be asked. He cannot solve for us the mystery of the child and neither would he want to (though he does suggest we must continue to puzzle over this). As I have emphasised, Bakhtin has no interest in providing us with a 'how to' manual for practice or for understanding children through and through. To do so would be to violate the very principles of dialogism. Please note: I did warn you of this when you began reading this book!

Yet all is not lost. As we have seen, dialogism provides important routes into the revised understanding of learning and, by association, teaching as a relationship event. The fundamental power of Bakhtin's theory of dialogism is its creativity – a gift that sets the scene for lively engagement and thoughtful attunement. An agency for agency, in other words.

Summarising dialogic pedagogy in the early years

In drawing this book to a close it is timely to synthesize each provocation revealed through its pages. As you consider each of these you are invited to contemplate its significance for you – as a teacher in the early years and perhaps, too, as a learner in life. These principles are by no means limited to formal settings but they are espe-cially relevant for this context because so much pedagogical harm is done in the name of 'education' to children in these spaces:

Dialogue *is* learning. Knowledge is gained as a by-product of experience with others. Central to dialogic pedagogy is the encounter and its generated meanings to those involved. For very young children dialogue is much more than words and the body plays a central role. It is in dialogue, in its broadest sense, that learning is situated because it is here where ideas are revealed (or concealed).

Teaching is a dialogic imperative. Frame clashes, disagreements and differ-ences are welcome in early years contexts where growth and creativity is valued. Dialogic pedagogy is characterised by teachers who exercise intellectual courage, honesty and restraint in pedagogical relationships that prioritise dialogue as learn-ing. This means that they are willing to engage in events as opportunities to learn more about the internally persuasive discourses that learners bring to the topic of inquiry. These are not only made up of scientific 'working theories' but may be imaginary, creative and illusive moments of insight that are difficult (or even pain-ful) for adults to 'see'.

Teachers *are* the curriculum. There are no programmes, curricula, objects or activities that can substitute for the teacher-child learning relationship. Teachers are implicated mind, body and soul. Every intonation, look or movement is laden with meanings that will be interpreted by learners in the moment of their delivery (and not in the aftermath of evaluation). Nonresponses play a vital role too – what is privileged through a response lays the foundation for what is valued. Children are highly capable of tuning in to these subtleties.

Pedagogy is an appreciative process. Lingering lovingly with the child is the most important work an early years teacher can do. It is aesthetic *and* architectronic (*arkhitektonika*); therefore teachers need to maintain an evaluative eye at the same time as recognising the potential one has to speak into the life of another. In this sense, pedagogy is an answerable act.

Pedagogy is interactive, responsive and oriented toward other. Learning is a process of meaning-making that occurs in the between-ness of dialogues that are conceptualised well beyond one- or two-way exchanges or sustained dialogues in the moment. Learning can take place across time, in events that may not seem significant to adults at all but which hold ontological significance for learners. Paying attention to the genres employed by young children provides insight into different routes to meaning-making and engagement.

Children are the authors of their own learning. Adults don't need to 'teach' young children agency, but effective pedagogy can promote it within the early years setting. Teachers can and do play an authoring role but they, too, are authored in the dialogic event – sometimes in unpredictable, destabilising ways. What this pedagogy might look like will depend on the extent to which adults can work with uncertainty and challenge.

Meaning is never fixed. Every child has the capacity to exercise their dialogic loophole – and does. Play, playfulness and humour are all a vital part of the discovery process and provide opportunities for testing, trialling and altering meanings. Dialogic pedagogy recognises that the contestability of meanings is central to learning.

Learning is a transgradient process. Creative growth occurs when people who reside in different chronotopic spaces are able to meet at the thresholds of encounter – not to create sameness but greater understanding. Opportunities to glimpse into the world of another are not only illuminating but they represent a chance to see our own world differently, perhaps even anew.

Ideology underpins practice. Even when it is unexamined or unknown ideology impacts on what takes place in the early years setting. Dialogic pedagogy takes ideologies very seriously, finding ways to open up spaces for people to share and for teachers to maintain vigilance about the extent to which their practice is shaped by ideologies – their own, and others.

Pedagogy can now speak boldly of love! As a deed, love represents an aesthetic encounter of understanding and acting ethically. This loving contemplation lies at the centre of dialogic pedagogy for the early years. Teachers can legitimately claim this kind of love for their students as an authorial gift rather than a form of manipulation when they are open to the priorities of learners alongside their own.

I can think of no better principles and practices for teachers to acquire than these. Indeed, I propose they are also qualities through which we might live life to its fullest extent. I think this is what Bakhtin means when he uses the term *Lebensphilosophie* – a philosophy of life. By posing these important provocations (and others that have yet to be considered) dialogic pedagogy gives us permission to pause in the busyness of our everyday practice to consider the impact of ourselves on others and the potential for others to impact on us when we take the time to try and understand deeply, creatively, with love and respect for learners and their endless potentiality. With this attitude early years pedagogy can resist tendencies to manipulate learning in ways that squeeze young children into a monologic mould. The emphasis in dialogic pedagogy is on the learner and their priorities. Hence we are no longer concerned with how teachers can impart knowledge but how knowledge can be generated in mutual dialogues. In consideration of the increasingly diverse world young children occupy, I believe that this is where the greatest riches will be found.

Ongoing dialogue

In summarising these provocations so neatly it might seem as if there is very little else to say about dialogic pedagogy in the early years. In fact nothing could be further from the truth. If this book has merely provided you with yet another set of helpful methods, given you further justification for current practice or presented a highly certain set of uncontestable claims, then I have failed in my dialogic quest. This book is merely the beginning of a dialogue based on my interpretations thus far. There is much more to be said, by many different voices across time and space, that will continue to provoke and extend those of us engaged with early years pedagogy – if we allow it to. In my view the ideas within these pages will only have their true impact, in a dialogic sense, if they remain open to ongoing debate in the early years sector, in practice and, of course, in pedagogy. From a dialogic standpoint pedagogy can only be interpreted by those who are living in the event, alongside others. That means you, me and all those who work within and beyond these spaces.

Thus I end this book in the expectation there will be further dialogue on the ideas it contains, whether in classrooms, staffrooms, study groups, on Facebook (https://www.facebook.com/DialogicPedagogyJournal) or other electronic sites (see for example, http://dpj.pitt.edu/ojs/index.php/dpj1/index). I have a specific dialogue space for the early years in mind, however, and I invite you to join me there to continue our conversation. You can register at https://education.waikato.ac.nz/dialogicpedagogy/

In this space I hope to learn about your interpretations of the ideas presented in this book and their relationship and significance to your experiences as an early years teacher or student, and to engage in lively conversations about what all this might mean for those of us who seek to learn, love, live and laugh with young children as social partners in the educational settings we share. In the meantime, I hope this book has tantalised you sufficiently to continue the dialogue and, in doing so, to remain open to the potential of dialogic pedagogy to 'see' more. As Bakhtin reminds us, it is in these open spaces of uncertainty that dialogue thrives and maintains the potential for creativity and growth. This is a message that is as important for adults as it is for children – we are all implicated in the early years heteroglot we now call 'education'.

GLOSSARY

addressivity the unavoidable state as a human being engages in dialogue with the world as it appears to themselves in relation to others

aesthetic the dialogic interaction between two or more noncoinciding consciousnesses, or ethical co-being

alterity the potential to alter or change through dialogue

answerability an ethical obligation or accountability to other

architectronics the science of relations that explores how parts make up the whole

author a person interacting with the consciousness of others (at its extreme it may be a form of assessment)

authoritative discourse ideas that are passed down to us and are fixed

axiology A branch of philosophy that encompasses ethics and aesthetics. In relation to a language act, it is its given aesthetic and ethical value.

becoming a lifelong dialogic process of becoming; see also *Bildungsroman*

being co-being as an event

carnivalesque genres that act to de-crown or mock hierarchy

chronotope an optic for reading discourses and their value

circumfusion a term to describe the relationship between language, its use and establishing an atmosphere that supports meaningful dialogue

dialogism a study of subjectivities encountering one another in the social act

heteroglossia the battleground between different social forces (see *raznorecie* and *raznogolosie*)

ideology Less political than the Marxist meaning typically given in the West because it is concerned with the way a given social group views the world. This is betrayed through utterance, according to Bakhtin.

internally persuasive discourse the evolving ideas people bring from their personal experience of life

loophole deliberately altering the finalised meaning of one's own words by others

monologism a singular way of engaging in dialogue and interpreting meaning that does not pay heed to alternative approaches or perspectives. There is only one voice.

outsidedness the quality 'I' bring to the evaluation of other

polyphony a chorus of voices who speak for themselves

speech genre combinations of language forms and their meaning in dialogue

transgradience perceiving beyond the limited perspective of a particular chronotope

underground voices that speak outside the official discourse

utterance answered language

visual surplus the additional insights offered by another

voice includes all kinds of language and its use (seen and unseen; verbal and nonverbal) including intonation, which reflects the values behind a consciousness

Key Russian (and German) terms

arkitektonika architectronics

Bildungsroman A type of a novel created in Germany where character's growth and development over time is at the novel's blueprint. An example of such a novel is Goethe's novel *Wilhelm Meister* where the character develops over time.

dolzhestvovanie oughtness or obligation (a purpose of consciousness)

dukh I-for-myself (spirit)

dusha I-for-another (soul)

Einfühlung a German term meaning empathy

emotsionalaniy no volevoi emotional-volitional

esteticheskii aesthetical

golos voice

izbytok visual surplus

khronotop chronotope

Lebensphilosophie A German term meaning 'philosophy of life' that emerged as a reaction to positivism and inspired by the critique by Schopenhauer, Kierkegaard, and Nietzsche. This school of philosophy positions all forms of life as relevant to meaning as philosophy of life that positions all forms of life as relevant to meaning.

nezavershennost unfinalisation or open potential

obrazovanie A process of education and up-bringing. For Bakhtin the real *obrazovanie* is a formation through encounters that give rise to creative spirit emergence or formation through encounters that give rise to creative spirit.

otvetstvennost see answerability

perezhivanie (for Bakhtin) an inner emotional and cognitive process that emerges as a reaction to an encounter or *postupok*

postupok an action or act that I myself choose to perform and am answerable for

poznanie a process of understanding

pravda lived knowing (as opposed to truth – *istina*)

raznogolosie the diversity of voices

raznojazyycie linguistic variation or multiplicity of languages

raznorecie diversity of voices

slovo language use or discourse

sobytie the event or eventness (i.e. a social event or full of event potential)

soznanie conciseness

uznanie a process of recognising something

ver'nost truthfulness in relation to meaning

vnenakhodimost outsidedness

vyskazyvanie utterance

vzhivanie living into through relationships with others

zhanr speech genre

znachenie a spark of meaning

znachimost a level of influence and importance of something the living interpretation of a language event

For further examination of these terms see:

Hirschkop, K. (1989). Glossary: Alternative translation of key terms. In K. Hirschkop & D. Shepherd (Eds.), *Bakhtin and cultural theory* (pp. 190–194). Manchester: Manchester University Press.

Morris, P. (1994). *The Bakhtin reader: Selected writings of Bakhtin, Medvedev, Voloshinov*. London: E. Arnold.

INDEX

Note: Page numbers with *f* indicate figures; those with *t* indicate tables.

Lightning Source UK Ltd.
Milton Keynes UK
UKOW06f1901140616

276307UK00016B/249/P

9 780415 819855